SLOW
COOKER
500
RECIPES

SLOW COOKER 500 RECIPES

SARA LEWIS

hamlyn

An Hachette UK Company
www.hachette.co.uk

First published in Great Britain in 2015 by Hamlyn, a division of
Octopus Publishing Group Ltd, Carmelite House
50 Victoria Embankment, London EC4Y 0DZ
www.octopusbooks.co.uk

Some of this material previously appeared in *200 Slow Cooker Recipes*,
200 More Slow Cooker Recipes, *200 Light Slow Cooker Recipes* and
200 Family Slow Cooker Recipes.

ISBN 978-0-600-63104-0

A CIP catalogue record for this book is available from the British Library

Printed and bound in China

10 9 8 7 6 5 4 3 2 1

♥ Recipes with this symbol are under 500 calories.

Follow the manufacturer's instructions for your slow cooker and
adjust the cooking time or temperature if necessary.

Both imperial and metric measurements have been given in
all recipes. Use one set of measurements only and not a mixture
of both.

Standard level spoon measurement are used in all recipes.

1 tablespoon = one 15 ml spoon

1 teaspoon = one 5 ml spoon

Eggs should be medium unless otherwise stated. The Department
of Health advises that eggs should not be consumed raw. This book
contains dishes made with raw or lightly cooked eggs. It is prudent
for more vulnerable people such as pregnant and nursing mothers,
invalids, the elderly, babies and young children to avoid uncooked or
lightly cooked dishes made with eggs. Once prepared these dishes
should be kept refrigerated and used promptly.

Milk should be full fat unless otherwise stated.

Fresh herbs should be used unless otherwise stated. If unavailable,
use dried herbs as an alternative but halve the quantities stated.

Ovens should be preheated to the specific temperature – if using
a fan-assisted oven, follow manufacturer's instructions for adjusting
the time and the temperature.

All microwave information is based on a 650 watt oven. Follow
manufacturer's instructions for an oven with a different wattage.

Pepper should be freshly ground black pepper unless otherwise stated.

This book includes dishes made with nuts and nut derivatives. It is
advisable for customers with known allergic reactions to nuts and
nut derivatives and those who may be potentially vulnerable to these
allergies, such as pregnant and nursing mothers, invalids, the elderly,
babies and children, to avoid dishes made with nuts and nut oils. It is
also prudent to check the labels of pre-prepared ingredients for the
possible inclusion of nut derivatives.

CONTENTS

INTRODUCTION

Whether you are new to slow cooking or a seasoned pro, you probably have a handful of favourite recipes that you keep going back to. It's true that some classics taste absolutely delicious when slow cooked, time after time: lamb stews, beef casseroles, coq au vin.

But a slow cooker isn't just for casseroles and stews, great though they are. You can make a huge variety of other dishes with this gadget, including lighter meals, delicious fish recipes and child-pleasing suppers. Try warming main meal soups, children's favourites such as pasta bakes, everyday favourites like chilli and chicken, easy cheats such as tortillas and curries and food to impress for easy dinner parties.

When water is added to the slow cooker pot it can be used as a bain-marie, or water bath, to cook baked custards, pâtés or terrines. Or you can pour alcoholic or fruit juice mixtures into the pot and make warming hot party punches or hot toddies.

The slow cooker pot can also be used to make chocolate or cheese fondues and preserves such as lemon curd or simple chutneys, and you can even boil up meat bones or a chicken carcass to make them into homemade stock.

In order to explore the wide range of versatile dishes on offer, this bumper cookbook offers 500 recipes to cover any occasion.

NEW TO SLOW COOKING? YOUR QUESTIONS ANSWERED

WILL IT REALLY MAKE MY LIFE EASIER?

If you're unfamiliar with using a slow cooker, the redistribution of time involved may seem odd. Early on in the day, you spend 15 minutes in the kitchen doing a little prep, then add everything to the slow cooker and walk away and get on with something else. While cooking before you rush out to work in the morning may not be for everyone, getting a lovely supper on to cook before you head out to the golf course or for a day of shopping, or before doing the Saturday taxi run to and from the kids' clubs may seem more manageable.

As the slow cooker cooks so gently, there is no need to stir or check on the food because there is no danger of it drying out or spoiling. Just enjoy the welcoming aroma of a delicious supper ready and waiting when you walk back through the door.

ARE ALL SLOW COOKERS THE SAME?

All slow cookers cook food slowly, though they do vary slightly. Oval-shaped slow cookers offer the most flexibility when it comes to cooking joints or desserts.

Generally, slow cookers come in three sizes:

- a two-portion size with a capacity of 1.5 litres (2½ pints)

- a four-portion size with a capacity of 2.5 litres (4 pints)

- a six- to eight-portion size with a capacity of 4 litres (7 pints) or 4.5 litres (8 pints)

Newer models might come with cooking pots that can be used on the hob, so you can fry off meat and onions prior to slow cooking in the slow cooker pot itself, saving on washing-up. These types of slow cookers do tend to cost more. A good nonstick frying pan in conjunction with a slow cooker works just as well.

As with all things, price varies considerably. The larger models are very often on special offer, but unless your family is large or you plan to cook larger quantities in order to freeze half the batch, you may find that, while the machine itself is a good price, you have to cook larger quantities than you had expected in order to just half-fill it. When selecting a slow cooker, choose a machine with a high and low setting and an on/off light at the front of the machine so that you can easily see that it is on.

WHAT TO DO BEFORE I START?
Dull though it sounds, once you have purchased a slow cooker, make sure you read the handbook. The majority of models should not be preheated with an empty slow

cooker pot. If you part-prep supper the night before and put the earthenware slow cooker pot in the refrigerator, all manufacturers agree that you should leave it at room temperature for 20 minutes before adding it to the slow cooker machine and turning it on. There are set-up notes on page 10.

IS IT SAFE TO LEAVE IT ON ALL DAY?
Yes, the slow cooker runs on such a small amount of power (the equivalent of two light bulbs) that it is safe to leave it on all day – even if you go out. Because the heat is so low and the lid forms a seal, there is no danger of the food boiling dry. The sides of the slow cooker will feel warm to the touch, so ensure you leave the machine on a non-cluttered part of the work surface.

DO I HAVE TO FRY FOODS BEFORE I ADD THEM TO THE SLOW COOKER POT?
Frying onions and browning meat adds colour and flavour to the finished casserole, but it isn't essential – it's very much a matter of personal taste. Foods will not brown in a slow cooker. The idea of frying before you rush out in the morning can be a bit off-putting, especially if are wearing your smart work clothes, so there are plenty of recipes in the book that can be made without pre-cooking. Boost colour and flavour with spices or herbs, red wine or beer or tomato purée.

DOES LIQUID HAVE TO BE HOT BEFORE GOING IN THE SLOW COOKER?
The slow cooker works by building up heat to just below boiling point, then safely maintaining the heat so that food cooks gently but without any danger of allowing the bacteria that cause food poisoning to proliferate. If you add all cold ingredients, this will extend the heating-up process, so add 2–3 hours to the cooking time, with the first hour on high, especially if the recipe states to use hot stock. But it is much quicker and very simple to dissolve a stock cube in boiling water and add the hot stock to the slow cooker pot. Always add hot liquid when cooking large joints.

HOW FULL SHOULD THE POT BE?
Ideally, the slow cooker pot should be filled half-full and up to three-quarters full for it to work efficiently. For soups, fill it so that the liquid is 5 cm (2 inches) from the top. If you have a very large slow cooker, make up amounts to serve six to eight people, then freeze the extra in single portions or portion sizes that will suit your family on another day. As the slow cooker heats up, the steam generated will condense and make a water seal between the lid and top of the slow cooker pot – this is perfectly normal.

CAN I USE MY ORDINARY RECIPES?

Yes, of course – stews, casseroles and pot roast recipes can all be made in the slow cooker with the same ingredients. However, because the slow cooker creates a seal during cooking, the liquid doesn't evaporate, so you will find that you need to reduce the liquid in your recipes by one-third, and sometimes even by half. For stews or casseroles, just cover the meat or vegetables with stock. Bear in mind, if using fresh tomatoes, that you will need slightly less stock because the tomatoes will pulp down as they cook.

Depending on the size of your slow cooker pot, you may need to cut down or size up the quantities of ingredients given in the recipes. A medium-sized slow cooker pot comfortably makes four portions, while a large one makes six to eight portions. Many of the recipes in this book are designed to feed four people – ideal for a medium-sized slow cooker pot.

The slow cooker can also be used as a bain-marie or steamer. Making steamed puddings works very well and you don't need to top up with boiling water during cooking, as there is no chance the water will boil dry.

As a rough guide, if a recipe takes 1–2 hours on the hob or in the oven, you should cook it in a slow cooker for 3–4 hours on the high setting, or 6–8 hours on the low setting. If a recipe takes 2–4 hours on the hob or in the oven, cook it in the slow cooker for 4–6 hours on high, or for 8–12 hours on low.

CAN I COOK RICE AND PASTA?

Yes, but as they are both starchy foods they can go sticky and gluey if overcooked. Choose easy-cook rice over ordinary rice where available, as some of the starch has been removed during manufacturing, making it less sticky. If making a risotto, add the stock all in one go rather than a ladleful at a time.

Cook pasta in a saucepan of boiling water, then drain and stir it into the slow cooker pot just before serving. For lasagne, use 'no pre-cook' dried lasagne sheets and cook for no more than 5–6¼ hours. Tiny pasta shapes can be added to soups, without cooking first, for the final 15–30 minutes of cooking time.

WHAT ABOUT DAIRY FOODS AND SHELLFISH?

Dairy foods, such as milk, double cream and grated Cheddar-style cheeses, are fine for recipes with short cooking times or in baked dishes that are cooked for up to 3–5 hours on a low setting, or they can be stirred into a dish towards the end of cooking so that they have the final 15–30 minutes to add richness and flavour. If you cook them too long, they will separate rather unattractively.

Shellfish can be added to a dish, but in small quantities only and again towards the end of the cooking time, when the other ingredients are already piping hot. Make sure that the shellfish is also piping hot before serving, so cook it on high, preferably for 15 minutes, then serve. Do not keep dishes containing shellfish warm. If you are using frozen fish, ensure that it is fully thawed before adding it to the slow cooker.

REMEMBER THE BASICS

• Always add liquid to a slow cooker pot, ideally hot or boiling water.

• Test food before serving it to ensure it is thoroughly cooked before serving. Chicken or pork should have no pink juices when they are pierced with a small, sharp knife. Beef and lamb should be tender. Fish should flake into even-coloured flakes when pressed in the centre with a knife.

• Remove the slow cooker pot from the housing when the dish is cooked using oven gloves to serve.

• Cover any remaining food, leave it to cool, then transfer it to the refrigerator as soon as possible.

• If using raw frozen food other than peas or sweetcorn, thaw before use.

• Do not reheat food in a slow cooker (Christmas pudding is the exception).

HEAT SETTINGS

All slow cookers have a 'high', 'low' and 'off' setting, and some also have either 'medium', 'warm' or 'auto' settings. In general, the 'high' setting will take half the time of the 'low' setting when you are cooking a diced meat or vegetable casserole. This can be useful if you plan to eat at lunchtime or are delayed in starting the casserole. Both settings will reach just below 100°C (212°F), boiling point, during cooking, but when it is set to 'high', the temperature is reached more quickly.

A combination of settings can be useful and is recommended by some manufacturers at the beginning of cooking. See your manufacturer's handbook for more details.

WHAT IS BEST AT WHAT SETTING?
The following is a general guide to what you should cook at which temperature:

Low
• Diced meat or vegetable casseroles
• Chops or chicken joints
• Soups
• Egg custard desserts
• Rice dishes
• Fish dishes

High
• Sweet or savoury steamed puddings or sweet dishes that include a raising agent (either self-raising flour or baking powder)
• Pâtés or terrines
• Whole chicken, guinea fowl or pheasant, gammon joint or half a shoulder of lamb

CAN I REHEAT FOODS IN THE SLOW COOKER?

All manufacturers recommend that you only cook foods from raw in the slow cooker pot. To reheat a casserole or stew, put it in a saucepan, set it on the hob and bring it up to the boil, stirring, then cook for at least 10 minutes until thoroughly reheated and piping hot throughout. Only reheat cooked food once.

TIMINGS

All the recipes in the book have variable timings, which means that they will be tender and ready to eat at the lower time but can be left without spoiling for an extra hour or two, which is perfect if you get delayed at work or stuck in traffic.

If you want to speed up or slow down casseroles based on diced meat or vegetables so that the cooking fits around your plans accordingly, adjust the heat settings and timings as suggested below:

Low	Medium	High
6–8 hours	4–6 hours	3–4 hours
8–10 hours	6–8 hours	5–6 hours
10–12 hours	8–10 hours	7–8 hours

The above timings were taken from the Morphy Richards slow cooker instruction manual.
Note: do not change timings or settings for fish, whole joints or dairy dishes.

USING YOUR SLOW COOKER FOR THE FIRST TIME

Before you start to use the slow cooker, put it on the work surface, somewhere out of the way, and make sure that the flex is tucked around the back of the machine and not trailing over the front of the work surface.

The outside of the slow cooker does get hot, so warn young members of the family and don't forget to wear oven gloves when you are lifting the pot out of the housing. Set it on to a heatproof mat on the table or work surface to serve the food.

If your slow cooker lid has a vent in the top, make sure that the slow cooker is not put under an eye-level cupboard or the steam may catch someone's arm as they reach into the cupboard.

Always check that the joint, pudding basin, soufflé dish or individual moulds will fit into your slow cooker pot before you begin work on a recipe to avoid frustration when you get to a critical point.

PREPARING FOOD FOR THE SLOW COOKER

MEAT
Cut meat into equal-sized pieces so that cooking is even, and fry off meat before adding to the slow cooker pot.

A whole guinea fowl or pheasant, a small gammon joint or half a shoulder of lamb can be cooked in an oval slow cooker pot, but make sure that it does not fill more than the lower two-thirds of the pot. Cover it with boiling liquid and cook on high.

Check that it is cooked either by using a meat thermometer or by inserting a skewer through the thickest part and making sure the juices run clear.

Add boiling stock or sauce to the slow cooker pot and press the meat beneath the surface of the liquid before cooking begins.

FISH
Whether you cut the fish into pieces or cook it in a larger piece of about 500 g (1 lb), the slow, gentle cooking will not cause the fish to break up or overcook. Make sure the fish is covered by the hot liquid so that it cooks evenly right through to the centre.

Do not add shellfish until the last 15 minutes of cooking, and ensure that the slow cooker is set to high. If the fish was frozen, it must be thoroughly thawed, rinsed with cold water and drained before use.

VEGETABLES
Root vegetables can (surprisingly) take longer to cook than meat. If you are adding vegetables to a meat casserole, make sure you cut them into pieces that are a little smaller than the meat and try to keep all the vegetable chunks the same size so that they cook evenly. Press the vegetables and the meat below the surface of the liquid before cooking begins. When you are making soup, purée it while it is still in the slow cooker pot by using a stick blender if you have one.

DRIED PULSES

Make sure you soak dried beans and peas in plenty of cold water overnight.

Drain them, then put them into a saucepan with fresh cold water and bring to the boil. Boil rapidly for 10 minutes, then drain or add with the cooking liquid to the slow cooker pot. See the recipes for details.

Pearl barley and lentils – red, Puy or green – do not need soaking overnight. If you are unsure, check the instructions on the packet.

RICE

Easy-cook rice is preferable to use for slow cookers because it has been partially cooked during manufacture and some of the starch has been washed off, making it less sticky.

When you are cooking rice in the slow cooker, allow a minimum of 250 ml (8 fl oz) water for each 100 g (3½ oz) easy-cook rice or up to 500 ml (17 fl oz) for risotto rice.

PASTA

For best results, cook the pasta separately in a saucepan of lightly salted boiling water according to the packet instructions until just tender, then mix with the sauce just before serving.

Small pasta shapes, such as macaroni or shells, can be added to soups 30–45 minutes before the end of cooking. Pasta can be soaked in boiling water for short-cook recipes, such as macaroni cheese.

CREAM AND MILK

Both cream and milk are generally added at the beginning of cooking only when you are making rice pudding or baked egg custard-style dishes.

Use full-fat milk where milk is cooked directly in the cooker pot rather than pudding moulds, as it is less likely to separate.

If you are making soup, add the milk at the very end, after the soup has been puréed. Stir cream into soups just 15 minutes before the end of cooking.

THICKENING STEWS AND CASSEROLES

Casseroles can be thickened in just the same way as if you were cooking conventionally. You can do it either before slow cooking, by adding the flour after searing meat or frying onions, or you can thicken the casserole with cornflour mixed with a little cold water 30–60 minutes before the end of cooking.

GETTING THE MOST FROM YOUR SLOW COOKER

DON'T BE TEMPTED TO PEEK

As a slow cooker cooks so gently, there really is no need for you to stir the food because it won't stick or boil dry as it cooks. Don't be tempted to lift open the lid – every time you do so you release some of the heat and can add up to 10–15 minutes to the cooking time. It is much better to peer through the glass lid, and stir just once before serving or when adding extra ingredients towards the end of the cooking time.

TIPS

- As foods cook so slowly in a slow cooker, you can make use of cheaper beef cuts – such as blade, skirt, cheek or oxtail – without compromising on flavour. Don't forget neck of lamb on the bone or lamb breast, too. And bear in mind that chicken thighs taste better in the slow cooker than the more expensive chicken breasts.

- Foods will not brown in the slow cooker, so add colour to your stews by frying onions and meats first, adding various spices or herbs, tomatoes or tomato purée, wine or beer, gravy browning or even Marmite (yeast extract).

- Save on washing-up by puréeing soups while they are still in the slow cooker pot using a stick blender.

- Getting a steamed pudding out of the slow cooker pot can be tricky, especially if the basin is quite a snug fit in the pot. Tie string around the basin to make a handle and use it to lift the pudding dish out of the slow cooker pot. Alternatively, fold two pieces of foil individually to make two long straps. Form a cross with the straps and place them on the work surface, then place the pudding dish on the cross and use the lengths of foil to lift up and lower the dish into the slow cooker pot. Tuck the straps over the top of the basin, then use them to lift out the pudding dish at the end of the cooking time.

- Food at the bottom of the slow cooker pot will cook more quickly than the rest, so add diced potatoes to the pot first, as these can take longer to cook than meat. Or, if you are adding lots of root vegetables, cut them into chunks the same size or slightly smaller than the meat you are using and mix up the meat and vegetable chunks.

- Short of time? Then cheat! Add a jar or can of ready-made sauce instead of making your own.

FOR THE FREEZER

The majority of soups and stews in this book can be frozen successfully, and if you don't have a large family or if you live on your own, freezing individual portions for another meal can be a great time saver.

After all, it requires only a little extra effort to make a larger casserole for four people than it does to make one for two. Thaw portions in the refrigerator overnight or at room temperature for 4 hours, then reheat thoroughly in a saucepan on the hob or in the microwave on full power.

If you are using raw frozen foods make sure that they are thoroughly thawed before you add them to the slow cooker. Exceptions to this rule are frozen peas and sweetcorn. Raw food that was frozen and is then thawed and cooked in the slow cooker can be refrozen in its cooked and cooled state.

CARING FOR YOUR SLOW COOKER

If you look after it carefully, you may find that your machine will last for 20 years or more. Because the heat of a slow cooker is so controllable, it is not like a saucepan with burned-on grime to contend with. Simply lift the slow cooker pot out of the housing, fill it with hot soapy water and leave to soak for a while. Although it is tempting to pop the slow cooker pot and lid into the dishwasher, they do take up a lot of space, and check with your manual first, because not all are dishwasher-proof.

Allow the machine itself to cool down before cleaning. Turn it off at the controls and pull out the plug. Wipe the inside with a damp dishcloth, removing any stubborn marks with a little cream cleaner. The outside of the machine and the controls can be wiped with a dishcloth, then buffed up with a duster or, if it has a chrome-effect finish, sprayed with a little multi-surface cleaner and polished with a duster. Never immerse the machine in water to clean it. If you are storing the slow cooker in a cupboard, make sure it is completely cold before you put it away.

BREAKFASTS & BRUNCHES

BREAKFAST BAKED TOMATOES ♥

Serves **4**
Preparation time **10 minutes**
Cooking temperature **low**
Cooking time **8–10 hours**
   or **overnight**

500 g (1 lb) **plum tomatoes**,
   halved lengthways
leaves from 2–3 **thyme sprigs**
1 tablespoon **balsamic vinegar**
salt and **pepper**
chopped **parsley**, to garnish
4 slices of **wholemeal bread**,
   40 g (1½ oz) each, to serve

Preheat the slow cooker if necessary. Arrange the tomatoes, cut sides up, in the slow cooker pot, packing them in tightly in a single layer. Sprinkle with the thyme, drizzle with the vinegar and season to taste. Cover and cook on low for 8–10 hours or overnight.

Toast the bread the next morning and place on 4 serving plates. Top with the tomatoes and a little of the juice and serve sprinkled with parsley.

FOR BALSAMIC TOMATOES WITH SPAGHETTI, follow the recipe above to cook the tomatoes, then chop them and mix with the cooking juices. Cook 200 g (7 oz) dried spaghetti in a large saucepan of lightly salted boiling water according to the packet instructions until just tender, then drain and toss with the tomatoes. Sprinkle each portion with 1 tablespoon freshly grated Parmesan cheese.

EGGS EN COCOTTE WITH SALMON

Serves **4**
Preparation time **10 minutes**
Cooking temperature **high**
Cooking time **40–45 minutes**

25 g (1 oz) **butter**
4 **eggs**
4 tablespoons **double cream**
2 teaspoons chopped **chives**
1 teaspoon chopped **tarragon**
200 g (7 oz) **sliced smoked salmon**
salt and **pepper**
4 **lemon** wedges, to garnish
4 slices of **toast**, halved diagonally,
    to serve

Preheat the slow cooker if necessary. Liberally butter the inside of 4 ramekins, each 150 ml (¼ pint), checking first that they will fit in the slow cooker pot.

Break an egg into each dish. Drizzle the cream over the eggs and sprinkle over the herbs and a little salt and pepper. Transfer the ramekins to the slow cooker pot and pour boiling water into the pot to come halfway up the sides of the ramekins.

Cover with the lid (there is no need to cover the dishes with foil) and cook on high for 40–45 minutes or until the egg whites are set and the yolks still slightly soft.

Lift the dishes carefully out of the slow cooker pot with a tea towel and transfer to plates with the smoked salmon. Garnish with the lemon wedges and serve with the triangles of toast.

FOR SPICED EGGS EN COCOTTE, break the eggs into buttered dishes and drizzle over each 1 tablespoon double cream, a few drops of Tabasco sauce and some salt and pepper. Sprinkle 3 teaspoons finely chopped coriander over the dishes and cook as above. Serve with toast and thin slices of pastrami.

BIG BREAKFAST BONANZA

Serves **4**
Preparation time **20 minutes**
Cooking temperature **low**
Cooking time **9–10 hours** or **overnight**

1 tablespoon **sunflower oil**
12 **herby chipolata sausages**, about 400 g (13 oz) in total
1 **onion**, thinly sliced
500 g (1 lb) **potatoes**, cut into 2.5 cm (1 inch) chunks
375 g (12 oz) **tomatoes**, roughly chopped
125 g (4 oz) **black pudding**, skinned and cut into chunks
250 ml (8 fl oz) **vegetable stock**
2 tablespoons **Worcestershire sauce**
1 teaspoon **English mustard**
2–3 **thyme sprigs**, plus extra to garnish
salt and **pepper**

Preheat the slow cooker if necessary. Heat the oil in a frying pan, add the sausages and brown on one side, then turn and add the onion. Fry, turning the sausages and stirring the onions, until the sausages are browned but not cooked.

Add the potatoes, tomatoes and black pudding to the slow cooker pot. Lift the sausages and onion from the pan with a slotted spoon and transfer to the slow cooker pot. Pour off the excess fat, then add the stock, Worcestershire sauce and mustard. Tear the leaves from the thyme sprigs and add to the pan with some salt and pepper. Bring to the boil and pour over the sausages.

Press the potatoes down so that the liquid covers them. Cover with the lid and cook on low for 9–10 hours or overnight. Stir before serving and garnish with extra thyme leaves.

FOR A VEGETARIAN BIG BREAKFAST, fry 400 g (13 oz) meat-free sausages in the oil with the onion as above. Add the potatoes and tomatoes to the slow cooker pot with 125 g (4 oz) halved button mushrooms instead of the black pudding. Heat the stock with the mustard and thyme and add 1 tablespoon tomato purée instead of the Worcestershire sauce. Season with salt and pepper, then pour the mixture over the sausages in the slow cooker. Cover and cook as above.

EASY SAUSAGE & BEANS

Serves **4**
Preparation time **15 minutes**
Cooking temperature **low**
Cooking time **9–10 hours** or **overnight**

1 tablespoon **sunflower oil**
1 **onion**, chopped
½ teaspoon **smoked paprika**
2 × 410 g (13½ oz) cans **baked beans**
2 teaspoons **wholegrain mustard**
2 tablespoons **Worcestershire sauce**
6 tablespoons **vegetable stock**
2 **tomatoes**, roughly chopped
½ **red pepper**, cored, deseeded and diced
350 g (11½ oz) **frankfurters**, chilled and thickly sliced
salt and **pepper**

Preheat the slow cooker if necessary. Heat the oil in a frying pan, add the onion and fry, stirring, for 5 minutes or until softened and just beginning to turn golden.

Stir in the paprika and cook for 1 minute, then mix in the beans, mustard, Worcestershire sauce and stock. Bring to the boil, then stir in the tomatoes, red pepper and a little salt and pepper.

Add the frankfurters to the slow cooker pot and tip the baked bean mixture over the top. Cover with the lid and cook on low for 9–10 hours or overnight.

Stir well, then spoon into shallow bowls and serve with hot buttered toast fingers, if liked.

FOR CHILLIED SAUSAGE & BEANS, fry the onion in the oil as above, then add ½ teaspoon crushed dried red chillies, ¼ teaspoon cumin seeds, roughly crushed in a pestle and mortar, and a pinch of ground cinnamon with the smoked paprika. Omit the mustard and Worcestershire sauce, then continue as above, adding the beans, stock, tomatoes, red pepper and frankfurters. Cook on low for 9–10 hours or overnight.

BAKED EGGS WITH TOAST FINGERS

Serves **4**
Preparation time **15 minutes**
Cooking temperature **high**
Cooking time **40–50 minutes**

25 g (1 oz) **butter**
4 wafer-thin slices of **honey roast ham**, about 65 g (2½ oz) in total
4 teaspoons **spicy tomato chutney**
4 **eggs**
2 **cherry tomatoes**, halved
1 **spring onion**, finely sliced
salt and **pepper**
4 slices of **buttered toast**, cut into fingers, to serve

Preheat the slow cooker if necessary. Grease 4 heatproof dishes, each 150 ml (¼ pint), with a little of the butter, checking first that they will fit in the slow cooker pot, then press a slice of ham into each to line the base and sides, leaving a small overhang of ham above the dish.

Add 1 teaspoon of chutney to the base of each dish, then break an egg on top. Add a cherry tomato half to each, sprinkle with the spring onion and a little salt and pepper, then dot with the remaining butter.

Cover each dish with a square of foil and put them into the slow cooker pot. Pour boiling water into the pot to come halfway up the sides of the dishes. Cover with the lid and cook on high for 40–50 minutes or until the egg whites are set and the yolks still slightly soft.

Lift the dishes out of the slow cooker pot using a tea towel and remove the foil. Loosen between the ham and the edge of the dishes with a knife and turn out. Quickly turn the baked eggs the right way up and arrange each one on a plate with the hot buttered toast fingers.

FOR EGGS BENEDICT, butter 4 dishes as above, then break an egg into each one, sprinkle with salt and pepper and the spring onion and dot with the remaining butter. Cover with foil and cook as above. To serve, grill 8 back bacon rashers until golden. Spread 4 toasted, halved English breakfast muffins with butter, divide the bacon between the bottom halves and arrange on serving plates. Top with the baked eggs and remaining muffin halves and serve drizzled with 150 ml (¼ pint) warmed ready-made hollandaise sauce.

BRUNCH POACHED EGGS & HADDOCK ♥

Serves **2**
Preparation time **5 minutes**
Cooking temperature **high**
Cooking time **1–1¼ hours**

low-calorie cooking oil spray
2 eggs
1 teaspoon chopped **chives**, plus
    extra to garnish
2 **smoked haddock steaks**, 125 g
    (4 oz) each
450 ml (¾ pint) boiling **water**
125 g (4 oz) **baby spinach**
salt and **pepper**

Preheat the slow cooker if necessary. Spray the insides of 2 small ovenproof dishes or ramekins with a little low-calorie cooking oil spray, then break an egg into each. Sprinkle with a few chives and season to taste.

Place the egg dishes in the centre of the slow cooker pot, then arrange a fish steak on each side. Pour the measurement boiling water over the fish so that the water comes halfway up the sides of the dishes. Cover and cook on high for 1–1¼ hours until the eggs are done to your liking and the fish flakes easily when pressed in the centre with a small knife.

Rinse the spinach with a little water, drain and place in a microwave-proof dish. Cover and cook in a microwave on full power for 1 minute until just wilted. Divide between 2 serving plates, and top with the fish steaks. Loosen the eggs with a knife and turn out of their dishes on top of the fish. Sprinkle with extra chopped chives, season with salt and pepper and serve.

FOR BRUNCH POACHED EGGS WITH SALMON, follow the recipe above, using 2 wild salmon steaks, 100 g (3½ oz) each, instead of the smoked haddock. Arrange 2 sliced tomatoes on the serving plates, top with the cooked salmon and eggs and serve.

BANANA & CINNAMON PORRIDGE

Serves **4**
Preparation time **5 minutes**
Cooking temperature **low**
Cooking time **1** or **2 hours**

600 ml (1 pint) boiling **water**
300 ml (½ pint) **UHT milk**
150 g (5 oz) **porridge oats**
2 **bananas**
4 tablespoons **light** or **dark
    muscovado sugar**
¼ teaspoon **ground cinnamon**

Preheat the slow cooker if necessary. Pour the measurement boiling water and milk into the slow cooker pot, then stir in the oats.

Cover with the lid and cook on low for 1 hour for 'runny' porridge or 2 hours for 'thick' porridge.

Spoon into bowls, then slice the bananas and divide between the bowls. Mix together the sugar and cinnamon and sprinkle over the top.

FOR HOT SPICED MUESLI, follow the recipe as above, adding 175 g (6 oz) Swiss-style muesli. When cooked, stir in ¼ teaspoon ground cinnamon and top with 100 g (3½ oz) diced ready-to-eat dried apricots. Drizzle over 2 tablespoons clear honey before serving.

OATMEAL & MIXED SEED GRANOLA ♥

Serves **4**
Preparation time **10 minutes**
Cooking temperature **high**
Cooking time **2½–3 hours**

125 g (4 oz) **medium oatmeal**
50 g (2 oz) **jumbo porridge oats**
25 g (1 oz) **pumpkin seeds**
25 g (1 oz) **sunflower seeds**
15 g (½ oz) **golden linseeds**
¼ teaspoon **ground cinnamon**
1 tablespoon **olive oil**
3 tablespoons **date syrup**
juice of ½ **orange**
25 g (1 oz) **dried goji berries**

TO SERVE
600 ml (1 pint) **skimmed milk**
sliced **banana**
sliced **strawberries**
raspberries

Preheat the slow cooker if necessary. Place the oatmeal, porridge oats and seeds in the slow cooker pot and stir well. Add the cinnamon, olive oil, date syrup and orange juice and mix again until thoroughly combined. Cover and cook on high for 1½–2 hours, stirring once or twice with a fork to break the mixture into clumps.

Remove the lid and cook for 1 hour more until the granola is crisp. Break up once more with a fork, add the goji berries, then leave to cool. Store in an airtight jar in the refrigerator until ready to serve.

Serve in bowls, topped with the skimmed milk and fruit.

FOR HONEYED OATMEAL & FRUIT GRANOLA, follow the recipe above, omitting the pumpkin seeds and using 3 tablespoons clear honey instead of the date syrup. Add 25 g (1 oz) dried cranberries and 25 g (1 oz) dried cherries instead of the goji berries and serve as above.

VANILLA BREAKFAST PRUNES & FIGS

Serves **4**
Preparation time **5 minutes**
Cooking temperature **low**
Cooking time **8–10 hours**
  or **overnight**

1 **English breakfast teabag**
600 ml (1 pint) boiling **water**
150 g (5 oz) **ready-to-eat**
  pitted prunes
150 g (5 oz) **dried figs**
75 g (3 oz) **caster sugar**
1 teaspoon **vanilla extract**
pared rind of ½ **orange**

TO SERVE
natural yogurt
muesli

Preheat the slow cooker if necessary. Put the teabag into a jug or teapot, add the measurement boiling water and leave to brew for 2–3 minutes. Remove the teabag and pour the tea into the slow cooker pot.

Add the whole prunes and figs, the sugar and vanilla extract to the hot tea, sprinkle with the orange rind and mix together. Cover with the lid and cook on low for 8–10 hours or overnight.

Serve hot with spoonfuls of natural yogurt and a sprinkling of muesli.

FOR BREAKFAST APRICOTS IN ORANGE, put 300 g (10 oz) ready-to-eat dried apricots, 50 g (2 oz) caster sugar, 300 ml (½ pint) boiling water and 150 ml (¼ pint) orange juice in the slow cooker. Cover and cook as above.

BERRY COMPOTE WITH SYLLABUB CREAM

Serves **4**
Preparation time **20 minutes,**
   plus cooling
Cooking temperature **low**
Cooking time **1½–2 hours**

500 g (1 lb) **strawberries**, hulled and
   halved or quartered if large
200 g (7 oz) **blueberries**
grated rind and juice of 1 **lemon**
3 tablespoons **caster sugar**
3 tablespoons **water**
lemon rind curls or small **herb** or
   pansy flowers, to decorate

SYLLABUB CREAM
150 ml (¼ pint) **double cream**
2 tablespoons **caster sugar**
grated rind of ½ **lemon**
2 tablespoons **dry white wine**

Preheat the slow cooker if necessary. Put the strawberries, blueberries, lemon rind and juice, sugar and measurement water into the slow cooker pot. Cover with the lid and cook on low for 1½–2 hours or until the fruit is tender but still holds its shape.

Lift the pot out of the housing using oven gloves and leave the compote to cool. Just before serving, make the syllabub cream. Pour the cream into a bowl, add the sugar and lemon rind and whisk until it forms soft swirls. Add the white wine and whisk for a further 1–2 minutes or until thick again.

Spoon the fruit into tall champagne-style glasses and top with spoonfuls of the syllabub cream. Decorate with lemon rind curls or small herb or pansy flowers and serve immediately.

FOR PEACH COMPOTE WITH VANILLA, halve and stone 6 firm, ripe peaches, then add to the slow cooker pot with 75 g (3 oz) caster sugar, 150 ml (¼ pint) Marsala or sweet sherry, 150 ml (¼ pint) water and a slit vanilla pod. Cover and cook as above. Transfer the peaches to a serving dish. Scrape the seeds from the vanilla pod and add to the syrup, then discard the pod. Mix 2 teaspoons cornflour with a little cold water to make a smooth paste, stir into the syrup in the slow cooker pot, replace the lid and cook on high for 15 minutes. Stir well, then pour over the peaches. Sprinkle with 125 g (4 oz) raspberries and leave to cool. Serve with spoonfuls of crème fraîche.

TOFFEE APPLE PANCAKES

Serves **4–6**
Preparation time **10 minutes**
Cooking temperature **high**
Cooking time **1–1½ hours**

50 g (2 oz) **butter**
75 g (3 oz) **light muscovado sugar**
2 tablespoons **golden syrup**
4 **dessert apples**, cored and each cut
   into 8 slices
juice of 1 **lemon**
375 g (12 oz) pack or 6
   ready-made pancakes
vanilla ice cream, to serve

Preheat the slow cooker if necessary. Heat the butter, sugar and syrup in a saucepan or in a microwave-proof bowl in the microwave until the butter has just melted.

Add the apples and lemon juice to the slow cooker pot and toss together. Stir the butter mixture and pour it over the apples. Cover with the lid and cook on high for 1–1½ hours or until the apples are tender but still holding their shape.

Heat the pancakes in a frying pan or the microwave according to the pack instructions. Fold in half and arrange on serving plates. Stir the apple mixture, then spoon it on to the pancakes. Top with scoops of vanilla ice cream.

FOR TOFFEE BANANA PANCAKES, make up the recipe as above, replacing the apples with 6 small, thickly sliced bananas and adding 150 ml (¼ pint) boiling water. When ready to serve, reheat 6 pancakes, spread with 3 tablespoons chocolate and hazelnut spread, then top with the bananas and ice cream.

PANCAKES WITH FRUIT COMPOTE ♥

Serves **4**
Preparation time **15 minutes**
Cooking temperature **high** and **low**
Cooking time **2–2½ hours**

300 g (10 oz) **ripe red plums**, halved,
   stoned and diced
1 **dessert apple**, quartered, cored
   and diced
150 g (5 oz) **blackberries**
¼ teaspoon **ground cinnamon**, plus
   extra to decorate
1 tablespoon **granular sweetener**
3 tablespoons **water**
150 g (5 oz) **fromage frais**, to serve

PANCAKES
75 g (3 oz) **plain flour**
1 **egg** and 1 **egg yolk**
200 ml (7 fl oz) **skimmed milk**
sunflower or **vegetable oil**, for oiling

Preheat the slow cooker if necessary. Place all the compote ingredients in the slow cooker pot, stir well, cover and cook on high for 2–2½ hours until the fruits have softened.

Meanwhile, make the pancake batter. Place the flour in a large bowl, create a well in the middle and add the whole egg, egg yolk and milk. Whisk, starting from the centre and gradually drawing the flour into the eggs and milk. Once all the flour is incorporated, beat until you have a smooth, thick batter. Leave to stand for 30 minutes.

When ready to serve, heat an 18 cm (7 inch) frying pan over a medium heat, wipe it with oiled kitchen paper and ladle some of the pancake batter into the pan, tilting the pan to move the batter around for a thin and even layer. Leave to cook for at least 30 seconds before flipping the pancake over to cook on the other side. Transfer to a plate and keep warm. The batter will make 4 pancakes. Alternatively, use 4 ready-made pancakes, 50 g (2 oz) each and heat in a frying pan or microwave according to the pack instructions.

Place each pancake on a serving plate. Top with the fruit compote, then fold the pancakes in half and spoon the fromage frais on top. Sprinkle with a little extra cinnamon and serve immediately.

FOR ORCHARD FRUIT SUNDAES, follow the recipe above to make the fruit compote and leave to cool. Spoon into 4 glasses, top with 250 g (8 oz) fromage frais and drizzle each portion with 2 teaspoons maple syrup.

STARTERS

LETTUCE WRAPPERS

Serves **4**
Preparation time **20 minutes**
Cooking temperature **low**
Cooking time **8–9 hours**

1 tablespoon **sunflower oil**
750 g (1½ lb) **stewing beef**, cut into
    small cubes
1 **onion**, chopped
2 **garlic cloves**, finely chopped
2 tablespoons **plain flour**
350 ml (12 fl oz) **beef stock**
1 teaspoon **crushed dried red chillies**
½ teaspoon **chilli powder**
2 tablespoons **soy sauce**
2 tablespoons **hoisin sauce**
2 tablespoons **rice vinegar**
1 tablespoon **dark muscovado sugar**
pepper

TO SERVE
1 **iceberg lettuce**
1 small **red onion**, thinly sliced
small handful of **coriander**,
    roughly chopped

Preheat the slow cooker if necessary. Heat the oil in a large frying pan, add the beef a few pieces at a time, then fry over a high heat, stirring, until browned.

Add the onion and garlic and fry for 3–4 minutes until softened. Sprinkle over the flour and mix it in, then gradually mix in the stock. Sprinkle over the chillies and chilli powder, then stir in the soy and hoisin sauces, vinegar and sugar. Season with a little pepper.

Bring to the boil, then transfer to the slow cooker pot. Press the meat beneath the liquid, cover with the lid and cook on low for 8–9 hours until the beef is tender.

Separate the lettuce leaves, spoon a little of the beef into each lettuce cup, then sprinkle with the red onion and coriander. To eat, you fold the leaves over the beef filling to pick up the parcels or eat them with a knife and fork.

FOR BEEF 'PEKING DUCK' WRAPPERS, make and cook the beef as above. Warm 16 Chinese pancakes in a steamer according to the packet instructions. Separate the pancakes, then top with spoonfuls of the hot beef, ½ cucumber, cut into matchstick strips, and a bunch of spring onions, cut into matchstick strips. Roll up and serve immediately.

AUBERGINE TIMBALE

Serves **2**
Preparation time **25 minutes**
Cooking temperature **high**
Cooking time **1½–2 hours**

4 tablespoons **olive oil**, plus extra
   for oiling
1 large **aubergine**, thinly sliced
1 small **onion**, chopped
1 **garlic clove**, finely chopped
½ teaspoon **ground cinnamon**
¼ teaspoon grated **nutmeg**
25 g (1 oz) **pistachio nuts**,
   roughly chopped
25 g (1 oz) **pitted dates**,
   roughly chopped
25 g (1 oz) **ready-to-eat dried
   apricots**, roughly chopped
75 g (3 oz) **easy-cook white
   long-grain rice**
300 ml (½ pint) boiling
   vegetable stock
salt and **pepper**

Preheat the slow cooker if necessary. Lightly oil the base of 2 soufflé dishes, each 350 ml (12 fl oz), and base-line each with a circle of nonstick baking paper, checking first that they will fit in the slow cooker pot.

Heat 1 tablespoon of the oil in a large frying pan, add one-third of the aubergines and fry on both sides until softened and golden. Scoop out of the pan with a slotted spoon and transfer to a plate. Repeat with the rest of the aubergines using 2 more tablespoons of oil.

Heat the remaining 1 tablespoon of oil in the pan, add the onion and fry for 5 minutes or until softened. Stir in the garlic, spices, nuts, fruit and rice. Add a little salt and pepper and mix well.

Arrange one-third of the aubergine slices in the base of the 2 dishes, overlapping the slices. Spoon one-quarter of the rice mixture into each dish, add a second layer of aubergine slices, then divide the remaining rice equally between the dishes. Top with the remaining aubergine slices. Pour the stock into the dishes, cover with lightly oiled foil and put in the slow cooker pot.

Pour boiling water into the pot to come halfway up the sides of the dishes. Cover with the lid and cook on high for 1½–2 hours or until the rice is tender. Lift the dishes out of the slow cooker pot using a tea towel and remove the foil. Loosen the edges of the timbales with a knife, turn out on to plates and peel off the lining paper. Serve hot with a green salad and baked tomatoes, if liked.

STICKY RIBS

Serves **4**
Preparation time **20 minutes**
Cooking temperature **high**
Cooking time **5–6 hours**

1.4 kg (2¾ lb) **pork ribs**
1 **onion**, quartered
2 **carrots**, thickly sliced
1 teaspoon **dried mixed herbs**
2 tablespoons **malt vinegar**
1 litre (1¾ pints) boiling **water**
salt and **pepper**

GLAZE
2 tablespoons **tomato ketchup**
2 tablespoons **thick-set honey**
2 tablespoons **Worcestershire sauce**
1 teaspoon **Dijon mustard**

Preheat the slow cooker if necessary. Add the ribs, onion and carrots to the slow cooker pot, then scatter over the dried herbs. Mix the vinegar into the measurement boiling water, pour the mixture into the pot, then season with salt and pepper.

Cover and cook on high for 5–6 hours or until the meat is almost falling off the bone.

Line a grill pan with foil, lift the ribs out of the slow cooker pot with a draining spoon, arrange them in a single layer on the foil, then add a ladleful of the cooking liquid.

Mix the ingredients for the glaze together, then brush the mixture over the ribs. Cook under a preheated medium grill for 10 minutes, turning and brushing once or twice, until covered with a sticky glaze.

Arrange the ribs on serving plates and serve with coleslaw and baked beans, if liked.

FOR COLA RIBS, bring 1 litre (1¾ pints) cola to the boil in a saucepan, then pour it over the ribs and vegetables instead of the vinegar and boiling water. Cover, cook and glaze as above.

BRANDIED DUCK & WALNUT TERRINE

Serves **6**

Preparation time **45 minutes**, plus **cooling** and **overnight chilling**

Cooking temperature **high**

Cooking time **5–6 hours**

175 g (6 oz) **rindless smoked streaky bacon rashers**

1 tablespoon **olive oil**

1 **onion**, chopped

2 **boneless spare rib pork chops**, about 275 g (9 oz) in total

2 **boneless duck breasts**, about 375 g (12 oz) in total, fat removed

2 **garlic cloves**, chopped

3 tablespoons **brandy**

75 g (3 oz) **fresh breadcrumbs**

50 g (2 oz) **sun-dried tomatoes in oil**, drained and chopped

3 **pickled walnuts**, drained and roughly chopped

1 **egg**, beaten

1 tablespoon **green peppercorns**, roughly crushed

salt

Preheat the slow cooker if necessary. Lay the bacon rashers on a chopping board and stretch each one with the flat of a large cook's knife until half as long again. Line the base and sides of a 15 cm (6 inch) diameter, deep soufflé dish with the bacon, checking first that the dish will fit in the slow cooker pot.

Heat the oil in a frying pan, add the onion and fry, stirring, for 5 minutes. Finely chop or mince the pork and 1 of the duck breasts. Cut the second duck breast into long, thin slices and set aside. Stir the garlic and minced or chopped meat into the pan and cook for 3 minutes. Add the brandy, flame with a match and stand well back until the flames subside.

Stir in the remaining ingredients. Mix well, then press half the mixture into the bacon-lined dish. Top with the sliced duck, then add the remaining mixture. Fold the bacon ends over the top, adding any leftover rashers to cover the gaps. Cover with foil.

Place the dish on an upturned saucer in the base of the slow cooker pot. Pour boiling water around the dish to come halfway up the sides. Cover with the lid and cook on high for 5–6 hours or until the meat juices run clear when the centre of the terrine is pierced with a knife.

Lift the dish carefully out of the pot using a tea towel, stand on a plate, remove the foil top and replace with greaseproof paper. Weigh down the top of the terrine with measuring weights set on a small plate. Transfer to the refrigerator when cool enough and chill overnight.

To serve, remove the greaseproof paper, then loosen the edge of the terrine with a knife, turn out on to a chopping board and cut into thick slices.

BAKED PEPPERS WITH CHORIZO ♥

Serves **4**
Preparation time **20 minutes**
Cooking temperature **high**
Cooking time **3–4 hours**

2 large **red peppers**, halved
   lengthways, cored
   and deseeded
2 **spring onions**, thinly sliced
50 g (2 oz) **chorizo**, skinned and
   finely diced
200 g (7 oz) **cherry tomatoes**, halved
1–2 **garlic cloves**, finely chopped
small handful of **basil**, torn, plus extra
   to garnish
4 pinches of **smoked hot paprika**
1 tablespoon **balsamic vinegar**
salt and **pepper**

Preheat the slow cooker if necessary. Arrange the peppers, cut sides up, in a single layer in the base of the slow cooker pot. Divide the spring onions and chorizo between the peppers, then pack in the cherry tomatoes.

Sprinkle with the garlic and torn basil, then add a pinch of paprika and a drizzle of balsamic vinegar to each one. Season to taste, cover and cook on high for 3–4 hours until the peppers have softened.

Transfer to a platter and sprinkle with extra basil leaves. Serve hot or cold as a light lunch with salad, if liked.

FOR BAKED PEPPER PIZZAS, follow the recipe above, omitting the chorizo and paprika. When cooked, transfer the peppers to a shallow ovenproof dish. Tear 150 g (5 oz) mozzarella cheese into small pieces, sprinkle over the peppers, then place under a preheated hot grill for 1–2 minutes until the cheese is bubbling and golden. Garnish with extra torn basil and 4 pitted black olives.

TOMATO, PEPPER & GARLIC BRUSCHETTA ♥

Serves **4**
Preparation time **20 minutes**
Cooking temperature **high**
Cooking time **3–5 hours**

1 large **red pepper**, quartered, cored and deseeded
500 g (1 lb) **plum tomatoes**, halved
4 large **garlic cloves**, unpeeled
leaves from 2–3 **thyme sprigs**
1 teaspoon **granular sweetener**
1 tablespoon **virgin olive oil**
8 slices of **French bread**, 175 g (6 oz) in total
8 **pitted black olives in brine**, drained
salt and **pepper**

Preheat the slow cooker if necessary. Arrange the pepper pieces, skin side down, in the base of the slow cooker pot, arrange the tomatoes on top, then tuck the garlic cloves in among them. Scatter the thyme leaves on top, reserving a little to garnish. Sprinkle with the sweetener and drizzle with the oil.

Season to taste, cover and cook on high for 3–5 hours until the vegetables are tender but the tomatoes still hold their shape.

Lift the vegetables out of the slow cooker pot with a slotted spoon. Peel the skins off the peppers, tomatoes and garlic, then roughly chop the vegetables and toss together. Adjust the seasoning if necessary.

Toast the bread on both sides, arrange on a serving plate, then spoon the tomato mixture on top. Arrange the olives and reserved thyme on the bruschetta and serve as a light lunch or starter.

FOR QUICK TOMATO & PEPPER PIZZAS, follow the recipe above to cook the tomato and pepper mixture, then spoon on to 2 halved and toasted ciabatta rolls. Sprinkle with 50 g (2 oz) grated reduced-fat Cheddar cheese and place under a preheated hot grill to melt the cheese. Serve with salad.

BEERY CHEESE FONDUE

Serves **4**
Preparation time **15 minutes**
Cooking temperature **high**
Cooking time **40–60 minutes**

15 g (½ oz) **butter**
2 **shallots** or ½ small **onion**, finely chopped
1 **garlic clove**, finely chopped
3 teaspoons **cornflour**
200 ml (7 fl oz) **blonde beer** or **lager**
200 g (7 oz) **Gruyère cheese** (rind removed), grated
175 g (6 oz) **Emmental cheese** (rind removed), grated
grated **nutmeg**
salt and **pepper**

TO SERVE
½ **wholemeal French stick**, cubed
2 **celery sticks**, cut into short lengths
8 small **pickled onions**, drained and halved
bunch of **radishes**, tops trimmed
1 **red pepper**, cored, deseeded and cubed
2 **endives**, leaves separated

Preheat the slow cooker if necessary. Butter the inside of the slow cooker pot, then add the shallots or onion and garlic.

Put the cornflour in a small bowl and mix with a little of the beer to make a smooth paste, then blend with the remaining beer. Add to the slow cooker with both cheeses, nutmeg and some salt and pepper.

Stir together, then cover with the lid and cook on high for 40–60 minutes, whisking once during cooking. Whisk again and serve with the dippers arranged on a serving plate, with long fondue or ordinary forks for dunking the dippers into the fondue.

FOR CLASSIC CHEESE FONDUE, omit the beer from the above ingredients and add 175 ml (6 fl oz) dry white wine and 1 tablespoon kirsch. Cook as above and serve with bread to dip.

DUCK, PORK & APPLE RILLETTES

Serves **4**
Preparation time **30 minutes, plus
cooling** and **overnight chilling**
Cooking temperature **high**
Cooking time **5–6 hours**

2 **duck legs**
500 g (1 lb) **rindless belly pork
rashers**, halved
1 **onion**, cut into wedges
1 **tart dessert apple**, such as
Granny Smith, peeled, cored
and thickly sliced
2–3 **thyme sprigs**
250 ml (8 fl oz) **chicken stock**
150 ml (¼ pint) **dry cider**
salt and **pepper**

Preheat the slow cooker if necessary. Put the duck and belly pork into the base of the slow cooker pot. Tuck the onion and apple between the pieces of meat and add the thyme.

Pour the stock and cider into a saucepan and add plenty of salt and pepper. Bring to the boil, then pour into the slow cooker pot. Cover with the lid and cook on high for 5–6 hours or until the duck and pork are cooked through and tender.

Lift the meat out of the slow cooker pot with a slotted spoon and transfer to a large plate, then leave to cool for 30 minutes. Peel away the duck skin and remove the bones. Shred the meat into small pieces and discard the thyme sprigs. Scoop out the apple and onion with a slotted spoon, finely chop and mix with the meat, then taste and adjust the seasoning, if needed.

Pack the chopped meat mix into 4 individual dishes or small preserving jars and press down firmly. Spoon over the juices from the slow cooker pot to cover and seal the meat. Leave to cool, then transfer to the refrigerator and chill overnight.

When the fat has solidified on the top, cover each dish with a lid or clingfilm and store in the refrigerator for up to 1 week. Serve the rillettes with warm crusty bread, a few radishes and pickled shallots, if liked.

FOR CHICKEN, PORK & PRUNE RILLETTES, omit the duck and put 2 chicken leg joints into the slow cooker pot with the belly pork rashers, onion and thyme, replacing the apple with 75 g (3 oz) ready-to-eat pitted prunes. Continue as above.

GARLICKY PORK & SAGE PÂTÉ

Serves **6–8**
Preparation time **30 minutes, plus
    cooling** and **overnight chilling**
Cooking temperature **high**
Cooking time **5–6 hours**

bunch of **sage**
1 tablespoon **olive oil**, plus extra
    for oiling
1 small **onion**, chopped
400 g (13 oz) or 6 **Toulouse
    sausages**, skins slit and removed
75 g (3 oz) **smoked streaky bacon
    rashers**, diced
200 g (7 oz) **boneless belly pork
    rashers**, finely diced
150 g (5 oz) **chicken livers**, rinsed
    with cold water and drained
1 **egg**, beaten
2 tablespoons **sherry vinegar**
salt and **pepper**

Preheat the slow cooker if necessary. Oil a 900 ml (1½ pint) rectangular heatproof dish and line the base and 2 long sides with nonstick baking paper, checking first that it will fit in the slow cooker pot. Cover the base with sage leaves, reserving the remainder.

Heat the oil in a frying pan, add the onion and fry until softened. Transfer to a bowl and add the sausages, bacon and diced pork. Chop the drained chicken livers, discarding the white cores. Add to the bowl with the egg, vinegar and plenty of salt and pepper. Mix together, then spoon half the mixture into the dish and press down firmly.

Arrange more sage leaves over the pâté, then cover with the remaining mixture. Press down firmly and arrange any remaining sage leaves on the top. Cover loosely with foil and stand the dish in the slow cooker pot. Pour boiling water into the pot to come halfway up the sides of the dish. Cover with the lid or foil, and cook on high for 5–6 hours or until the meat juices run clear when the centre of the pâté is pierced with a knife.

Lift the dish out of the slow cooker pot using a tea towel, pour off the excess fat, stand the dish on a plate, then cover the top with a second plate and weigh down with measuring weights. Leave to cool, then transfer to the refrigerator overnight.

To serve, remove the weights, plate and foil. Loosen the edges of the pâté with a knife, then turn out on to a chopping board and peel off the lining paper. Cut into slices and serve with toasted bread and salad, if liked.

FISH TERRINE

Serves **6–8**
Preparation time **30 minutes,
  plus cooling**
Cooking temperature **high**
Cooking time **3–4 hours**

sunflower or **vegetable oil**, for oiling
375 g (12 oz) **skinless haddock** or
  cod loin, cubed
2 **egg whites**
grated rind of ½ **lemon**
juice of 1 **lemon**
250 ml (8 fl oz) **double cream**
125 g (4 oz) **sliced smoked salmon**
  or **trout**
150 g (5 oz) **salmon** or **trout fillet**,
  thinly sliced
salt and **pepper**

Preheat the slow cooker if necessary. Lightly oil a 1 litre (1¾ pint) soufflé dish and base-line with a circle of nonstick baking paper, checking first that the dish will fit in the slow cooker pot. Blend the haddock or cod loin, egg whites, lemon rind, half the lemon juice and salt and pepper in a food processor until roughly chopped, then gradually add the cream and blend until just beginning to thicken.

Arrange half the smoked fish slices over the base of the dish. Spoon in half the fish mousse and spread it level. Mix the fish fillet with a little remaining lemon juice and some pepper, then arrange on top. Top with the remaining fish mousse, then the smoked fish slices.

Cover the top with foil and lower into the slow cooker pot. Pour boiling water into the pot to come halfway up the sides of the dish. Cover with the lid and cook on high for 3–4 hours or until the fish is cooked through and the terrine is set.

Lift the dish out of the slow cooker pot using a tea towel and leave to cool for 2 hours. Loosen the edge, turn out on to a plate and peel off the lining paper. Cut into thick slices and serve with salad and toast, if liked.

FOR SMOKED HADDOCK & CHIVE TERRINE, make up the white fish mousse as above and flavour with 4 tablespoons chopped chives, 2 tablespoons chopped capers and the grated rind and juice of ½ lemon. Omit the smoked fish and arrange 1 sliced tomato over the base of the dish. Cover with half the fish mousse, 150 g (5 oz) thinly sliced smoked cod fillet, then the remaining fish mousse. Continue as above.

TURKEY & CRANBERRY MEATLOAF

Serves **4–6**
Preparation time **30 minutes, plus
  cooling** and **overnight chilling**
Cooking temperature **high**
Cooking time **5–6 hours**

200 g (7 oz) **rindless smoked streaky
  bacon rashers**
115 g (3¾ oz) pack **dried orange and
  cranberry stuffing mix**
25 g (1 oz) **dried cranberries**
1 tablespoon **sunflower oil**, plus extra
  for oiling
1 **onion**, finely chopped
500 g (1 lb) **skinless turkey
  breast steaks**
1 **egg**, beaten
salt and **pepper**

Preheat the slow cooker if necessary. Lightly oil a soufflé dish 14 cm (5½ inches) in diameter and 9 cm (3½ inches) deep, and base-line with nonstick baking paper, checking first that the dish will fit in the slow cooker pot. Lay the bacon rashers on a chopping board and stretch each one with the flat of a large cook's knife until half as long again. Use about three-quarters of the rashers to line the base and sides of the dish, trimming to fit.

Put the stuffing mix in a bowl, add the cranberries and mix with boiling water according to the pack instructions. Heat the oil in a frying pan, add the onion and fry for 5 minutes, stirring, until softened. Set aside. Finely chop the turkey steaks in a food processor or pass through a coarse mincer.

Mix the stuffing with the fried onion, chopped turkey and egg. Season well and spoon into the bacon-lined dish. Press flat and cover with the remaining bacon rashers. Cover the top of the dish with foil and lower into the slow cooker pot. Pour boiling water into the pot to come halfway up the sides of the dish. Cover with the lid and cook on high for 5–6 hours or until the juices run clear when the centre of the meatloaf is pierced with a knife.

Lift the dish out of the slow cooker pot using a tea towel and leave to cool. Transfer to the refrigerator to chill overnight until firm. Loosen the edge of the meatloaf with a knife, turn out on to a plate and peel off the lining paper. Cut into thick slices and serve with salad and spoonfuls of cranberry sauce or sweet chutney, if liked.

SMOKED SALMON TIMBALES

Serves **4**
Preparation time **30 minutes, plus
cooling** and **chilling**
Cooking temperature **low**
Cooking time **3–3½ hours**

butter, for greasing
200 ml (7 fl oz) **full-fat crème fraîche**
4 **egg yolks**
grated rind and juice of ½ **lemon**
1 small growing pot of **basil**
100 g (3½ oz) **sliced smoked salmon**
salt and **pepper**
lemon wedges, to garnish

Preheat the slow cooker if necessary. Lightly butter 4 individual metal moulds, each 150 ml (¼ pint), and base-line with circles of nonstick baking or greaseproof paper, checking first that they will fit in the slow cooker pot.

Put the crème fraîche in a bowl and gradually beat in the egg yolks. Add the lemon rind and juice and season with salt and pepper. Chop half the basil and 75 g (3 oz) of the smoked salmon, then stir both into the crème fraîche mixture.

Pour the mixture into the prepared moulds. Stand the moulds in the slow cooker pot (there is no need to cover them with foil). Pour hot water around the moulds to come halfway up the sides, cover with the lid and cook on low for 3–3½ hours or until the mixture is set.

Remove the moulds carefully from the slow cooker using a tea towel and leave to cool at room temperature. Transfer to the refrigerator and chill for at least 4 hours or overnight.

Loosen the edges of the timbales with a knife dipped in hot water, then invert on to serving plates and remove the moulds. Smooth any rough areas with the side of the knife and remove the lining discs. Top with the remaining smoked salmon and basil leaves and garnish with lemon wedges.

FOR SMOKED MACKEREL TIMBALES, omit the basil and smoked salmon and stir in 3 tablespoons freshly chopped chives, ½ teaspoon hot horseradish and 75 g (3 oz) skinned, flaked smoked mackerel fillets. Continue as above. Serve with salad.

LUNCHES &
LIGHT BITES

MUSHROOM & WHEATBERRY PILAU ♥

Serves **4**
Preparation time **20 minutes**
Cooking temperature **high**
Cooking time **3½–4 hours**

1 tablespoon **olive oil**
1 **onion**, thinly sliced
2 **garlic cloves**, finely chopped
325 ml (11 fl oz) **brown ale**
450 ml (¾ pint) **vegetable stock**
3 **sage sprigs**
¼ teaspoon grated **nutmeg**
5 cm (2 inch) **cinnamon stick**
1 tablespoon **sun-dried tomato paste**
200 g (7 oz) **wheatberries**
250 g (8 oz) **chestnut mushrooms**, halved
250 g (8 oz) large **closed-cap mushrooms**, quartered
salt and **pepper**
15 g (½ oz) **parsley**, roughly chopped, to garnish

Preheat the slow cooker if necessary. Heat the oil in a large frying pan over a medium heat until hot. Add the onion and fry for 4–5 minutes, stirring, until just beginning to soften. Add the garlic, brown ale, stock, sage, nutmeg and cinnamon. Stir in the tomato paste and season well, then bring to the boil.

Place the wheatberries and mushrooms in the slow cooker pot. Pour over the hot ale mixture, then cover and cook on high for 3½–4 hours until the wheatberries are tender and nearly all the liquid has been absorbed. Stir well, then sprinkle with the parsley. Spoon into shallow bowls to serve.

FOR RED PEPPER WHEATBERRY PILAU, fry 1 sliced red onion in the oil as above, then add 2 finely chopped garlic cloves and 2 cored, deseeded and sliced red peppers. Stir in 200 ml (7 fl oz) red wine, 600 ml (1 pint) vegetable stock, a small handful of basil leaves and 1 tablespoon sun-dried tomato paste. Season to taste and bring to the boil, then pour over the wheatberries in the slow cooker pot and cook as above.

WARM LENTIL & FETA SALAD

Serves **4**
Preparation time **20 minutes**
Cooking temperature **high**
Cooking time **3–4 hours**

150 g (5 oz) **dried Puy lentils**
1 **onion**, chopped
1 **red pepper**, cored, deseeded
 and sliced
250 g (8 oz) **cherry tomatoes**
600 ml (1 pint) boiling
 vegetable stock
2 tablespoons **tomato purée**
2 **thyme sprigs**
4 tablespoons **olive oil**
2 tablespoons **balsamic vinegar**
100 g (3½ oz) bag **watercress,
 spinach and rocket salad**
150 g (5 oz) **feta cheese**, crumbled
leaves from a small bunch of **mint**
salt and **pepper**

Preheat the slow cooker if necessary. Put the lentils into a sieve, rinse well with cold water, drain and add to the slow cooker pot along with the onion, red pepper and tomatoes.

Mix the boiling stock with the tomato purée, thyme and a generous amount of salt and pepper. Pour over the lentils, cover with the lid and cook on high for 3–4 hours or until the lentils are tender.

When almost ready to serve, fork the oil and balsamic vinegar together in a bowl, add the salad leaves and toss gently. Spoon the hot lentils into shallow bowls, draining off any excess cooking liquid. Pile the salad on top and sprinkle with the feta, mint leaves and a little extra pepper. Serve immediately with warmed pitta breads, if liked. Alternatively, lift the pot out of the housing using oven gloves, leave the lentils to go cold, then make the dressing and toss together with the salad leaves, feta and mint.

FOR LENTIL SALAD WITH SARDINES & PEAS, cook the lentils as above, adding 100 g (3½ oz) frozen peas for the last 15 minutes of cooking time. Drain 2 x 120 g (3¾ oz) cans sardines in tomato sauce, reserving the sauce. Flake the fish into chunky pieces, discarding the bones. Stir the sauce into the lentils. Shred 2 little gem lettuces and mix with ½ finely chopped red onion, then toss with the juice of 1 lemon, a small bunch of mint, roughly chopped, and salt and pepper. Spoon the hot lentils into shallow bowls and top with the sardines and the lettuce salad. Serve immediately.

WARM BEETROOT & BEAN SALAD

Serves **4–5**
Preparation time **25 minutes**
Cooking temperature **low**
Cooking time **3½–4½ hours**

1 tablespoon **olive oil**
1 large **onion**, chopped
500 g (1 lb) **raw beetroot**, peeled and finely diced
2 × 410 g (13½ oz) cans **borlotti beans**, rinsed and drained
450 ml (¾ pint) **vegetable stock**
salt and **pepper**

TO SERVE
¼ **cucumber**, finely diced
200 ml (7 fl oz) **natural yogurt**
1 **cos** or **iceberg lettuce**
4 **red** or **white-stemmed spring onions**, thinly sliced
4 tablespoons chopped **coriander** or **mint leaves**

Preheat the slow cooker if necessary. Heat the oil in a frying pan, add the onion and fry, stirring, for 5 minutes or until pale golden. Add the beetroot to the pan with the drained beans, stock and plenty of salt and pepper. Bring to the boil, stirring.

Transfer the beetroot mixture to the slow cooker pot. Cover with the lid and cook on low for 3½–4½ hours or until the beetroot is tender. Stir well and lift the pot out of the housing using oven gloves.

Stir the cucumber into the yogurt and season with salt and pepper. Arrange the lettuce leaves on 4–5 individual plates. Top with the warm beetroot salad, then add spoonfuls of the cucumber yogurt. Scatter the spring onions and coriander or mint over the top and serve at once.

FOR WARM BEETROOT SALAD WITH FETA & TOMATOES, prepare the salad as above. Mix 125 g (4 oz) crumbled feta cheese with 2 diced tomatoes. Core, deseed and dice ½ red or orange pepper and combine with the cheese and tomatoes. Add 4 tablespoons chopped mint and 2 tablespoons olive oil. Spoon over the warm salad and top with 50 g (2 oz) rocket leaves.

CHILLIED BEEF WITH CHEESY TORTILLAS

Serves **4–5**
Preparation time **20 minutes**
Cooking temperature **low**
Cooking time **8–10 hours**

1 tablespoon **sunflower oil**
500 g (1 lb) **extra-lean minced beef**
1 **onion**, chopped
2 **garlic cloves**, finely chopped
1 teaspoon **smoked paprika**
½ teaspoon **crushed dried
    red chillies**
1 teaspoon **ground cumin**
1 tablespoon **plain flour**
400 g (13 oz) can **chopped tomatoes**
410 g (13½ oz) can **red kidney
    beans**, drained
150 ml (¼ pint) **beef stock**
1 tablespoon **dark muscovado sugar**
salt and **pepper**

TOPPING
100 g (3½ oz) **tortilla chips**
½ **red pepper**, cored, deseeded
    and diced
chopped **coriander**
100 g (3½ oz) **mature Cheddar
    cheese**, grated

Preheat the slow cooker if necessary. Heat the oil in a frying pan, add the mince and onion and fry, stirring and breaking up the mince with a wooden spoon, for 5 minutes until it is browned.

Stir in the garlic, paprika, chillies and cumin and cook for 2 minutes. Stir in the flour. Mix in the tomatoes, kidney beans, stock and sugar, season with salt and pepper and pour the mixture into the slow cooker pot. Cover with the lid and cook on low for 8–10 hours.

Stir the chilli, then arrange the tortilla chips on top. Sprinkle over the remaining ingredients, lift the pot out of the housing using oven gloves and place under a preheated hot grill until the cheese just melts. Spoon into bowls to serve.

FOR TURKEY FAJITAS WITH GUACAMOLE, make up the chilli as above, using 500 g (1 lb) minced turkey instead of the beef. For the guacamole, halve, stone and peel 1 avocado, then mash the flesh with the juice of 1 lime, a small bunch of torn coriander and some salt and pepper. Spoon the turkey mixture on to 8 warmed, medium soft flour tortillas, top with spoonfuls of the guacamole and 8 tablespoons soured cream, if liked, and roll up to serve.

COURGETTE & BROAD BEAN FRITTATA

Serves **4**
Preparation time **15 minutes**
Cooking temperature **high**
Cooking time **1½–2 hours**

40 g (1½ oz) **butter**
4 **spring onions**, sliced
1 **courgette**, about 200 g (7 oz), thinly sliced
100 g (3½ oz) podded **fresh broad beans**
6 **eggs**
250 ml (8 fl oz) **crème fraîche**
2 teaspoons chopped **tarragon**
2 tablespoons chopped **parsley**
salt and **pepper**

Preheat the slow cooker if necessary. Heat the butter, spring onions and courgette in a saucepan or in a microwave-proof bowl in the microwave until the butter has melted.

Line the slow cooker pot with nonstick baking paper, tip in the courgette and butter mixture, then add the broad beans. Fork together the eggs, crème fraîche, herbs and a little salt and pepper in a bowl, then pour into the pot. Cover with the lid and cook on high for 1½–2 hours or until set in the middle.

Lift the pot out of the housing using oven gloves. Loosen the edge of the frittata with a knife, carefully turn out on to a large plate and peel off the lining paper. Cut into wedges and serve with salad, if liked.

FOR COURGETTE, SALMON & ASPARAGUS FRITTATA, add 100 g (3 ½ oz) sliced asparagus tips to the butter, spring onions and courgette when heating and replace the broad beans with 100 g (3½ oz) chopped smoked salmon. Continue as above.

HOT QUINOA & PEPPER SALAD ♥

Serves **4**
Preparation time **15 minutes**
Cooking temperature **high**
Cooking time **3–4 hours**

3 **peppers**, cored, deseeded, and cut into chunks
2 **celery sticks**, sliced
2 **courgettes**, halved lengthways and thickly sliced
250 g (8 oz) **plum tomatoes**, roughly chopped
2 **garlic cloves**, finely chopped
125 g (4 oz) **quinoa and bulgar wheat grain mix**
4 tablespoons **red wine**
300 ml (½ pint) hot **vegetable stock**
1 tablespoon **tomato purée**
1 teaspoon **granular sweetener**
15 g (½ oz) **basil leaves**, roughly torn
salt and **pepper**

Preheat the slow cooker if necessary. Place the peppers, celery, courgettes and tomatoes in the slow cooker pot and sprinkle over the garlic and grain mix.

Mix the red wine with the stock, tomato purée and sweetener, season to taste and pour into the slow cooker pot. Stir the ingredients together, then cover and cook on high for 3–4 hours until the vegetables have softened and the grains have absorbed the liquid.

Stir the salad, then divide between 4 shallow bowls and serve topped with the torn basil leaves.

FOR HOT QUINOA & PRAWN SALAD, follow the recipe above to make the quinoa salad and divide between 4 bowls. Omit the basil and divide 100 g (3½ oz) mixed spinach, watercress and rocket leaves and 175 g (6 oz) cooked peeled prawns between the bowls.

BEETROOT & CARAWAY RISOTTO ♥

Serves 4
Preparation time 15 minutes
Cooking temperature low
Cooking time 5–6 hours

200 g (7 oz) **easy-cook brown
   long-grain rice**
300 g (10 oz) **raw beetroot**, peeled
   and diced
1 **red onion**, finely chopped
2 **garlic cloves**, finely chopped
1 teaspoon **caraway seeds**
2 teaspoons **tomato purée**
1.2 litres (2 pints) hot **vegetable stock**
salt and **pepper**

TO SERVE
4 tablespoons **Greek yogurt**
125 g (4 oz) **smoked salmon slices**
handful of rocket leaves

Preheat the slow cooker if necessary. Place the rice in a sieve, rinse well under cold running water and drain well.

Place the beetroot, onion and garlic in the slow cooker pot, add the drained rice, caraway seeds and tomato purée, then stir in the hot stock and season generously. Cover and cook on low for 5–6 hours until the rice and beetroot are tender.

Stir the risotto, spoon into shallow bowls and top each portion with a spoonful of the yogurt, some of the smoked salmon and a few rocket leaves. Serve immediately.

FOR PUMPKIN & SAGE RISOTTO, place 300 g (10 oz) peeled, deseeded and diced pumpkin in the slow cooker pot with 1 finely chopped white onion and 2 chopped garlic cloves. Mix in 250 g (8 oz) rinsed easy-cook brown long-grain rice and flavour with 2 sage sprigs, 1 teaspoon paprika and 2 teaspoons tomato purée. Add 1.2 litres (2 pints) hot vegetable stock, season and cook as above. Serve sprinkled with 75 g (3 oz) finely grated Parmesan cheese.

SPINACH & COURGETTE TIAN

Serves **4**
Preparation time **20 minutes**
Cooking temperature **high**
Cooking time **1½–2 hours**

50 g (2 oz) **easy-cook white long-grain rice**
butter, for greasing
1 **tomato**, sliced
1 tablespoon **olive oil**
½ **onion**, chopped
1 **garlic clove**, finely chopped
1 **courgette**, about 175 g (6 oz), coarsely grated
125 g (4 oz) **spinach**, rinsed, well drained and thickly shredded
3 **eggs**
6 tablespoons **milk**
pinch of grated **nutmeg**
4 tablespoons chopped **mint**
salt and **pepper**

Preheat the slow cooker if necessary. Bring a small saucepan of water to the boil, add the rice, bring back to the boil, then simmer for 8–10 minutes or until tender. Meanwhile, butter the inside of a soufflé dish 14 cm (5½ inches) in diameter and 9 cm (3½ inches) deep and base-line with a circle of nonstick baking paper. Arrange the tomato slices, overlapping, on top.

Heat the oil in a frying pan, add the onion and fry, stirring, for 5 minutes or until softened and just beginning to turn golden. Stir in the garlic, then add the courgette and spinach and cook for 2 minutes or until the spinach is just wilted.

Beat together the eggs, milk, nutmeg and a little salt and pepper. Drain the rice and stir into the spinach mixture with the egg mixture and mint. Mix well, then spoon into the dish. Cover loosely with buttered foil and lower into the slow cooker pot.

Pour boiling water into the slow cooker pot to come halfway up the sides of the dish. Cover and cook on high for 1½–2 hours or until the tian is set in the middle. Lift the dish out of the slow cooker using a tea towel, leave to stand for 5 minutes, then remove the foil, loosen the edge and turn out on to a plate. Cut into wedges and serve warm with salad, if liked.

FOR CHEESY SPINACH & PINE NUT TIAN, omit the courgette and instead stir in 50 g (2 oz) freshly grated Parmesan cheese, a small bunch of chopped basil and 4 tablespoons toasted pine nuts.

ROASTED VEGETABLE TERRINE

Serves **4**
Preparation time **30 minutes,**
 plus cooling
Cooking temperature **high**
Cooking time **2–3 hours**

375 g (12 oz) **courgettes**, thinly sliced
1 **red pepper**, quartered, cored
 and deseeded
1 **orange pepper**, quartered, cored
 and deseeded
2 tablespoons **olive oil**, plus extra
 for oiling
1 **garlic clove**, finely chopped
2 **eggs**
150 ml (¼ pint) **milk**
25 g (1 oz) **Parmesan cheese**,
 freshly grated
3 tablespoons chopped **basil**
salt and **pepper**

Preheat the slow cooker if necessary. Line a grill rack with foil. Arrange all the vegetables on the foil in a single layer, with the peppers skin side up. Drizzle with the oil and sprinkle with the garlic and salt and pepper. Cook under a preheated medium grill for 10 minutes or until softened and browned. Transfer the courgette slices to a plate and wrap the peppers in the foil. Leave to stand for 5 minutes to loosen the skins.

Oil a 500 g (1 lb) loaf tin and line the base and 2 long sides with nonstick baking paper, checking first it will fit in the slow cooker pot. Beat together the eggs, milk, Parmesan, basil and salt and pepper in a bowl. Unwrap the peppers and peel away the skins with a knife.

Arrange one-third of the courgette slices over the base of the tin. Spoon in a little of the custard, then add the peppers and a little more custard. Repeat, ending with a layer of courgettes and custard. Cover the top with foil and put in the slow cooker pot. Pour boiling water into the pot to come halfway up the sides of the tin. Cover with the lid and cook on high for 2–3 hours or until the custard is set.

Lift the tin out of the slow cooker using a tea towel and leave to cool. Loosen the edges with a knife, turn out on to a chopping board and peel off the lining paper. Cut into slices and serve with Romesco Sauce (*see* below), if liked.

FOR ROMESCO SAUCE TO ACCOMPANY THE TERRINE, fry 1 chopped onion in 1 tablespoon olive oil until softened. Mix in 2 chopped garlic cloves, 4 skinned and chopped tomatoes, ½ teaspoon paprika and 40 g (1½ oz) finely chopped almonds. Simmer for 10 minutes until thick.

BABA GANOUSH ♥

Serves **4**
Preparation time **20 minutes**
Cooking temperature **high**
Cooking time **3–4 hours**

1 large **aubergine**, 300 g (10 oz),
    halved lengthways
1 tablespoon **olive oil**
2 tablespoons **0% fat Greek yogurt**
3 tablespoons chopped
    coriander leaves
1 large **garlic clove**, finely chopped
juice of ½ **lemon**
seeds from ¼ **pomegranate**
salt and **pepper**

TO SERVE
4 **pitta breads**
1 **red pepper**, cored, deseeded
    and cut into batons
½ **cucumber**, deseeded and cut
    into batons

Preheat the slow cooker if necessary. Cut criss-cross lines over the cut side of each aubergine half, rub with salt and pepper, then drizzle with the oil. Arrange, cut sides down, in the base of the slow cooker pot, cover and cook on high for 3–4 hours or until the aubergine is soft. Leave to cool.

Use a spoon to scoop the flesh out of the aubergine skins and chop it roughly. Place in a mixing bowl with the yogurt, coriander, garlic and lemon juice. Season to taste, spoon into a serving dish and scatter with the pomegranate seeds.

Warm the pitta breads under a preheated hot grill, then cut into thick strips. Arrange on a serving plate with the pepper and cucumber batons, and serve with the baba ganoush.

FOR GRILLED STEAKS WITH AUBERGINE SAUCE, make the baba ganoush following the recipe above. Trim the fat from 4 sirloin steaks, 125 g (4 oz) each, and season to taste. Spray with a little low-calorie cooking oil spray and cook on a preheated hot ridged griddle pan for 2–3 minutes, turning once, or until cooked to your liking. Serve the steaks with the baba ganoush and a rocket salad tossed with lemon juice.

RED PEPPER & CHORIZO TORTILLA

Serves 4
Preparation time 20 minutes
Cooking temperature high
Cooking time 2–2½ hours

1 tablespoon **olive oil**, plus extra
    for oiling
1 small **onion**, chopped
75 g (3 oz) **chorizo**, skinned
    and diced
6 **eggs**
150 ml (¼ pint) **milk**
100 g (3½ oz) **roasted red pepper**
    (from a jar), drained and sliced
250 g (8 oz) cooked **potatoes**, sliced
salt and **pepper**

Preheat the slow cooker if necessary. Lightly oil a 1.2 litre (2 pint) soufflé dish and base-line with a circle of nonstick baking paper, checking first that the dish will fit in the slow cooker pot.

Heat the oil in a frying pan, add the onion and chorizo and fry for 4–5 minutes until the onion is softened. Beat the eggs, milk and a little salt and pepper in a bowl, then add the onion and chorizo, the red pepper and sliced potatoes and mix together.

Tip the mixture into the oiled dish, cover the top with foil and stand the dish in the slow cooker pot. Pour boiling water into the pot to come halfway up the sides of the dish. Cover with the lid and cook on high for 2–2½ hours or until the egg mixture has set in the centre.

Lift the dish out of the slow cooker pot using a tea towel and remove the foil. Loosen the edge of the tortilla with a knife, turn it out on to a plate and peel off the lining paper. Cut the tortilla into slices and serve hot or cold with salad, if liked.

FOR CHEESY BACON & ROSEMARY TORTILLA, replace the chorizo with 75 g (3 oz) diced smoked streaky bacon rashers and fry with the onion as above. Beat the eggs and milk in a bowl with the chopped leaves from 2 small rosemary sprigs and 4 tablespoons freshly grated Parmesan or Cheddar cheese and salt and pepper. Replace the red pepper with 75 g (3 oz) sliced button mushrooms and continue as above.

CHILLIED SWEETCORN

Serves **4**
Preparation time **15 minutes**
Cooking temperature **high**
Cooking time **2–3 hours**

1 tablespoon **sunflower oil**
1 **onion**, finely chopped
1 **orange pepper**, cored, deseeded
  and diced
100 g (3½ oz) **frozen**
  sweetcorn, thawed
1 **garlic clove**, finely chopped
large pinch of **crushed dried**
  red chillies
½ teaspoon **ground cumin**
1 teaspoon **ground coriander**
410 g (13½ oz) can **mixed**
  pulses, drained
400 g (13 oz) can **chopped tomatoes**
150 ml (¼ pint) **vegetable stock**
2 teaspoons **brown sugar**
salt and **pepper**

TO SERVE
8 tablespoons **crème fraîche**
grated **Cheddar cheese**

Preheat the slow cooker if necessary. Heat the oil in a large frying pan, add the onion and fry for 5 minutes, stirring, until softened.

Stir in the orange pepper, sweetcorn, garlic and spices and cook for 1 minute. Add the pulses, tomatoes, stock, sugar and a little salt and pepper and bring to the boil.

Pour the mixture into the slow cooker pot, cover with the lid and cook on high for 2–3 hours or until cooked through. Spoon into bowls and serve with the crème fraîche and cheese.

FOR CHILLIED MUSHROOMS, fry the onion as above, then add 250 g (8 oz) quartered closed-cup mushrooms instead of the pepper and sweetcorn. Fry for 2–3 minutes, then add the garlic and spices and continue as above.

SOUPS

CARAMELIZED ONION SOUP

Serves **4**
Preparation time **25 minutes**
Cooking temperature **low**
Cooking time **4–5 hours**

25 g (1 oz) **butter**
2 tablespoons **olive oil**
500 g (1 lb) **onions**, thinly sliced
1 tablespoon **caster sugar**
2 tablespoons **plain flour**
250 ml (8 fl oz) **brown ale**
750 ml (1¼ pints) **beef stock**
2 **bay leaves**
1 tablespoon **Worcestershire sauce**
salt and **pepper**

CHEESY CROUTES
8 slices of **French bread**
75 g (3 oz) **mature Cheddar
cheese**, grated
2 teaspoons **Worcestershire sauce**

Preheat the slow cooker if necessary. Heat the butter and oil in a large frying pan, add the onions and fry over a medium heat, stirring occasionally, for 15 minutes or until softened and just beginning to turn golden. Stir in the sugar and fry for 10 minutes, stirring frequently as the onions begin to caramelize and turn a deep golden brown.

Stir in the flour, then add the ale, stock, bay leaves and Worcestershire sauce. Add a little salt and pepper and bring to the boil, stirring. Pour into the slow cooker pot, cover with the lid and cook on low for 4–5 hours or until the onions are very soft.

When almost ready to serve, toast the French bread slices on both sides under a preheated medium grill. Sprinkle with the cheese and drizzle with the Worcestershire sauce, then grill until the cheese is bubbling. Ladle the soup into shallow bowls and float the croutes on top.

FOR FRENCH ONION SOUP, fry the onions as above and stir in the flour. Replace the ale with 250 ml (8 fl oz) red wine and add with the stock, bay leaves and salt and pepper, omitting the Worcestershire sauce. Continue as above. For the croutes, toast the French bread, then rub one side of each piece with a cut garlic clove, sprinkle with 75 g (3 oz) grated Gruyère cheese and grill. Serve as above.

MULLIGATAWNY SOUP

Serves **4–6**
Preparation time **15 minutes**
Cooking temperature **low**
Cooking time **6–8 hours**

1 **onion**, chopped
1 **carrot**, diced
1 **dessert apple**, cored and
    coarsely grated
2 **garlic cloves**, finely chopped
400 g (13 oz) can
    chopped tomatoes
75 g (3 oz) **dried red lentils**, rinsed
    and drained
50 g (2 oz) **sultanas**
3 teaspoons **mild curry paste**
1.2 litres (2 pints) boiling **vegetable**
    or **chicken stock**
salt and **pepper**

CROUTES
50 g (2 oz) **butter**
2 **garlic cloves**, finely chopped
3 tablespoons chopped **coriander**
8–12 slices of **French bread**,
    depending on size

Preheat the slow cooker if necessary. Put the vegetables, apple, garlic, tomatoes, lentils and sultanas into the slow cooker pot.

Add the curry paste, then stir in the boiling stock and add a little salt and pepper. Cover and cook on low for 6–8 hours or until the lentils are soft and the carrots are tender.

When almost ready to serve, make the croutes. Beat together the butter, garlic and chopped coriander in a bowl. Toast the bread on both sides, then spread with the butter. Ladle the hot soup into soup bowls and serve with the croutes.

FOR GINGERED CARROT SOUP, put 500 g (1 lb) diced carrots and a 3.5 cm (1½ inch) piece of peeled and finely chopped fresh root ginger into the slow cooker pot with the onion, lentils and curry paste as above, omitting the other ingredients. Pour over 1.2 litres (2 pints) boiling vegetable stock and continue as above. Purée with a stick blender, mix in 300 ml (½ pint) milk and cook on high for 15 minutes until piping hot. Ladle into bowls and serve with swirls of natural yogurt.

CHICKEN NOODLE BROTH ♥

Serves **4**
Preparation time **10 minutes**
Cooking temperature **high**
Cooking time **5 hours 20 minutes–7½ hours**

1 **chicken carcass**
1 **onion**, cut into wedges
2 **carrots**, sliced
2 **celery sticks**, sliced
1 **bouquet garni**
1.2 litres (2 pints) boiling **water**
75 g (3 oz) **dried vermicelli**
4 tablespoons chopped **parsley**
salt and **pepper**

Preheat the slow cooker if necessary. Place the chicken carcass in the slow cooker pot, breaking it in half if necessary to make it fit. Add the onion, carrots, celery and bouquet garni. Pour over the measurement boiling water and season to taste. Cover and cook on high for 5–7 hours.

Strain the soup through a large sieve, then return the liquid to the slow cooker pot. Remove any meat from the carcass and add to the pot. Adjust the seasoning if necessary, add the vermicelli pasta and cook for a further 20–30 minutes until the pasta is just cooked. Sprinkle with the parsley, ladle into bowls and serve.

FOR CHICKEN & MINTED PEA SOUP, follow the recipe above to make the soup, then strain and pour it back into the slow cooker pot. Add 200 g (7 oz) finely sliced leeks, 375 g (12 oz) frozen peas and a small bunch of mint, cover and cook for a further 30 minutes. Purée the soup while still in the slow cooker with a stick blender. Alternatively, transfer to a freestanding blender and purée, in batches if necessary, until smooth, then return to the pot and reheat on high for 15 minutes. Stir in 150 g (5 oz) mascarpone cheese until melted. Ladle into bowls and sprinkle with extra mint, if liked.

CHUNKY BEEF & BARLEY BROTH ♥

Serves **4**
Preparation time **15 minutes**
Cooking temperature **high**
Cooking time **5¼–6¼ hours**

300 g (10 oz) **lean stewing beef**, diced
250 g (8 oz) **swede**, finely diced
250 g (8 oz) **carrot**, finely diced
1 **onion**, finely chopped
50 g (2 oz) **pearl barley**
50 g (2 oz) **dried red lentils**, rinsed and drained
900 ml (1½ pints) hot **beef stock**
1 teaspoon **dried mixed herbs**
1 teaspoon **mustard powder**
1 tablespoon **Worcestershire sauce**
125 g (4 oz) **green cabbage**, finely shredded
salt and **pepper**

Preheat the slow cooker if necessary. Place the beef, swede, carrot and onion in the slow cooker pot, then add the pearl barley and lentils.

Mix the hot stock with the herbs, mustard powder and Worcestershire sauce, then pour over the meat and vegetables. Stir well, season to taste, cover and cook on high for 5–6 hours until the beef and barley are tender.

Stir, then add the cabbage. Cover again and cook for 15 minutes until the cabbage is just tender. Ladle into bowls and serve.

FOR CHICKEN & BARLEY BRO, follow the recipe above, using 300 g (10 oz) boneless, skinless diced chicken thighs and 1 sliced leek instead of the beef and onion. Use 900 ml (1½ pints) chicken stock instead of the beef stock, and 50 g (2 oz) diced ready-to-eat pitted prunes instead of the Worcestershire sauce. Cook as above, adding the cabbage for the last 15 minutes.

CALDO VERDE

CORN & SMOKED COD CHOWDER ♥

Serves **6**
Preparation time **20 minutes**
Cooking temperature **low** and **high**
Cooking time **6¼ hours–8 hours 20 minutes**

2 tablespoons **olive oil**
2 **onions**, chopped
2 **garlic cloves**, finely chopped
150 g (5 oz) **chorizo** in one piece, skinned and diced
625 g (1¼ lb) or 3 small **baking potatoes**, cut into 1 cm (½ inch) dice
1 teaspoon **smoked paprika**
1.2 litres (2 pints) hot **chicken stock**
125 g (4 oz) **green cabbage**, finely shredded
salt and **pepper**

Preheat the slow cooker if necessary. Heat the oil in a large frying pan, add the onions and fry, stirring, for 5 minutes or until lightly browned. Add the garlic, chorizo, potatoes and paprika and cook for 2 minutes.

Transfer the mixture to the slow cooker pot, add the hot stock and season to taste with salt and pepper. Cover with the lid and cook on low for 6–8 hours.

Add the cabbage, replace the lid and cook on high for 15–20 minutes or until the cabbage is tender. Ladle into bowls and serve with warm crusty bread, if liked.

FOR CALDO VERDE WITH PUMPKIN, prepare the soup as above, reducing the baking potatoes to 375 g (12 oz) and adding 250 g (8 oz) peeled, deseeded and diced pumpkin. Reduce the chicken stock to 900 ml (1½ pints) and add a 400 g (13 oz) can chopped tomatoes.

Serves **4**
Preparation time **20 minutes**
Cooking temperature **high**
Cooking time **2¼–3¼ hours**

low-calorie cooking oil spray
1 **leek**, thinly sliced, white and green parts kept separate
50 g (2 oz) **smoked back bacon rashers**, trimmed of fat and diced
200 g (7 oz) **potato**, finely diced
175 g (6 oz) **celeriac**, finely diced
75 g (3 oz) **frozen sweetcorn**
450 ml (¾ pint) **fish stock**
1 **bay leaf**
250 g (8 oz) **smoked cod fillet**
200 ml (7 fl oz) **skimmed milk**
50 g (2 oz) **reduced-fat cream cheese**
salt and **pepper**
chopped **parsley**, to garnish

Preheat the slow cooker if necessary. Spray a large frying pan with a little low-calorie cooking oil spray and place over a medium heat until hot. Add the white leek slices and the bacon and cook for 3–4 minutes until the leeks have softened and the bacon is just beginning to brown.

Add the potato, celeriac, sweetcorn and stock. Bring to the boil, stirring, then add the bay leaf and season to taste. Transfer to the slow cooker pot, arrange the fish on top and press the fish into the liquid. Cover and cook on high for 2–3 hours until the potatoes and celeriac are tender and the fish flakes easily when pressed with a small knife. Transfer the fish to a plate, remove the skin and bones and break into pieces.

Stir the milk and cream cheese into the slow cooker pot, then stir in the reserved green leek slices and the flaked fish. Cover again and cook for 15 minutes until the leeks are tender. Ladle into bowls and serve garnished with chopped parsley.

FOR SALMON & CRAB CHOWDER, follow the recipe above, using 250 g (8 oz) salmon fillet instead of the smoked cod. Cook as above, stirring in a 40 g (1½ oz) can brown crab meat for the last 15 minutes of cooking time.

OLD ENGLISH PEA & HAM SOUP

Serves **4–6**
Preparation time **15 minutes**
Cooking temperature **high**
Cooking time **5–6 hours**

175 g (6 oz) **dried green split peas**,
  soaked overnight in cold water
2 **onions**, chopped
2 **celery sticks**, diced
1 **carrot**, diced
1.5 litres (2½ pints) **water**
3 teaspoons **English mustard**
1 **bay leaf**
500 g (1 lb) **unsmoked boneless
  bacon joint**
4 tablespoons chopped **parsley**
salt and **pepper**

Preheat the slow cooker if necessary. Drain the peas and add to a large saucepan with the onions, celery, carrot and measurement water. Bring to the boil, skim off any scum that rises to the surface and boil for 10 minutes.

Pour the mixture into the slow cooker pot, then stir in the mustard, bay leaf and some pepper. Rinse the bacon joint in several changes of cold water, then add to the pot and press below the surface of the liquid. Cover and cook on high for 5–6 hours or until the peas are soft and the bacon cooked through and tender.

Lift the bacon joint out of the slow cooker pot with a carving fork, drain well, then cut away the rind and fat. Cut the meat into bite-sized pieces. Purée the soup with a stick blender or leave chunky, if preferred. Stir the bacon back into the pot and mix in the parsley. Taste and adjust the seasoning, adding salt, if needed. Ladle the soup into bowls and serve with crusty bread, if liked.

FOR SPLIT PEA & PARSNIP SOUP, soak 175 g (6 oz) dried yellow split peas as above. Drain and put into a saucepan with 1 chopped onion, 300 g (10 oz) diced parsnips and 1.5 litres (2½ pints) chicken or vegetable stock. Boil for 10 minutes, then transfer to the slow cooker pot. Cover and cook as above. Purée and adjust the seasoning, if needed. Beat 75 g (3 oz) butter with 2 finely chopped garlic cloves, 3 tablespoons chopped coriander and 1 teaspoon each roughly crushed cumin seeds and coriander seeds. Ladle the soup into bowls and top with spoonfuls of the butter.

TOMATO & RED PEPPER SOUP

Serves **4–6**
Preparation time **15 minutes**
Cooking temperature **high**
Cooking time **2½–3¼ hours**

2 tablespoons **olive oil**
1 **onion**, chopped
1 **red pepper**, cored, deseeded
    and diced
750 g (1½ lb) **tomatoes**,
    roughly chopped
1 **garlic clove**, finely chopped
600 ml (1 pint) **vegetable stock**
1 tablespoon **tomato purée**
2 teaspoons **caster sugar**
1 tablespoon **balsamic vinegar**,
    plus extra to garnish
salt and **pepper**

Preheat the slow cooker if necessary. Heat the oil in a large frying pan, add the onion and fry until softened. Stir in the red pepper, tomatoes and garlic and fry for 1–2 minutes.

Pour in the stock, add the tomato purée, sugar, balsamic vinegar and a little salt and pepper and bring to the boil, stirring. Pour into the slow cooker pot, cover with the lid and cook on high for 2½–3 hours or until the vegetables are tender.

Purée the soup while still in the slow cooker pot with a stick blender. Alternatively, transfer to a freestanding blender and purée, in batches if necessary, until smooth, then return to the slow cooker pot and reheat on high for 15 minutes.

Taste and adjust the seasoning, if needed, then ladle the soup into bowls and garnish with a drizzle of extra balsamic vinegar or stir in spoonfuls of Spring Onion & Basil Pesto (*see* below).

FOR SPRING ONION & BASIL PESTO TO GARNISH THE SOUP, roughly chop 4 spring onions, then finely chop with a stick blender in a jug, or in a freestanding blender, with 4 basil sprigs, 25 g (1 oz) freshly grated Parmesan cheese, 4 tablespoons olive oil and a little pepper until a coarse paste. Spoon over the top of the soup just before serving.

THAI COCONUT & PUMPKIN SOUP

Serves **4–6**
Preparation time **20 minutes**
Cooking temperature **low** and **high**,
  if necessary
Cooking time **7–8¼ hours**

1 tablespoon **sunflower oil**
1 **onion**, chopped
4 teaspoons **Thai red curry paste**
1 teaspoon **galangal paste**
2 **garlic cloves**, finely chopped
1 **butternut squash**, about 1 kg (2 lb),
  peeled, deseeded and cut into
  2 cm (¾ inch) chunks
250 ml (8 fl oz) carton
  coconut cream
750 ml (1¼ pints) **vegetable stock**
1 tablespoon **soy sauce**
small bunch of **coriander**
salt and **pepper**

Preheat the slow cooker if necessary. Heat the oil in a large frying pan, add the onion and fry until softened. Stir in the curry paste, galangal paste and garlic and cook for 1 minute, then mix in the squash.

Pour in the coconut cream and stock, then add the soy sauce and bring to the boil, stirring. Pour into the slow cooker pot, cover with the lid and cook on low for 7–8 hours or until the squash is tender. (You may find that the coconut cream separates slightly, but this will disappear after puréeing.)

Purée the soup while still in the slow cooker pot with a stick blender. Alternatively, transfer to a freestanding blender and purée, in batches if necessary, until smooth, then return it to the slow cooker pot and reheat on high for 15 minutes.

Reserve a few coriander sprigs, chop the rest and stir into the soup. Ladle the soup into bowls and garnish with the reserved coriander sprigs.

FOR PUMPKIN & ORANGE SOUP, fry the onion in 25 g (1 oz) butter, then add the diced butternut squash with the grated rind and juice of 2 small oranges, 900 ml (1½ pints) vegetable stock and 3 whole star anise. Bring to the boil, stirring, add a little salt and pepper and continue as above. Remove the star anise before puréeing and serve with swirls of double cream.

HADDOCK & BACON CHOWDER

Serves **4**
Preparation time **15 minutes**
Cooking temperature **high**
Cooking time **2½–3½ hours**

25 g (1 oz) **butter**
1 **onion**, finely chopped
300 g (10 oz) **potatoes**, cut into
    small dice
4 **smoked streaky bacon
    rashers**, diced
750 ml (1¼ pints) boiling **fish stock**
125 g (4 oz) **frozen
    sweetcorn**, thawed
1 **bay leaf**
500 g (1 lb) **smoked haddock
    fillet**, skinned
150 ml (¼ pint) **double cream**
salt and pepper
chopped **parsley**, to garnish

Preheat the slow cooker if necessary. Heat the butter in a large frying pan, add the onion, potatoes and bacon and fry gently, stirring, until just beginning to colour.

Transfer the potato mixture to the slow cooker pot. Pour over the boiling stock, then add the sweetcorn, bay leaf and a little salt and pepper. Cover with the lid and cook on high for 2–3 hours or until the potatoes are tender.

Add the fish and press it just below the surface of the stock, cutting the pieces in half, if needed. Replace the lid and cook on high for 30 minutes or until the fish flakes easily when pressed in the centre with a knife.

Lift the fish on to a plate with a fish slice and break it into flakes with a knife and fork, checking for and removing any bones. Stir the cream into the soup, then return the fish. Ladle the soup into bowls and sprinkle with parsley.

FOR SALMON & CRAB CHOWDER, fry the onion and potatoes, omitting the bacon, and continue to cook for 2–3 hours as above. Replace the smoked haddock with a 43 g (1¾ oz) can dressed brown crab meat, stirred into the potato mixture, and 500 g (1 lb) salmon fillet, skinned, cut into 4 strips and pressed below the surface of the stock. Cook for 30–40 minutes until the salmon flakes easily, then continue as above.

CHICKEN & TORTELLONI SOUP

Serves **4**
Preparation time **15 minutes**
Cooking temperature **high**
Cooking time **5 hours**
    20 minutes–7½ hours

1 **chicken carcass**
1 **onion**, quartered
2 **celery sticks**, sliced
2 **carrots**, thinly sliced
2 **thyme** or **basil sprigs**
1.25 litres (2¼ pints) boiling **water**
½ teaspoon **black peppercorns**,
    roughly crushed
100 g (3½ oz) **spinach**, rinsed,
    drained and roughly torn
3 **tomatoes**, diced
250 g (8 oz) **fresh**
    spinach tortelloni
salt
freshly grated **Parmesan cheese**,
    to serve

Preheat the slow cooker if necessary. Put the chicken carcass into the slow cooker pot, breaking it in half if necessary to make it fit. Add the vegetables, thyme or basil sprigs and measurement boiling water, then add the peppercorns and salt to taste.

Cover with the lid and cook on high for 5–7 hours. Lift the carcass out of the slow cooker pot and remove any meat; cut this into small pieces and reserve. Strain the stock, discarding the bones, vegetables and herbs, then pour the hot stock back into the slow cooker pot.

Add the shredded chicken, spinach, tomatoes and tortelloni. Replace the lid and cook for 20–30 minutes, still on high, until piping hot. Ladle the soup into bowls and serve sprinkled with a little grated Parmesan.

FOR PESTO & LEMON SOUP, cook the chicken carcass as above, then stir 2 teaspoons pesto sauce and the grated rind and juice of 1 lemon into the strained stock. Mix in 125 g (4 oz) finely chopped broccoli, 125 g (4 oz) frozen peas and 125 g (4 oz) rinsed, drained and roughly chopped spinach with the shredded chicken, omitting the tomatoes and tortelloni. Cook as above and serve topped with extra pesto and grated Parmesan.

LAMB & BARLEY BROTH

Serves **4–6**
Preparation time **15 minutes**
Cooking temperature **low**
Cooking time **8–10 hours**

25 g (1 oz) **butter**
1 tablespoon **sunflower oil**
1 **lamb rump chop** or 125 g (4 oz)
    lamb fillet, diced
1 **onion**, chopped
1 small **leek**, chopped
500 g (1 lb) mixed **parsnip**,
    swede, **turnip** and **carrot**,
    cut into small dice
50 g (2 oz) **pearl barley**
1.2 litres (2 pints) **lamb** or
    chicken stock
¼ teaspoon **ground allspice**
2–3 **rosemary sprigs**
salt and **pepper**
chopped **parsley** or **chives**,
    to garnish (optional)

Preheat the slow cooker if necessary. Heat the butter and oil in a large frying pan, add the lamb, onion and leek and fry, stirring, until the lamb is lightly browned.

Stir in the root vegetables and barley, then add the stock, allspice, rosemary and plenty of salt and pepper and bring to the boil, stirring. Pour into the slow cooker pot, cover with the lid and cook on low for 8–10 hours or until the barley is tender.

Stir well, taste and adjust the seasoning, if needed, then ladle the soup into bowls. Garnish with chopped herbs and serve with warm bread, if liked.

FOR HUNGARIAN CHORBA, fry the lamb and vegetables as above, omitting the pearl barley. Stir in 1 teaspoon smoked paprika, then add 50 g (2 oz) easy-cook white long-grain rice and a few dill sprigs. Stir in 1.2 litres (2 pints) lamb stock, 2 tablespoons red wine vinegar and 1 tablespoon light muscovado sugar. Add salt and pepper, bring to the boil and continue as above. Garnish with extra chopped dill and serve with rye bread.

CARROT & CUMIN SOUP

Serves **4–6**
Preparation time **20 minutes**
Cooking temperature **low** and **high**,
   if necessary
Cooking time **7–8¼ hours**

1 tablespoon **sunflower oil**
1 large **onion**, chopped
625 g (1¼ lb) **carrots**, thinly sliced
1½ teaspoons **cumin seeds**,
   roughly crushed
1 teaspoon **ground turmeric**
50 g (2 oz) **easy-cook white
   long-grain rice**
1.2 litres (2 pints) **vegetable stock**
salt and **pepper**

TO SERVE
150 ml (¼ pint) **natural yogurt**
mango chutney
poppadums (optional)

Preheat the slow cooker if necessary. Heat the oil in a large frying pan, add the onion and fry over a medium heat, stirring, until softened. Stir in the carrots, crushed cumin seeds and turmeric and fry for 2–3 minutes to release the cumin flavour and colour the onions.

Stir in the rice, then add the stock and a little salt and pepper and bring to the boil. Pour into the slow cooker pot, cover with the lid and cook on low for 7–8 hours or until the carrots are tender.

Purée the soup while still in the slow cooker pot with a stick blender. Alternatively, transfer to a freestanding blender and purée, in batches if necessary, until smooth, then return to the slow cooker pot and reheat on high for 15 minutes.

Taste and adjust the seasoning, if needed, then ladle the soup into bowls. Top with spoonfuls of the yogurt and a little mango chutney, and serve with poppadums, if liked.

FOR SPICED PARSNIP SOUP, fry the onion as above, replacing the carrots with 625 g (1¼ lb) halved and thinly sliced parsnips and adding 1 teaspoon each ground turmeric, cumin and coriander and a 3.5 cm (1½ inch) piece of peeled and finely chopped fresh root ginger. Continue as above.

MINESTRONE SOUP

Serves **4**
Preparation time **25 minutes**
Cooking temperature **low** and **high**
Cooking time **6¼–8½ hours**

1 tablespoon **olive oil**
1 **onion**, chopped
1 **carrot**, diced
2 **smoked streaky bacon
  rashers**, diced
2 **garlic cloves**, finely chopped
4 **tomatoes**, skinned and chopped
2 **celery sticks**, diced
2 small **courgettes**, diced
3 teaspoons **pesto**, plus extra
  to serve
1.2 litres (2 pints) **chicken** or
  vegetable stock
75 g (3 oz) **purple sprouting
  broccoli** stems and florets
  cut into small pieces
40 g (1½ oz) **tiny dried soup pasta**
salt and **pepper**
freshly grated **Parmesan cheese**,
  to serve

Preheat the slow cooker if necessary. Heat the oil in a large frying pan, add the onion, carrot and bacon and fry, stirring, until lightly browned.

Add the garlic, then stir in the tomatoes, celery and courgettes and cook for 1–2 minutes. Stir in the pesto and stock, then add a little salt and pepper and bring to the boil, stirring.

Pour into the slow cooker pot, cover and cook on low for 6–8 hours or until the vegetables are tender. Add the broccoli and pasta, replace the lid and cook on high for 15–30 minutes or until the pasta is tender.

Stir well, taste and adjust the seasoning, if needed, then ladle the soup into bowls. Top with extra spoonfuls of pesto, to taste, and sprinkle with grated Parmesan. Serve with crusty bread, if liked.

FOR CURRIED VEGETABLE & CHICKEN SOUP, omit the bacon and add the diced meat from 2 chicken thighs when frying the onion and carrot. Add the garlic, tomatoes, celery and courgettes, then add 3 teaspoons mild curry paste instead of the pesto and 40 g (1½ oz) basmati rice. Add 1.2 litres (2 pints) chicken stock and continue as above, omitting the pasta. Garnish with chopped coriander and serve with warmed naan breads.

CHUNKY CHICKPEA & CHORIZO SOUP

Serves **4**
Preparation time **20 minutes**
Cooking temperature **low**
Cooking time **6–8 hours**

2 tablespoons **olive oil**
1 **onion**, chopped
2 **garlic cloves**, finely chopped
150 g (5 oz) **chorizo**, skinned
   and diced
¾ teaspoon **smoked paprika**
2–3 **thyme sprigs**
1 litre (1¾ pints) **chicken stock**
1 tablespoon **tomato purée**
375 g (12 oz) **sweet potatoes**, diced
410 g (13½ oz) can **chickpeas**, drained
salt and **pepper**
chopped **parsley** or **thyme leaves**,
   to garnish

Preheat the slow cooker if necessary. Heat the oil in a frying pan, add the onion and fry, stirring, for 5 minutes or until just beginning to turn golden.

Stir in the garlic and chorizo and cook for 2 minutes. Mix in the paprika, add the thyme sprigs, stock and tomato purée and bring to the boil, stirring, then add a little salt and pepper.

Add the sweet potatoes and chickpeas to the slow cooker pot and pour over the hot stock mixture. Cover with the lid and cook on low for 6–8 hours until the sweet potatoes are tender.

Ladle into bowls, sprinkle with a little chopped parsley or thyme leaves and serve with warmed pitta breads, if liked.

FOR TOMATO, CHICKPEA & CHORIZO SOUP, make the soup as above up to the point where the paprika and thyme have been added. Reduce the stock to 750 ml (1¼ pints) and add to the frying pan with the tomato purée and 2 teaspoons brown sugar. Bring to the boil. Omit the sweet potatoes but add 500 g (1 lb) skinned and diced tomatoes to the slow cooker pot along with the chickpeas. Pour over the stock mixture and continue as above.

CRAB GUMBO

Serves **4**
Preparation time **25 minutes**
Cooking temperature **high**
Cooking time **3 hours
20 minutes–4½ hours**

1 tablespoon **sunflower oil**
1 **onion**, finely chopped
1 **garlic clove**, chopped
2 **celery sticks**, sliced
1 **carrot**, cut into small dice
400 g (13 oz) can **chopped tomatoes**
600 ml (1 pint) **fish stock**
50 g (2 oz) **easy-cook white
long-grain rice**
1 **bay leaf**
2 **thyme sprigs**
¼ teaspoon **crushed dried
red chillies**
75 g (3 oz) **okra**, sliced
43 g (1¾ oz) can **dressed brown
crab meat**
salt and **pepper**
170 g (5¾ oz) can **white crab meat**,
to serve (optional)

Preheat the slow cooker if necessary. Heat the oil in a large frying pan, add the onion and fry for 5 minutes or until softened.

Stir in the garlic, celery and carrot, then mix in the tomatoes, stock, rice, thyme and chillies. Add a little salt and pepper and bring to the boil. Pour into the slow cooker pot, cover with the lid and cook on high for 3–4 hours or until the vegetables and rice are tender.

Stir the soup, then add the okra and dressed brown crab meat. Replace the lid and cook on high for 20–30 minutes. Ladle the soup into bowls and top with the flaked white crab meat and serve with warm crusty bread, if liked.

FOR MIXED VEGETABLE GUMBO, make up the soup as above, omitting the cans of brown and white crab meat. Garnish with croutons made by frying 2 slices of bread, cut into cubes, in 25 g (1 oz) butter, 3 tablespoons olive oil and ¼ teaspoon crushed dried red chillies until golden.

LEEK, POTATO & STILTON SOUP

Serves **4–6**
Preparation time **25 minutes**
Cooking temperature **low**
Cooking time **5½–6½ hours**

25 g (1 oz) **butter**
1 tablespoon **sunflower oil**
500 g (1 lb) **leeks**, thinly sliced, white
and green parts kept separate
1 **smoked back bacon rasher**, diced,
plus 4 grilled **rashers**, chopped,
to garnish
375 g (12 oz) **potatoes**, diced
900 ml (1½ pints) **chicken** or
vegetable stock
300 ml (½ pint) **milk**
150 ml (¼ pint) **double cream**
150 g (5 oz) **mature Stilton** (rind
removed), diced
salt and pepper

Preheat the slow cooker if necessary. Heat the butter and oil in a large frying pan, then add the white leek slices, the diced bacon and potatoes and fry over a medium heat, stirring, until just beginning to turn golden.

Pour in the stock, add a little salt and pepper and bring to the boil, stirring. Transfer to the slow cooker pot, cover with the lid and cook on low for 5–6 hours. Stir the reserved green leek slices and milk into the slow cooker pot. Replace the lid and cook, still on low, for 30 minutes or until the leeks are tender. Roughly purée the soup in the pot with a stick blender or use a masher, if preferred.

Mix in the cream and two-thirds of the Stilton cheese and continue stirring until the cheese has melted. Taste and adjust the seasoning, if needed, then ladle the soup into bowls and sprinkle with the remaining cheese and chopped grilled bacon.

FOR COCK-A-LEEKIE SOUP, heat the butter and oil as above, then add 2 chicken thighs on the bone and fry until golden, remove them from the pan and put into the slow cooker pot. Fry the white leek slices, bacon and potatoes as above, then mix in 1.2 litres (2 pints) chicken stock, 50 g (2 oz) chopped ready-to-eat pitted prunes and a thyme sprig. Season, bring to the boil, then transfer to the slow cooker pot. Cover and cook on low for 8–10 hours. Take the chicken off the bone, discarding the skin, then dice the meat and return it to the pot with the green leek slices. Cook for 30 minutes, then ladle into bowls, omitting the milk, cream, Stilton and bacon garnish.

THAI BROTH WITH FISH DUMPLINGS

Serves **4**
Preparation time **30 minutes**
Cooking temperature **low** and **high**
Cooking time **2¼–3¼ hours**

900 ml (1½ pints) boiling **fish stock**
2 teaspoons **Thai fish sauce**
1 tablespoon **Thai red curry paste**
1 tablespoon **soy sauce**
1 **carrot**, thinly sliced
2 **garlic cloves**, finely chopped
bunch of **asparagus**, trimmed and stems cut into 4
2 **pak choi**, thickly sliced

DUMPLINGS
bunch of **spring onions**, sliced
15 g (½ oz) **coriander leaves**
3.5 cm (1½ inch) piece of **fresh root ginger**,
   peeled and sliced
400 g (13 oz) **cod fillet**, skinned
1 tablespoon **cornflour**
1 **egg white**

Preheat the slow cooker if necessary. Make the dumplings. Put half the spring onions into a food processor with the coriander and ginger and chop finely. Add the cod, cornflour and egg white and process until the fish is finely chopped. With wetted hands, shape into 12 balls.

Pour the fish stock into the slow cooker pot, add the fish sauce, curry paste and soy sauce. Add the rest of the spring onions, the carrot and garlic, then add the dumplings. Cover with the lid and cook on low for 2–3 hours. When almost ready to serve, add the asparagus and pak choi to the broth. Replace the lid and cook on high for 15 minutes or until just tender. Ladle into bowls and serve.

FOR THAI BROTH WITH NOODLES & PRAWNS, prepare and cook the broth as above, omitting the dumplings. Add the asparagus, pak choi and 200 g (7 oz) frozen large cooked peeled prawns, fully thawed, and cook for 15 minutes on high. Meanwhile, soak 75 g (3 oz) dried rice noodles in boiling water according to the packet instructions. Drain and add to 4 soup bowls. Ladle the broth on top and garnish with chopped coriander.

CHEESY CAULIFLOWER SOUP

Serves **4**
Preparation time 20 minutes
Cooking temperature **low** and **high**
Cooking time **4¼–5¼ hours**

25 g (1 oz) **butter**
1 tablespoon **olive oil**
1 **onion**, chopped
1 small **baking potato**, about 150 g (5 oz), cut into
   small dice
1 **cauliflower**, trimmed and cut into pieces, about
   500 g (1 lb) prepared weight
600 ml (1 pint) **vegetable stock**
1 teaspoon **English mustard**
3 teaspoons **Worcestershire sauce**
50 g (2 oz) **Parmesan** or **mature Cheddar cheese**, grated
200 ml (7 fl oz) **milk**
grated **nutmeg**
salt and **pepper**

Preheat the slow cooker if necessary. Heat the butter and oil in a large frying pan, add the onion and potato and fry for 5 minutes or until softened but not coloured.

Stir in the cauliflower, stock, mustard, Worcestershire sauce, cheese and a little salt and pepper and bring to the boil. Pour into the slow cooker pot, cover with the lid and cook on low for 4–5 hours or until the vegetables are tender.

Purée the soup while still in the slow cooker pot with a stick blender. Alternatively, transfer to a freestanding blender and purée, in batches if necessary, until smooth, then return to the slow cooker pot.

Stir in the milk, replace the lid and cook on high for 15 minutes until reheated. Stir and add nutmeg to taste. Ladle the soup into bowls and serve.

FOR CHEESY PUMPKIN SOUP, omit the cauliflower and add 500 g (1 lb) peeled, deseeded and diced pumpkin or butternut squash to the fried onion and potato mixture. Continue as above.

FRAGRANT SPICED CHICKEN ♥

Serves **4**
Preparation time **15 minutes**
Cooking temperature **high**
Cooking time **5¼–6¼ hours**

1.5 kg (3 lb) **oven-ready chicken**
1 **onion**, chopped
200 g (7 oz) **carrots**, sliced
7.5 cm (3 inch) piece of **fresh root
    ginger**, peeled and sliced
2 **garlic cloves**, sliced
1 large **mild red chilli**, halved
3 large **star anise**
4 tablespoons **soy sauce**
4 tablespoons **rice vinegar**
1 tablespoon **light muscovado sugar**
900 ml (1½ pints) boiling **water**
small bunch of **coriander**
75 g (3 oz) **mangetout**, thickly sliced
150 g (5 oz) **pak choi**, thickly sliced
salt and **pepper**
200 g (7 oz) **dried egg noodles**,
    to serve

Preheat the slow cooker if necessary. Place the chicken, breast side down, in the slow cooker pot. Add the onion, carrots, ginger, garlic, chilli and star anise and spoon over the soy sauce, vinegar and sugar. Pour over the measurement boiling water.

Add the coriander stems, reserving the leaves, and season to taste. Cover and cook on high for 5–6 hours or until the chicken is thoroughly cooked and the meat juices run clear when the thickest parts of the leg and breast are pierced with a sharp knife.

Transfer the chicken to a chopping board and keep warm. Add the mangetout and pak choi to the pot, cover again and cook for about 10 minutes or until just wilted. Meanwhile, cook the noodles according to the packet instructions, drain well and divide between 4 bowls.

Carve the chicken into bite-sized pieces and arrange on top of the noodles with the reserved coriander leaves, then ladle over the hot broth. Serve immediately.

FOR ITALIAN SPICED CHICKEN WITH PESTO, put the chicken into the pot with 1 chopped onion, 200 g (7 oz) sliced carrots, 2 sliced garlic cloves, 1 sliced fennel bulb and 1 sliced lemon. Pour over the boiling water as above and replace the coriander with a small bunch of basil. Use 3 chopped tomatoes, 150 g (5 oz) chopped purple sprouting broccoli and 2 tablespoons pesto sauce instead of the mangetout and pak choi. Cook 250 g (8 oz) fresh tagliatelle in a large saucepan of lightly salted boiling water according to the packet instructions until just tender and serve with the chicken.

STEWS &
CASSEROLES

CHICKEN & SAGE HOTPOT

Serves **4**
Preparation time **30 minutes**
Cooking temperature **high**
Cooking time **4–5 hours**

1 tablespoon **sunflower oil**
6 **boneless, skinless chicken thighs**,
    about 550 g (1 lb 2 oz), each cut
    into 3 pieces
1 **onion**, sliced
4 **smoked streaky bacon**
    rashers, diced
2 tablespoons **plain flour**
600 ml (1 pint) **chicken stock** or
    a mix of **stock** and **dry cider**
2–3 **sage sprigs**
125 g (4 oz) **black pudding**, skinned
    and diced (optional)
200 g (7 oz) **carrots**, diced
200 g (7 oz) **swede**, diced
625 g (1¼ lb) **potatoes**, thinly sliced
25 g (1 oz) **butter**
salt and **pepper**

Preheat the slow cooker if necessary. Heat the oil in a large frying pan, add the chicken a few pieces at a time until all the meat is in the pan, then add the onion and bacon and fry, stirring, until the chicken is golden.

Stir in the flour, then gradually mix in the stock or stock and cider. Add the sage sprigs and a little salt and pepper and bring to the boil, stirring.

Add the black pudding, if using, carrots and swede to the slow cooker pot. Pour over the hot chicken mixture, then arrange the potatoes overlapping on the top and press below the surface of the liquid. Sprinkle with a little extra salt and pepper, then cover and cook on high for 4–5 hours or until the potatoes are tender and the chicken is cooked through.

Lift the pot out of the housing using oven gloves, dot the potatoes with butter and brown under a preheated hot grill. Spoon the hotpot into shallow dishes to serve.

FOR MUSTARDY BEEF HOTPOT, replace the chicken with 750 g (1½ lb) trimmed and diced stewing beef. Fry the beef in the oil and transfer to the slow cooker pot, then fry the onion, omitting the bacon. Stir in the flour, then mix in 600 ml (1 pint) beef stock, 2 teaspoons English mustard, 1 tablespoon Worcestershire sauce, 1 tablespoon tomato purée and salt and pepper and bring to the boil. Omit the black pudding and continue as above.

PORK STEW WITH SWEET POTATOES ♥

Serves **4**
Preparation time **20 minutes**
Cooking temperature **low** and **high**
Cooking time **8¼–9¼ hours**

low-calorie cooking oil spray
500 g (1 lb) **lean pork**, cubed
1 **onion**, chopped
125 g (4 oz) **closed-cap mushrooms**, sliced
450 ml (¾ pint) **chicken stock**
2 tablespoons **tomato purée**
2 tablespoons **soy sauce**
¼ teaspoon **chilli powder**
½ teaspoon **ground allspice**
¼ teaspoon **ground cinnamon**
1 teaspoon **granular sweetener**
150 g (5 oz) **carrots**, thinly sliced
2 **celery sticks**, thickly sliced
375 g (12 oz) **sweet potato**, cut into 2.5 cm (1 inch) chunks
125 g (4 oz) **curly kale**, shredded

Preheat the slow cooker if necessary. Spray a large frying pan with a little low-calorie cooking oil spray and place over a high heat until hot. Add the pork a few pieces at a time until all the pork is in the pan and cook for 3 minutes, stirring. Add the onion and cook for a further 2–3 minutes until the pork is golden.

Stir in the mushrooms, then add the stock, tomato purée and soy sauce. Add the chilli powder, allspice, cinnamon and sweetener, season to taste and bring to the boil, stirring.

Place the carrots, celery and sweet potato in the slow cooker pot, then pour over the pork and sauce. Press the meat into the liquid, cover and cook on low for 8–9 hours until the pork is tender.

Stir the stew, then add the kale. Cover again and cook on high for 15 minutes, then spoon into bowls and serve immediately.

FOR FRAGRANT SAUSAGE & SWEET POTATO STEW, place 500 g (1 lb) reduced-fat pork sausages under a preheated hot grill until browned but not cooked through. Transfer to the slow cooker pot. Continue with the recipe above, omitting the pork.

CHILLI BLACK BEAN STEW

Serves **4–6**
Preparation time **30 minutes, plus overnight soaking**
Cooking temperature **low**
Cooking time **8–10 hours**

250 g (8 oz) **dried black beans**, soaked overnight in cold water
2 tablespoons **olive oil**
1 large **onion**, chopped
2 **carrots**, diced
2 **celery sticks**, sliced
2–3 **garlic cloves**, chopped
1 teaspoon **fennel seeds**, crushed
1 teaspoon **cumin seeds**, crushed
2 teaspoons **coriander seeds**, crushed
1 teaspoon **chilli powder** or **smoked paprika**
400 g (13 oz) can **chopped tomatoes**
300 ml (½ pint) **vegetable stock**
1 tablespoon **brown sugar**
150 g (5 oz) **soured cream** or **natural yogurt** (optional)
salt and **pepper**
boiled **rice** or **crusty bread**, to serve

Preheat the slow cooker if necessary. Drain and rinse the soaked beans, then drain again. Place them in a saucepan, add fresh water to cover and bring to the boil. Boil vigorously for 10 minutes, then drain into a sieve.

Meanwhile, heat the oil in a saucepan, add the onion and fry, stirring, for 5 minutes or until softened. Add the carrots, celery and garlic and fry for 2–3 minutes. Stir the crushed fennel, cumin and coriander seeds into the vegetables with the chilli powder or paprika and cook for 1 minute.

Add the tomatoes, stock, sugar and a little pepper. Bring to the boil, then pour into the slow cooker pot. Mix in the beans, pressing them under the liquid, then cover with the lid and cook on low for 8–10 hours.

Season the cooked beans to taste with salt. Top with spoonfuls of soured cream or yogurt, if liked, and Avocado Salsa (*see* below), and serve accompanied by boiled rice or crusty bread.

FOR AVOCADO SALSA TO ACCOMPANY THE STEW, halve, stone and peel 1 avocado. Dice the flesh and toss with the grated rind and juice of 1 lime. Mix with ½ finely chopped red onion, 2 diced tomatoes and 2 tablespoons chopped coriander leaves. Make the salsa about 10 minutes before serving the stew.

SPICED BEEF & RED PEPPER STEW ♥

Serves **4**
Preparation time **20 minutes**
Cooking temperature **low**
Cooking time **8–10 hours**

low-calorie cooking oil spray
500 g (1 lb) **stewing beef**, trimmed of
    fat and cubed
2 **red onions**, cut into wedges
2 **celery sticks**, thickly sliced
2 **red peppers**, cored, deseeded and
    cut into chunks
2 **garlic cloves**, finely chopped
1 teaspoon **cumin seeds**,
    roughly crushed
1 teaspoon **chilli powder**
2 teaspoons **plain flour**
450 ml (¾ pint) **beef stock**
1 tablespoon **tomato purée**
salt and **pepper**

TO SERVE
4 tablespoons chopped **coriander**
250 g (8 oz) **long-grain rice**, boiled

Preheat the slow cooker if necessary. Spray a large frying pan with a little
low-calorie cooking oil spray and place over a high heat until hot. Add
the beef a few pieces at a time until all the beef is in the pan and cook for
5 minutes, stirring, until browned. Use a slotted spoon to transfer the beef
to the slow cooker pot.

Add a little more low-calorie cooking oil spray to the pan, add the onion
wedges and cook for 2–3 minutes, stirring. Add the celery and red peppers,
then stir in the garlic, crushed cumin seeds and chilli powder and cook for
1 minute.

Stir in the flour, then add the stock and tomato purée, season to taste and
bring to the boil, stirring. Spoon over the beef, cover and cook on low for
8–10 hours until the beef is tender.

Stir the chopped coriander into the cooked rice and spoon into shallow
bowls. Stir the beef casserole, spoon over the rice and serve.

FOR CHINESE GINGERED BEEF, follow the recipe above, replacing the
cumin seeds and chilli powder with 2 tablespoons soy sauce and
2 tablespoons finely chopped fresh root ginger. Serve with 250 g (8 oz)
dried egg noodles, cooked according to the packet instructions.

TURKEY & SAUSAGE STEW

Serves **4**
Preparation time **30 minutes**
Cooking temperature **high**
Cooking time **5½–6¾ hours**

1 **turkey drumstick**, about 700 g
(1 lb 6 oz)
2 tablespoons **sunflower oil**
4 **smoked streaky bacon
rashers**, diced
3 large **pork and herb sausages**,
about 200 g (7 oz) in total, each
cut into 4 pieces
1 **onion**, sliced
1 **leek**, sliced, white and green parts
kept separate
2 tablespoons **plain flour**
600 ml (1 pint) **chicken stock**
small bunch of mixed **herbs**
300 g (10 oz) **baby carrots**, halved
if large
2 **celery sticks**, sliced
65 g (2½oz) fresh **cranberries**
salt and **pepper**

PARSLEY DUMPLINGS
150 g (5 oz) **self-raising flour**
75 g (3 oz) **shredded suet**
4 tablespoons chopped **parsley**
5–7 tablespoons **water**

Preheat the slow cooker if necessary. If the turkey drumstick does not fit into the slow cooker pot, sever the knuckle end with a large heavy knife, hitting it with a rolling pin.

Heat the oil in a large frying pan, add the drumstick, bacon and sausage pieces and fry, turning, until browned all over. Transfer to the slow cooker pot. Add the onion and white leek slices to the pan and fry until softened. Stir in the flour, then mix in the stock. Add the herbs and salt and pepper and bring to the boil. Add the carrots, celery and cranberries to the pot and pour over the hot onion mixture.

Cover and cook on high for 5–6 hours or until the turkey is almost falling off the bone. Lift the turkey out of the slow cooker pot. Remove and discard the skin, then cut the meat into pieces, discarding the bones and tendons. Return the meat to the pot with the reserved green leek slices.

Make the dumplings. Mix the flour, suet, parsley and salt and pepper in a bowl. Stir in enough of the measurement water to make a soft dough. Knead, then shape into 12 small balls. Arrange over the turkey, replace the lid and cook, still on high, for 30–45 minutes or until the dumplings are cooked through. Spoon into shallow bowls to serve.

FOR TURKEY & CRANBERRY PUFF PIE, make the stew as above. Roll out 500 g (1 lb) puff pastry, thawed if frozen, trim to an oval a little larger than the top of the slow cooker pot and put on an oiled baking sheet. Brush the top with beaten egg, then bake in a preheated oven, 200°C (400°F), Gas Mark 6, for about 25 minutes until golden. Spoon the stew on to plates and top with wedges of the pastry.

POLISH SAUSAGE STEW ♥

Serves **4**
Preparation time **20 minutes**
Cooking temperature **low**
Cooking time **8–10 hours**

low-calorie cooking oil spray
325 g (11 oz) **boneless, skinless
    chicken thighs**, cubed
1 **onion**, chopped
2 teaspoons **mild paprika**
1 teaspoon **caraway seeds**
1 **dessert apple**, quartered, cored
    and thinly sliced
250 g (8 oz) **tomatoes**, diced
1 tablespoon **granular sweetener**
400 g (13 oz) **sauerkraut**, drained
200 g (7 oz) **smoked pork
    sausage**, sliced
100 g (3½ oz) **gherkins**, sliced
150 ml (¼ pint) hot chicken stock
salt and **pepper**

TO GARNISH
3 tablespoons chopped **dill**
3 tablespoons chopped **parsley**

Preheat the slow cooker if necessary. Spray a large frying pan with a little low-calorie cooking oil spray and place over a high heat until hot. Add the chicken a few pieces at a time until all the chicken is in the pan, then add the onion and cook for 5 minutes, stirring, until the chicken is golden.

Add the paprika, caraway, apple, tomatoes and sweetener to the pan and heat through. Place the sauerkraut in the slow cooker pot and pour the chicken mixture on top, then add the sliced sausage and gherkins.

Pour over the hot stock and season to taste. Stir well, cover and cook on low for 8–10 hours until the chicken is cooked through and tender. Serve in bowls, garnished with the chopped dill and parsley.

FOR POLISH PORK STEW, follow the recipe above, using 500 g (1 lb) diced lean pork instead of the chicken. Use 1 teaspoon mild paprika and 1 teaspoon smoked hot paprika or chilli powder instead of 2 teaspoons mild paprika, and continue with the recipe, omitting the smoked sausage.

ALL-IN-ONE CHICKEN CASSEROLE ♥

Serves **4**
Preparation time **20 minutes**
Cooking temperature **low**
Cooking time **8¼–10¼ hours**

low-calorie cooking oil spray
4 **skinless chicken legs**, 875 g
   (1¾ lb) in total
50 g (2 oz) **smoked back bacon
   rashers**, trimmed of fat
   and chopped
300 g (10 oz) **baby new potatoes**,
   scrubbed and thickly sliced
2 small **leeks**, thickly sliced, white
   and green parts kept separate
2 **celery sticks**, thickly sliced
2 **carrots**, sliced
2 teaspoons **plain flour**
1 teaspoon **dried mixed herbs**
1 teaspoon **mustard powder**
450 ml (¾ pint) **chicken stock**
50 g (2 oz) **curly kale**, sliced
salt and **pepper**

Spray a large frying pan with a little low-calorie cooking oil spray and place over a high heat until hot. Add the chicken and cook for 5 minutes, turning, until browned all over. Transfer to the slow cooker pot.

Add the bacon and potatoes to the frying pan with a little extra low-calorie cooking oil spray and cook for 4–5 minutes, stirring, until the bacon is beginning to brown. Stir in the white leek slices, celery and carrots. Add the flour, herbs and mustard and stir well.

Pour in the stock, season to taste and bring to the boil, stirring. Spoon over the chicken, cover and cook on low for 8–10 hours or until the chicken is tender and cooked through.

Add the reserved green leek slices and the kale to the slow cooker pot, cover and cook for 15 minutes, still on low, until the vegetables are just tender. Serve in shallow bowls.

FOR CHICKEN HOTPOT, follow the main recipe to make the chicken mixture, omitting the new potatoes and carrots. Transfer to the slow cooker pot and cover with 300 g (10 oz) scrubbed and thinly sliced baking potatoes and 2 thinly sliced carrots, arranging the slices alternately overlapping. Spray with low-calorie cooking oil spray, season to taste, then cook as above. Brown the top under a preheated hot grill, if liked.

CHUNKY CHICKEN & BASIL STEW ♥

Serves **4**
Preparation time **20 minutes**
Cooking temperature **low** and **high**
Cooking time **8½–10¾ hours**

low-calorie cooking oil spray
625 g (1¼ lb) **boneless, skinless chicken thighs**, each cut into 3 pieces
1 **onion**, chopped
2 small **carrots**, finely diced
2 teaspoons **plain flour**
350 ml (12 fl oz) **chicken stock**
15 g (½ oz) **basil leaves**, torn, plus extra to garnish
100 g (3½ oz) **frozen peas**, thawed
200 g (7 oz) **Tenderstem broccoli**, stems cut into 3 or 4 pieces
150 g (5 oz) **fine green beans**, thickly sliced
salt and **pepper**

Preheat the slow cooker if necessary. Spray a large frying pan with a little low-calorie cooking oil spray and place over a high heat until hot. Add the chicken a few pieces at a time until all the chicken is in the pan and cook for 5 minutes, stirring, until golden. Transfer to the slow cooker pot using a slotted spoon.

Add a little more low-calorie cooking oil spray to the pan if necessary, then cook the onion for 4–5 minutes until just beginning to soften. Stir in the carrots and flour, then add the stock and bring to the boil, stirring. Add the basil, season to taste and pour over the chicken. Cover and cook on low for 8–10 hours until the chicken is tender and cooked through.

Add the peas, broccoli and green beans, cover again and cook on high for 15–30 minutes until the vegetables are tender. Serve in bowls, garnished with extra basil.

FOR CHUNKY CHICKEN WITH 30 GARLIC CLOVES, brown 625 g (1¼ lb) boneless, skinless chicken thighs, each cut into 3 pieces, in a frying pan and place in the slow cooker pot with 30 unpeeled garlic cloves. Follow the recipe above, using 250 g (8 oz) small peeled shallots instead of the onion and carrot, and 3 thyme sprigs and 2 teaspoons Dijon mustard instead of the basil. Cook as above, omitting the green vegetables, and serve sprinkled with chopped parsley.

IRISH STEW

Serves **4**
Preparation time **20 minutes**
Cooking temperature **high**
Cooking time **6–7 hours**

2 tablespoons **sunflower oil**
1 kg (2 lb) **stewing lamb** or **budget lamb chops** of different sizes
1 **onion**, roughly chopped
3 **carrots**, sliced
250 g (8 oz) **swede**, diced
250 g (8 oz) **parsnips**, diced
2 tablespoons **plain flour**
400 g (13 oz) **potatoes**, cut into chunks no bigger than 3.5 cm (1½ inches)
800 ml (1 pint 7 fl oz) **lamb** or **chicken stock**
3 rosemary sprigs
salt and **pepper**
4 tablespoons mixed chopped **chives** and **rosemary**, to garnish

Preheat the slow cooker if necessary. Heat the oil in a large frying pan, add the lamb and fry until browned on both sides. Scoop out of the pan with a slotted spoon and transfer to a plate.

Add the onion to the pan and fry for 5 minutes or until softened. Add the carrots, swede and parsnips and cook for 1–2 minutes, then stir in the flour. Add the potatoes, stock, rosemary sprigs and plenty of salt and pepper and bring to the boil, stirring.

Pour into the slow cooker pot, add the lamb and press below the surface of the liquid. Cover with the lid and cook on high for 6–7 hours or until the lamb is falling off the bones and the potatoes are tender.

Spoon into shallow bowls, removing the lamb bones if liked, and sprinkle with the chopped chives and rosemary. Serve with a spoon and fork and crusty bread, if liked.

FOR LAMB STEW WITH DUMPLINGS, make up the stew as above. About 35–50 minutes before the end of cooking, mix 150 g (5 oz) self-raising flour, 75 g (3 oz) shredded vegetable suet, 2 teaspoons chopped rosemary leaves and a little salt and pepper in a bowl. Stir in 5–7 tablespoons water to make a soft but not sticky dough. Shape into 12 balls, add to the slow cooker pot, cover and cook on high for 30–45 minutes until well risen.

BALSAMIC BEEF HOTPOT ♥

Serves **4**
Preparation time **30 minutes**
Cooking temperature **high**
Cooking time **7–8 hours**

low-calorie cooking oil spray
600 g (1 lb) **lean stewing beef**,
   trimmed of fat and cubed
1 **onion**, chopped
250 g (8 oz) **swede**, cut into 2 cm
   (¾ inch) cubes
300 g (10 oz) **carrots**, sliced
150 g (5 oz) **mushrooms**, sliced
2 teaspoons **plain flour**
450 ml (¾ pint) **beef stock**
2 tablespoons **balsamic vinegar**
1 teaspoon **mustard powder**
500 g (1 lb) **potatoes**, sliced
salt and **pepper**
1 tablespoon chopped **parsley**,
   to garnish

TO SERVE
200 g (7 oz) **broccoli**
   florets, steamed
200 g (7 oz) **sugar snap**
   peas, steamed

Preheat the slow cooker if necessary. Spray a large frying pan with a little low-calorie cooking oil spray and place over a high heat until hot. Add the beef a few pieces at a time until all the beef is in the pan and cook for 5 minutes, stirring, until browned. Use a slotted spoon to transfer the beef to the slow cooker pot.

Add a little more low-calorie cooking oil spray to the pan, add the onion and cook for 4–5 minutes until beginning to brown. Add the swede, carrots and mushrooms and cook for 2 minutes. Add the flour and stir well.

Stir in the stock, vinegar and mustard, season to taste and bring to the boil. Pour over the beef in the slow cooker pot. Arrange the potato slices on top, slightly overlapping. Season lightly, then press the potatoes into the stock. Cover and cook on high for 7–8 hours until the potatoes and beef are tender.

Lift the pot out of the housing using oven gloves. Spray the potatoes with a little extra low-calorie cooking oil spray, then place under a preheated hot grill until the potatoes are golden. Sprinkle with the parsley and serve with the steamed vegetables.

FOR MUSTARD BEEF HOTPOT, follow the recipe above, using 1 tablespoon wholegrain mustard in place of the balsamic vinegar and mustard powder.

CHICKEN & HARICOT BEAN STEW

Serves **4**
Preparation time **20 minutes**
Cooking temperature **low**
Cooking time **8–9 hours**

2 tablespoons **olive oil**
625 g (1¼ lb) **boneless, skinless
  chicken thighs**, cubed
1 **onion**, sliced
2 **garlic cloves**, finely chopped
2 tablespoons **plain flour**
600 ml (1 pint) **chicken stock**
1 **red pepper**, cored, deseeded
  and sliced
200 g (7 oz) can **sweetcorn**, drained
410 g (13½oz) can **haricot
  beans**, drained
300 g (10 oz) small **new potatoes**,
  scrubbed and thinly sliced
2 **thyme sprigs**, plus extra leaves
  to garnish (optional)
salt and **pepper**

Preheat the slow cooker if necessary. Heat the oil in a large frying pan, add the chicken and onion and fry, stirring, until lightly browned.

Stir in the garlic and flour, then gradually mix in the stock. Add the red pepper, sweetcorn, haricot beans and new potatoes. Add the thyme and a little salt and pepper and bring to the boil, stirring.

Transfer the mixture to the slow cooker pot and press the chicken and potatoes below the surface of the liquid. Cover with the lid and cook on low for 8–9 hours or until the chicken is cooked through and the potatoes are tender.

Stir well, then spoon into shallow bowls and sprinkle with a few extra thyme leaves. Serve with hot garlic bread, if liked.

FOR SPANISH CHICKEN WITH CHORIZO, fry the chicken and onion as above with 75 g (3 oz) ready-diced chorizo until well coloured, then mix in 1 teaspoon smoked paprika, the garlic and flour. Continue as above, replacing the thyme sprigs with 2 rosemary sprigs. Serve sprinkled with chopped parsley.

HEARTY WINTER SAUSAGE STEW ♥

Serves **4**
Preparation time **20 minutes**
Cooking temperature **high**
Cooking time **5–6 hours**

low-calorie cooking oil spray
50 g (2 oz) **smoked back bacon rashers**, trimmed
   of fat and chopped
1 **red onion**, chopped
½ teaspoon **smoked hot paprika** or **chilli powder**
300 ml (½ pint) **chicken stock**
400 g (13 oz) can **reduced-sugar baked beans**
450 g (14½ oz) **extra-lean sausages**
1 **red pepper**, cored, deseeded and chopped
400 g (13 oz) peeled and deseeded **pumpkin**, diced
2 **celery sticks**, thickly sliced
2 sage sprigs or ½ teaspoon **dried sage**
salt and **pepper**

Preheat the slow cooker if necessary. Spray a large frying pan with a little low-calorie cooking oil spray and place over a high heat until hot. Add the bacon and onion and fry for 4–5 minutes, stirring, until just beginning to brown. Stir in the paprika or chilli powder, then pour in the stock and baked beans. Season to taste, then bring to the boil, stirring.

Arrange the sausages in a single layer in the base of the slow cooker pot, top with the red pepper, pumpkin, celery and sage, then pour over the hot stock and beans. Cover and cook on high for 5–6 hours. Stir the stew, spoon into shallow bowls and serve.

FOR BONFIRE NIGHT CHICKEN STEW, follow the recipe above, using 625 g (1¼ lb) boneless, skinless chicken thighs instead of the sausages, and browning it with the bacon and onion. Add to the slow cooker pot with the vegetables, pour over the hot stock and beans, cover and cook on low for 7–8 hours.

CIDERED GAMMON HOTPOT ♥

Serves **4**
Preparation time **25 minutes**
Cooking temperature **high**
Cooking time **6–7 hours**

500 g (1 lb) **unsmoked gammon joint**, trimmed of fat
625 g (1¼ lb) **baking potatoes**, cut into 2 cm
   (¾ inch) chunks
200 g (7 oz) small **shallots**, peeled
3 **carrots**, thickly sliced
2 **celery sticks**, thickly sliced
1 large **leek**, thickly sliced
2 **bay leaves**
200 ml (7 fl oz) **dry cider**
200 ml (7 fl oz) hot **chicken stock**
¼ teaspoon **cloves**
1 teaspoon **mustard powder**
pepper
3 tablespoons chopped **chives**, to garnish

Preheat the slow cooker if necessary. Rinse the gammon joint with cold water, drain and place in the slow cooker pot with the potatoes. Arrange the shallots, carrots, celery and leek slices around the gammon, then tuck in the bay leaves.

Pour the cider and stock into a saucepan, add the cloves and mustard powder, then season with pepper (gammon joints can be salty, so don't be tempted to add salt). Bring to the boil, then pour around the gammon. Cover and cook on high for 6–7 hours until the gammon is cooked through.

Cut the gammon into pieces and serve in shallow bowls with the vegetables and stock, garnished with chopped chives.

FOR GAMMON IN COLA, follow the recipe above, using 450 ml (¾ pint) diet cola instead of the cider and stock and omitting the potatoes. Serve with 625 g (1¼ lb) boiled baby new potatoes and 150 g (5 oz) steamed green beans.

SKINNY CASSOULET ♥

Serves **4**
Preparation time **20 minutes**
Cooking temperature **low**
Cooking time **8–10 hours**

low-calorie cooking oil spray
500 g (1 lb) **lean pork**, diced
75 g (3 oz) **chorizo**, sliced
1 **onion**, chopped
3 **garlic cloves**, finely chopped
1 **red pepper**, cored, deseeded
   and diced
2 **celery sticks**, sliced
1 **carrot**, diced
500 g (1 lb) **passata**
1 teaspoon **dried
   Mediterranean herbs**
2 x 375 g (12 oz) cans **cannellini
   beans**, drained
3 tablespoons **fresh breadcrumbs**
salt and **pepper**

Preheat the slow cooker if necessary. Spray a large frying pan with a little low-calorie cooking oil spray and place over a high heat until hot. Add the pork a few pieces at a time until all the meat is in the pan and cook for 5 minutes, stirring, until browned. Use a slotted spoon to transfer the pork to the slow cooker pot.

Add the chorizo and onion to the frying pan and cook for 4–5 minutes until the onion has softened. Stir in the garlic, red pepper, celery, carrot, passata and herbs. Season to taste and bring to the boil, stirring.

Place the beans in the slow cooker pot, pour over the passata mixture and stir well. Level the surface with the back of a spoon, then sprinkle over the breadcrumbs. Cover and cook on low for 8–10 hours until the pork is tender. Spoon into shallow bowls and serve with salad, if liked.

FOR CHICKEN CASSOULET, follow the recipe above, using 500 g (1 lb) boneless, skinless chicken thighs, diced, instead of the pork. Mix the breadcrumbs with 2 tablespoons chopped rosemary and 2 tablespoons chopped parsley, then spoon over the cassoulet and cook as above.

CHICKEN & POULTRY

LEMON CHICKEN

Serves **4**
Preparation time **20 minutes**
Cooking temperature **high**
Cooking time **3¼–4¼ hours**

1 tablespoon **olive oil**
4 **boneless, skinless chicken breasts**,
   about 550 g (1 lb 2 oz) in total
1 **onion**, chopped
2 **garlic cloves**, finely chopped
2 tablespoons **plain flour**
450 ml (¾ pint) **chicken stock**
½ **lemon** (cut in half lengthways), cut
   into 4 wedges
2 **pak choi**, thickly sliced
125 g (4 oz) **sugar snap peas**,
   halved lengthways
4 tablespoons **crème fraîche**
2 tablespoons mixed chopped **mint**
   and **parsley**
salt and **pepper**

TO SERVE
couscous mixed with finely chopped
   tomato, **red onion** and **red pepper**

Preheat the slow cooker if necessary. Heat the oil in a large frying pan, add the chicken breasts and fry over a high heat until browned on both sides. Remove from the pan and transfer to a plate. Add the onion to the pan and fry, stirring, for 5 minutes or until lightly browned.

Stir in the garlic and flour, then mix in the stock and lemon wedges. Season with salt and pepper and bring to the boil.

Put the chicken breasts in the slow cooker pot, pour the hot stock mixture over them and press the chicken below the surface of the liquid. Cover and cook on high for 3–4 hours until tender and cooked through.

Add the pak choi and sugar snap peas and cook, still on high, for 15 minutes or until just tender. Lift out the chicken, slice the pieces and arrange them on plates. Stir the crème fraîche and herbs into the sauce, then spoon it and the vegetables over the chicken. Serve with couscous mixed with finely chopped tomato, red onion and red pepper.

FOR LEMON CHICKEN WITH HARISSA, add 4 teaspoons harissa to the frying pan with the chicken stock and wedges cut from ½ lemon. Continue as above. Omit the pak choi at the end, adding instead 125 g (4 oz) broccoli, the florets cut into small pieces and stems sliced, and ½ sliced courgette. Reduce the sugar snap peas to just 50 g (2 oz).

TARRAGON CHICKEN WITH MUSHROOMS ♥

Serves **4**
Preparation time **20 minutes**
Cooking temperature **low** and **high**
Cooking time **8¼–9½ hours**

low-calorie cooking oil spray
4 **skinless chicken legs**, 1.2 kg
(2 lb 6 oz) in total
2 **leeks**, sliced, white and green
parts kept separate
175 g (6 oz) **closed-cap**
mushrooms, sliced
1 tablespoon **plain flour**
1 teaspoon **mustard powder**
450 ml (¾ pint) **chicken stock**
2 tablespoons chopped **tarragon**,
plus extra to garnish
3 tablespoons **sherry** (optional)
125 g (1 oz) fine green beans
salt and **pepper**

Preheat the slow cooker if necessary. Spray a large frying pan with a little low-calorie cooking oil spray and place over a high heat until hot. Add the chicken legs and cook for 4–5 minutes, turning once, until golden. Transfer to the slow cooker pot.

Add a little extra low-calorie cooking oil spray to the pan if necessary, then add the white leek slices and the mushrooms and cook for 2–3 minutes. Stir in the flour, then add the mustard powder, stock, tarragon and sherry, if using. Season to taste and bring to the boil, stirring.

Pour the liquid and vegetables over the chicken, cover and cook on low for 8–9 hours until the chicken is tender and cooked through.

Stir the casserole, then add the reserved green leek slices and the green beans. Cover again and cook on high for 15–30 minutes until the vegetables are tender. Spoon into shallow bowls and serve garnished with a little extra tarragon, accompanied by Low-cal Garlicky Mash (*see* below), if liked.

FOR LOW-CAL GARLICKY MASH TO ACCOMPANY THE TARRAGON CHICKEN, cut 625 g (1¼ lb) potatoes into chunks, then cook in a saucepan of lightly salted boiling water for about 15 minutes until tender. Drain and mash with 3 tablespoons chicken stock, 2 crushed garlic cloves and a little salt and pepper.

FRENCH-STYLE CHICKEN POT ROAST ♥

Serves **4**
Preparation time **20 minutes**
Cooking temperature **high**
Cooking time **5–6 hours**

1.35 kg (2 lb 10 oz) **oven-ready chicken**
225 g (7½ oz) **baby new potatoes**,
   scrubbed and halved
1 **red pepper**, cored, deseeded
   and diced
1 **yellow pepper**, cored, deseeded
   and diced
4 **garlic cloves**, halved
200 g (7 oz) **cherry tomatoes**, halved
½ **lemon**, sliced
small bunch of **basil**
300 ml (½ pint) hot **chicken stock**
1 tablespoon **tomato purée**
3 teaspoons **granular sweetener**
40 g (1½ oz) **pitted green olives in**
   brine, drained and halved
salt and **pepper**

Preheat the slow cooker if necessary. Put the chicken into the slow cooker pot, then tuck the potatoes, peppers, garlic and tomatoes around it. Season the chicken, then arrange the lemon slices over the breast. Tear half the basil into pieces and sprinkle over the chicken and vegetables.

Mix the hot stock with the tomato purée and sweetener, then pour into the slow cooker pot and add the olives. Cover and cook on high for 5–6 hours or until the chicken is thoroughly cooked and the meat juices run clear when the thickest parts of the leg and breast are pierced with a sharp knife.

Lift the pot out of the housing with over gloves and place under a preheated hot grill until the chicken is golden. Cut the meat off the bones and arrange it in shallow bowls with the vegetables and stock, garnished with the remaining basil. If you prefer a thicker sauce, drain the stock into a small saucepan and boil rapidly to reduce by half.

FOR LEMON & TARRAGON POT-ROASTED CHICKEN, place the chicken in the slow cooker pot and tuck 225 g (7½ oz) halved, scrubbed baby new potatoes, 3 chopped carrots, 3 chopped celery sticks and 2 tarragon sprigs around it. Season the chicken and cover the breast with ½ sliced lemon. Mix 300 ml (½ pint) hot chicken stock with 1 tablespoon tomato purée and 3 teaspoons Dijon mustard and pour over the chicken. Cook as above and serve garnished with extra tarragon.

POT-ROASTED CHICKEN WITH LEMON

Serves **4–5**
Preparation time **25 minutes**
Cooking temperature **high**
Cooking time **5–6 hours**

2 tablespoons **olive oil**
1.5 kg (3 lb) **oven-ready chicken**
1 large **onion**, cut into 6 wedges
500 ml (17 fl oz) **dry cider**
3 teaspoons **Dijon mustard**
2 teaspoons **caster sugar**
900 ml (1½ pints) hot **chicken stock**
3 **carrots**, cut into chunks
3 **celery sticks**, thickly sliced
1 **lemon**, cut into 6 wedges, plus
    extra to garnish (optional)
20 g (¾ oz) **tarragon**
3 tablespoons **crème fraîche**
salt and **pepper**

Preheat the slow cooker if necessary. Heat the oil in a large frying pan, add the chicken, breast side down, and fry for 10 minutes, turning the chicken several times until browned all over.

Put the chicken, breast side down, in the slow cooker pot. Fry the onion wedges in the remaining oil in the pan until lightly browned. Add the cider, mustard and sugar and season with salt and pepper. Bring to the boil, then pour over the chicken. Add the hot stock, then the vegetables, lemon wedges and 3 sprigs of the tarragon, making sure that the chicken and all the vegetables are well below the level of the stock so that they cook evenly and thoroughly.

Cover with the lid and cook on high for 5–6 hours or until the chicken is thoroughly cooked and the meat juices run clear when the thickest parts of the leg and breast are pierced with a sharp knife. Turn the chicken after 4 hours, if liked.

Lift the chicken out of the stock, drain well and transfer to a large serving plate. Remove the vegetables with a slotted spoon and arrange them around the chicken. Measure 600 ml (1 pint) of the hot cooking stock from the slow cooker pot into a jug. Reserve a few tarragon sprigs to garnish, chop the remainder and whisk into the jug with the crème fraîche to make a gravy. Adjust the seasoning to taste. Carve the chicken in the usual way and serve with the gravy and vegetables. Garnish with extra lemon wedges, if liked, and the reserved tarragon sprigs, torn into pieces.

CARIBBEAN CHICKEN WITH RICE & PEAS

Serves **4**
Preparation time **20 minutes**
Cooking temperature **low** and **high**
Cooking time **7–9 hours**

8 **chicken thigh**s, about 1 kg (2 lb)
   in total
3 tablespoons **Jerk Marinade**
   (*see* below)
2 tablespoons **sunflower oil**
2 large **onions**, chopped
2 **garlic cloves**, finely chopped
400 ml (14 fl oz) can **full-fat
   coconut milk**
300 ml (½ pint) **chicken stock**
410 g (13½ oz) can **red kidney
   beans**, drained
200 g (7 oz) **easy-cook white
   long grain rice**
125 g (4 oz) **frozen peas**
salt and **pepper**

TO GARNISH
lime wedges
coriander sprigs

Preheat the slow cooker if necessary. Remove the skin from the chicken thighs, slash each thigh 2–3 times and rub with the jerk marinade.

Heat 1 tablespoon of the oil in a large frying pan, add the chicken and fry over a high heat until browned on both sides. Lift out with a slotted spoon and transfer to a plate. Add the remaining oil, the onions and garlic, reduce the heat and fry for 5 minutes or until softened and lightly browned. Pour in the coconut milk and stock, season to taste and bring to the boil.

Transfer half the mixture to the slow cooker pot, add half the chicken pieces, all the beans and then the remaining chicken, onions and coconut mixture. Cover and cook on low for 6–8 hours until the chicken is tender and cooked through.

Stir in the rice, replace the lid and cook on high for 45 minutes. Add the frozen peas (no need to thaw) and cook for a further 15 minutes. Spoon on to plates and serve garnished with lime wedges and coriander sprigs.

FOR JERK MARINADE, halve 1–2 Scotch bonnet chillies, depending on their size, discard the seeds and chop finely. Put in a sterilized screw-top jar with 1 tablespoon finely chopped thyme leaves, 1 teaspoon each ground allspice and cinnamon, ½ teaspoon grated nutmeg, ½ teaspoon salt, ½ teaspoon ground black pepper, 3 teaspoons brown sugar, 2 tablespoons sunflower oil and 4 tablespoons cider vinegar. Add the lid and shake to mix. Use 3 tablespoons of the marinade and store the remainder in the refrigerator for up to 2 weeks.

THAI GREEN CHICKEN CURRY ♥

Serves **4**
Preparation time **20 minutes**
Cooking temperature **low** and **high**
Cooking time **8¼–10¼ hours**

1 tablespoon **sunflower oil**
2 tablespoons **Thai green curry paste**
2 teaspoons **galangal paste**
2 **Thai green chillies**, deseeded and thinly sliced
1 **onion**, finely chopped
8 **chicken thighs**, about 1 kg (2 lb) in total, skinned, boned and cubed
400 ml (14 fl oz) **full-fat coconut milk**
150 ml (¼ pint) **chicken stock**
4 **dried kaffir lime leaves**
2 teaspoons **light muscovado sugar**
2 teaspoons **fish sauce**
100 g (3½ oz) **sugar snap peas**
100 g (3½ oz) **green beans**, halved
small bunch of **coriander**
boiled **rice**, to serve

Preheat the slow cooker if necessary. Heat the oil in a frying pan, add the curry paste, galangal paste and green chillies and cook for 1 minute.

Stir in the onion and chicken and cook, stirring, until the chicken is just beginning to turn golden. Pour in the coconut milk and stock, then add the lime leaves, sugar and fish sauce. Bring to the boil, stirring.

Transfer the mixture to the slow cooker pot, cover with the lid and cook on low for 8–10 hours or until the chicken is tender.

Stir in the peas and beans and cook on high for 15 minutes or until they are just tender. Tear the coriander leaves over the top, then spoon into bowls and serve with rice.

FOR THAI RED CHICKEN CURRY, make up the curry as above but omit the green curry paste and green chillies and instead add 2 tablespoons red curry paste and 2 finely chopped garlic cloves. Cook for 8–10 hours as above but omit the peas and beans, then spoon into bowls and sprinkle with some torn coriander leaves.

TURKEY WITH PUMPKIN & CRANBERRIES ♥

Serves **4**
Preparation time **20 minutes**
Cooking temperature **low**
Cooking time **6–8 hours**

low-calorie cooking oil spray
500 g (1 lb) **turkey breast**, diced
1 **onion**, chopped
2 teaspoons **plain flour**
300 ml (½ pint) **chicken stock**
juice of 1 large **orange**
½ teaspoon **ground mixed spice**
30 g (1¼ oz) **dried cranberries**
500 g (1 lb) peeled and deseeded **pumpkin**,
   cut into 2.5 cm (1 inch) cubes
salt and **pepper**

Preheat the slow cooker if necessary. Spray a large frying pan with a little low-calorie cooking oil spray and place over a high heat until hot. Add the turkey a few pieces at a time until all the turkey is in the pan. Add the onion and cook for 5 minutes, stirring and turning the turkey pieces, until golden.

Sprinkle in the flour and stir well. Add the stock, orange juice, mixed spice and cranberries and season to taste. Bring to the boil, stirring.

Place the pumpkin in the slow cooker pot and pour the turkey mixture on top, pushing the turkey pieces into the liquid. Cover and cook on low for 6–8 hours until the turkey is tender and cooked through. Spoon into shallow dishes and serve with steamed green beans and broccoli, if liked.

FOR TURKEY CURRY WITH SULTANAS & PUMPKIN, follow the recipe above but omit the mixed spice and cranberries and add 3 teaspoons medium-hot curry powder and 25 g (1 oz) sultanas instead.

ASIAN TURKEY WITH RAINBOW CHARD ♥

Serves **4**
Preparation time **20 minutes**
Cooking temperature **low** and **high**
Cooking time **8¼–9½ hours**

low-calorie cooking oil spray
500 g (1 lb) **turkey breast**, diced
1 **onion**, chopped
2 **garlic cloves**, finely chopped
200 g (7 oz) **closed-cap mushrooms**, sliced
450 ml (¾ pint) **chicken stock**
2.5 cm (1 inch) piece of **fresh root ginger**,
   peeled and chopped
2 tablespoons **soy sauce**
1 tablespoon **tamarind paste**
1 tablespoon **tomato purée**
1 tablespoon **cornflour**
200 g (7 oz) **rainbow chard**, thickly sliced
salt and **pepper**

Preheat the slow cooker if necessary. Spray a large frying pan with a little low-calorie cooking oil spray and place over a high heat until hot. Gradually add the turkey to the pan and cook for 5 minutes, stirring, until golden. Transfer to the slow cooker pot using a slotted spoon.

Add a little extra low-calorie cooking oil spray to the frying pan, if necessary, and cook the onion for 4–5 minutes until softened. Stir in the garlic and mushrooms and cook for 2–3 minutes more. Add the stock, ginger, soy sauce, tamarind and tomato purée, season to taste and bring to the boil, stirring. Pour over the turkey, cover and cook on low for 8–9 hours until the turkey is cooked through.

Mix the cornflour to a smooth paste with a little cold water and stir into the turkey mixture. Arrange the chard on top, cover again and cook on high for 15–30 minutes until tender. Spoon into bowls and serve with rice, if liked.

FOR BLACK BEAN TURKEY, follow the recipe above, adding the mushrooms to the frying pan with a 500 g (1 lb) jar of black bean sauce, then bring to the boil. Transfer to the slow cooker pot and cook as above. Stir-fry 275 g (9 oz) ready-prepared stir-fry vegetables in a little low-calorie cooking oil spray and serve.

CREAMY TARRAGON CHICKEN

Serves **4**
Preparation time **15 minutes**
Cooking temperature **high**
Cooking time **3–4 hours**

1 tablespoon **olive oil**
15 g (½ oz) **butter**
4 **boneless, skinless chicken breasts**,
    about 650 g (1 lb 6 oz) in total
200 g (7 oz) **shallots**, halved
1 tablespoon **plain flour**
300 ml (½ pint) **chicken stock**
4 tablespoons **dry vermouth**
2 **tarragon sprigs**, plus
    1 tablespoon chopped
3 tablespoons **double cream**
2 tablespoons chopped **chives**
salt and **pepper**
coarsely mashed **potato** mixed
    with **peas**, to serve

Preheat the slow cooker if necessary. Heat the oil and butter in a frying pan, add the chicken and fry over a high heat until golden on both sides but not cooked through. Drain and put into the slow cooker pot in a single layer.

Add the shallots to the frying pan and cook, stirring, for 4–5 minutes or until just beginning to turn golden. Stir in the flour, then gradually mix in the stock and vermouth. Add the tarragon sprigs and a little salt and pepper and bring to the boil, stirring.

Pour the sauce over the chicken breasts, cover and cook on high for 3–4 hours or until the chicken is tender and cooked through to the centre.

Stir the cream into the sauce and sprinkle the chicken with the chopped tarragon and chives. Serve with coarsely mashed potato mixed with peas.

FOR CREAMY PESTO CHICKEN, prepare the dish as above, but replace the vermouth with 4 tablespoons white wine and the tarragon with 1 tablespoon pesto. Sprinkle the chicken with some tiny basil leaves and a little freshly grated Parmesan cheese instead of the chives. Serve the chicken sliced, if liked, and mixed with cooked penne and drizzled with the creamy sauce.

TANGY TURKEY TAGINE ♥

Serves **4**
Preparation time **25 minutes**
Cooking temperature **low**
Cooking time **8–9 hours**

low-calorie cooking oil spray
400 g (13 oz) **turkey breast**, diced
1 **onion**, chopped
2 **garlic cloves**, finely chopped
1 tablespoon **plain flour**
450 ml (¾ pint) **chicken stock**
2 pinches of **saffron threads** or
   1 teaspoon **ground turmeric**
5 cm (2 inch) **cinnamon stick**
finely grated rind of 1 **lemon**
400 g (13 oz) can
   chickpeas, drained
25 g (1 oz) **sultanas**
salt and **pepper**

TO SERVE
175 g (6 oz) **couscous**
450 ml (¾ pint) boiling **water**
4 tablespoons chopped **mint** or
   mixed **mint** and **parsley**

Preheat the slow cooker if necessary. Spray a large frying pan with a little low-calorie cooking oil spray and place over a high heat until hot. Add the turkey a few pieces at a time until all the turkey is in the pan and cook for 5 minutes, stirring, until golden. Use a slotted spoon to transfer the turkey to a plate.

Add the onion to the frying pan and cook for 4–5 minutes until softened. Stir in the garlic and flour, then add the stock and mix well. Add the saffron or turmeric, cinnamon and lemon rind, then the chickpeas and sultanas. Season to taste and bring to the boil, stirring.

Pour into the slow cooker pot, add the turkey pieces and press into the liquid. Cover and cook on low for 8–9 hours until the turkey is tender and cooked through.

Meanwhile, place the couscous in a mixing bowl, pour over the boiling water, cover with a plate and leave to soak for 5 minutes until tender. Stir in the chopped herbs, season to taste and fluff up with a fork.

Divide the couscous between 4 plates and top with the tagine. Serve with warmed naan bread, if liked.

FOR HARISSA-BAKED TURKEY, follow the recipe above, using 300 ml (½ pint) chicken stock and 250 g (8 oz) diced tomatoes instead of 450 ml (¾ pint) chicken stock. Omit the saffron, cinnamon and lemon and add 2 teaspoons harissa and a 2.5 cm (1 inch) piece of fresh root ginger, peeled and chopped, instead. Cook as above and serve with the herby couscous.

CREAMY CHICKEN KORMA

Serves **4**
Preparation time **15 minutes**
Cooking temperature **low**
Cooking time **6¼–7¼ hours**

25 g (1 oz) **butter**
4 **boneless, skinless chicken breasts**,
about 150 g (5 oz) each
1 **onion**, finely chopped
2 **garlic cloves**, finely chopped
2.5 cm (1 inch) piece of **fresh root
ginger**, peeled and finely chopped
3 tablespoons **korma curry paste**
4 tablespoons **ground almonds**
200 ml (7 fl oz) **chicken stock**
3 tablespoons **double cream**
3 tablespoons chopped **coriander**
salt and **pepper**
3 tablespoons toasted **flaked
almonds**, to garnish
boiled **rice**, to serve

Preheat the slow cooker if necessary. Heat the butter in a large frying pan, add the chicken and fry on both sides until browned but not cooked through. Lift out of the pan with a slotted spoon and transfer to the slow cooker pot.

Add the onion, garlic and ginger to the pan and fry for 2–3 minutes, then stir in the curry paste and cook for 1 minute. Stir in the ground almonds, stock and salt and pepper and bring to the boil.

Pour the sauce over the chicken. Cover with the lid and cook on low for 6–7 hours or until the chicken is tender and cooked through.

Stir in the cream and chopped coriander, replace the lid and cook, still on low, for 15 minutes. Slice the chicken. Spoon on to rice-lined plates and sprinkle with the almonds.

FOR CREAMY PANEER KORMA, omit the chicken and fry 2 small, very finely chopped onions in 25 g (1 oz) butter until softened. Add the garlic, ginger and curry paste, then stir in the ground almonds and stock and bring to the boil as above. Drain and cut 450 g (14½ oz) paneer (Indian cheese) into 2 cm (¾ inch) cubes, then add to the slow cooker pot with the sauce. Continue as above.

SWEET & SOUR CHICKEN

Serves **4**
Preparation time **20 minutes**
Cooking temperature **low**
Cooking time **6¼–8¼ hours**

1 tablespoon **sunflower oil**
8 small **chicken thighs**, about
  1 kg (2 lb) in total, skinned,
  boned and cubed
4 **spring onions**, thickly sliced, white
  and green parts kept separate
2 **carrots**, halved lengthways and
  thinly sliced
2.5 cm (1 inch) piece of **fresh root
  ginger**, peeled and finely chopped
430 g (14¼ oz) can **pineapple chunks
  in natural juice**
300 ml (½ pint) **chicken stock**
1 tablespoon **cornflour**
1 tablespoon **tomato purée**
2 tablespoons **caster sugar**
2 tablespoons **soy sauce**
2 tablespoons **malt vinegar**
225 g (7½ oz) can **bamboo
  shoots**, drained
125 g (4 oz) **bean sprouts**
100 g (3½ oz) **mangetout**,
  thinly sliced
rice, to serve

Preheat the slow cooker if necessary. Heat the oil in a frying pan, add the chicken thighs and fry, stirring, until browned on all sides. Mix in the white spring onion slices, carrots and ginger and cook for 2 minutes.

Stir in the pineapple chunks and their juice and the stock. Put the cornflour, tomato purée and sugar into a small bowl, then gradually mix in the soy sauce and vinegar to make a smooth paste. Stir into the frying pan and bring to the boil, stirring.

Tip the chicken and sauce into the slow cooker pot, add the bamboo shoots and press the chicken beneath the surface of the sauce. Cover with the lid and cook on low for 6–8 hours.

When almost ready to serve, add the green spring onion slices, the bean sprouts and mangetout to the slow cooker pot and mix well. Replace the lid and cook, still on low, for 15 minutes or until the vegetables are just tender. Spoon into rice-filled bowls.

FOR LEMON CHICKEN, follow the recipe as above up until the addition of the chicken stock. Gradually mix the juice of 1 lemon into the cornflour to make a smooth paste, then stir into the stock with 2 tablespoons dry sherry and 4 teaspoons caster sugar. Bring to the boil, stirring, then add to the slow cooker pot and cook as above, adding the green spring onion slices, bean sprouts and mangetout at the end.

TANGY CHICKEN, FENNEL & LEEK BRAISE ♥

Serves **4**
Preparation time **20 minutes**
Cooking temperature **low**
Cooking time **8½–9½ hours**

low-calorie cooking oil spray
625 g (1¼ lb) **boneless, skinless
    chicken thighs**, halved
1 **fennel bulb**, cored and sliced, green
    fronds reserved
2 **leeks**, thinly sliced, white and green
    parts kept separate
350 ml (12 fl oz) **chicken stock**
finely grated rind and juice of
    ½ **orange**
2 teaspoons **cornflour**
salt and **pepper**

Preheat the slow cooker if necessary. Spray a large frying pan with a little low-calorie cooking oil spray and place over a high heat until hot. Add the chicken and cook for 3–4 minutes, turning once, until browned on both sides. Use a slotted spoon to transfer to a plate.

Add the fennel and white leek slices to the frying pan and cook for 2–3 minutes until just beginning to soften, then add the stock and orange rind and juice. Mix the cornflour to a smooth paste with a little cold water and stir into the pan. Season to taste and bring to the boil, stirring.

Transfer the mixture to the slow cooker pot, arrange the chicken pieces on top in a single layer and press into the liquid. Cover and cook on low for 8–9 hours until the chicken is cooked through.

Add the reserved green leek slices, stir into the sauce, cover again and cook, still on low, for 30 minutes. Serve garnished with the reserved fennel fronds.

FOR BRAISED MUSTARD CHICKEN & LEEKS, follow the recipe above, using 75 g (3 oz) diced lean back bacon rashers instead of the fennel. Use 1 teaspoon Dijon mustard instead of the orange rind and juice and cook as above. Garnish with chopped parsley.

KASHMIRI BUTTER CHICKEN ♥

Serves **4**
Preparation time **30 minutes**
Cooking temperature **low**
Cooking time **5–7 hours**

2 **onions**, quartered
3 **garlic cloves**
3.5 cm (1½ inch) piece of **fresh root ginger**, peeled
1 large **red chilli**, deseeded
8 **boneless, skinless chicken thighs**
1 tablespoon **sunflower oil**
25 g (1 oz) **butter**
1 teaspoon **cumin seeds**, crushed
1 teaspoon **fennel seeds**, crushed
4 **cardamom pods**, crushed
1 teaspoon **paprika**
1 teaspoon **ground turmeric**
¼ teaspoon **ground cinnamon**
300 ml (½ pint) **chicken stock**
1 tablespoon **brown sugar**
2 tablespoons **tomato purée**
5 tablespoons **double cream**
salt

TO GARNISH
toasted **flaked almonds**
coriander sprigs
boiled **rice**, to serve

Preheat the slow cooker if necessary. Blend the onions, garlic, ginger and chilli in a food processor or blender, or chop finely.

Cut each chicken thigh into 4 pieces. Heat the oil in a large frying pan and add the chicken a few pieces at a time until all the meat has been added. Cook over a high heat until browned. Drain and transfer to a plate.

Add the butter to the frying pan. When it has melted, add the onion paste and cook over a more moderate heat until it is just beginning to colour. Stir in the crushed cumin and fennel seeds, the cardamom pods and their black seeds and ground spices. Cook for 1 minute, then mix in the stock, sugar, tomato purée and salt. Bring to the boil, stirring.

Transfer the chicken to the slow cooker pot, pour the onion mixture and sauce over the top and press the pieces of chicken below the surface of the liquid. Cover with the lid and cook on low for 5–7 hours.

Stir in the cream. Garnish with toasted flaked almonds and coriander sprigs and serve with boiled rice and Coriander Flat Breads (*see below*), if liked.

FOR CORIANDER FLAT BREADS TO ACCOMPANY THE CURRY, mix together 200 g (7 oz) self-raising flour, ½ teaspoon baking powder, 3 tablespoons roughly chopped coriander leaves and a little salt in a bowl. Add 2 tablespoons sunflower oil, then gradually mix in 6–7 tablespoons water to make a soft dough. Cut the dough into 4 pieces and roll out each piece thinly on a lightly floured surface to form a rough oval. Cook on a preheated ridged griddle pan for 3–4 minutes on each side until singed and puffy.

BRAISED DUCK WITH ORANGE SAUCE

Serves **4**
Preparation time **15 minutes**
Cooking temperature **high**
Cooking time **4–5 hours**

4 **duck legs**, about 175 g (6 oz) each
1 **onion**, sliced
2 tablespoons **plain flour**
150 ml (¼ pint) **chicken stock**
150 ml (¼ pint) **dry white wine**
1 large **orange**, ½ squeezed juice, ½ sliced
1 **bay leaf**
1 teaspoon **Dijon mustard**
½ teaspoon **black peppercorns**, roughly crushed
salt

Preheat the slow cooker if necessary. Dry-fry the duck in a large frying pan over a low heat until the fat begins to run, then increase the heat until the duck is browned on both sides. Lift out of the pan with a slotted spoon and transfer to the slow cooker pot.

Pour off any excess fat to leave about 1 tablespoon. Fry the onion until softened. Stir in the flour, then mix in the stock, wine, orange juice, bay leaf, a little salt and the crushed peppercorns and bring to the boil, stirring. Add the orange slices.

Pour the sauce over the duck, cover with the lid and cook on high for 4–5 hours or until the duck is tender and almost falling off the bones. Serve with rice and steamed green beans, if liked.

FOR BRAISED DUCK WITH CRANBERRIES & PORT, fry the duck and onions as above. Mix in the flour and stock, then replace the wine with 150 ml (¼ pint) ruby port and 100 g (3½ oz) fresh cranberries. Add the orange slices and juice and continue as above.

MUSTARD CHICKEN & BACON

Serves **4**
Preparation time **15 minutes**
Cooking temperature **low**
Cooking time **8¼–10¼ hours**

15 g (½ oz) **butter**
1 tablespoon **sunflower oil**
4 **chicken thighs** and 4 **chicken drumstick joints**
4 **smoked back bacon rashers**, diced
400 g (13 oz) **leeks**, thinly sliced white and green parts kept separate
2 tablespoons **plain flour**
600 ml (1 pint) **chicken stock**
3 teaspoons **wholegrain mustard**
salt and **pepper**
mashed **potato**, to serve

Preheat the slow cooker if necessary. Heat the butter and oil in a frying pan, add the chicken joints and fry over a high heat until browned on all sides. Transfer to the slow cooker pot with a slotted spoon.

Add the bacon and white leek slices to the frying pan and fry, stirring, for 5 minutes or until just beginning to turn golden. Stir in the flour, then gradually mix in the stock, mustard and a little salt and pepper. Bring to the boil. Pour into the slow cooker pot, cover with the lid and cook on low for 8–10 hours.

Add the green leek slices and stir into the sauce, then replace the lid and cook, still on low, for 15 minutes or until the green leeks are just softened. Spoon into shallow serving bowls and serve with mashed potato.

FOR MUSTARD CHICKEN & FRANKFURTER CASSEROLE, fry the chicken as above, then drain and add to the slow cooker pot. Add 1 chopped onion to the pan, then mix in 4 chilled, sliced frankfurters and fry for 5 minutes. Stir in the flour, then mix in the stock, mustard and seasoning as above. Add a 200 g (7 oz) can drained sweetcorn, transfer to the slow cooker pot and cook on low for 8–10 hours.

TURKEY KEEMA MUTTER ♥

Serves **4**
Preparation time **20 minutes**
Cooking temperature **low** and **high**
Cooking time **8¼–10¼ hours**

low-calorie cooking oil spray
500 g (1 lb) **minced turkey breast**
1 **onion**, chopped
2 **garlic cloves**, finely chopped
2.5 cm (1 inch) piece of **fresh root ginger**, peeled
   and finely chopped
1 teaspoon **cumin seeds**, crushed
4 teaspoons **medium-hot curry powder**
500 g (1 lb) **passata**
2 teaspoons **granular sweetener**
150 g (5 oz) **frozen peas**
4 tablespoons chopped **coriander**
salt and **pepper**
½ **red onion**, thinly sliced, to garnish
4 small **chapatis**, 50 g (2 oz) each, to serve

Preheat the slow cooker if necessary. Spray a large
frying pan with a little low-calorie cooking oil spray
and place over a high heat until hot. Add the minced
turkey and onion and fry for 4–5 minutes, stirring and
breaking up the mince with a wooden spoon, until it is
just beginning to brown.

Stir in the garlic, ginger, cumin and curry powder and
cook for 1 minute, then add the passata and sweetener.
Season to taste and bring to the boil, stirring. Transfer
to the slow cooker pot, cover and cook on low for
8–10 hours until the turkey is cooked through.

Add the frozen peas to the slow cooker pot with
half the coriander. Cover again and cook on high for
15 minutes. Sprinkle with the remaining coriander
and the red onion and serve with the chapatis.

FOR KEEMA MUTTER JACKETS, follow the recipe above
to make and cook the turkey and pea mixture. Scrub
and prick 4 baking potatoes, 175 g (6 oz) each, place in
the microwave on a sheet of kitchen paper and cook on
full power for about 20 minutes until tender. Transfer
to serving plates, cut in half and top with the keema
mutter, remaining coriander and red onion.

POT-ROAST PHEASANT WITH CHESTNUTS

Serves **2–3**
Preparation time **15 minutes**
Cooking temperature **high**
Cooking time **3–4 hours**

25 g (1 oz) **butter**
1 tablespoon **olive oil**
750 g (1½ lb) **oven-ready pheasant**
200 g (7 oz) **shallots**, halved
50 g (2 oz) **smoked streaky bacon rashers**, diced,
   or **ready-diced pancetta**
2 **celery sticks**, thickly sliced
1 tablespoon **plain flour**
300 ml (½ pint) **chicken stock**
4 tablespoons **dry sherry**
100 g (3½ oz) **vacuum-packed prepared chestnuts**
2–3 **thyme sprigs**
salt and **pepper**

Preheat the slow cooker if necessary. Heat the butter
and oil in a frying pan, add the pheasant, breast side
down, the shallots, bacon or pancetta and celery and fry
until golden brown, turning the pheasant and stirring
the other ingredients. Transfer the pheasant to the slow
cooker pot, placing it breast side down.

Stir the flour into the onion mixture. Gradually add
the stock and sherry, then add the chestnuts, thyme
and a little salt and pepper. Bring to the boil, stirring,
then spoon over the pheasant. Cover with the lid and
cook on high for 3–4 hours until tender. Test with a
knife through the thickest part of the pheasant leg and
breast to make sure that the juices run clear. Carve the
pheasant breast into thick slices and cut the legs away
from the body.

FOR POT-ROAST GUINEA FOWL WITH PRUNES, fry
a 1 kg (2 lb) guinea fowl instead of the pheasant as
above. Transfer the fowl to the slow cooker, mix in
2 tablespoons plain flour, then add 450 ml (¾ pint)
chicken stock and the sherry. Omit the chestnuts and
add 75 g (3 oz) halved ready-to-eat pitted prunes
instead. Continue as above, but cook for 5–6 hours.

SUN-DRIED TOMATO & CHICKEN PILAF

Serves **4**
Preparation time **25 minutes**
Cooking temperature **high**
Cooking time **3–4 hours**

1 tablespoon **olive oil**
4 **boneless, skinless chicken breasts**
1 large **onion**, roughly chopped
2 **garlic cloves**, chopped (optional)
400 g (13 oz) can **chopped tomatoes**
50 g (2 oz) **sun-dried tomatoes in oil**,
    drained and sliced
2 teaspoons **pesto**
600 ml (1 pint) hot **chicken stock**
150 g (5 oz) **easy-cook brown
    long-grain rice**
50 g (2 oz) **wild rice**
salt and **pepper**

TO SERVE
rocket salad
olive oil and lemon dressing

Preheat the slow cooker if necessary. Heat the oil in a frying pan and fry the chicken breasts on one side only until browned. Remove from the pan with a slotted spoon and reserve on a plate.

Fry the onion and garlic, if using, in the pan, stirring, for 5 minutes or until lightly browned. Add the tomatoes, sun-dried tomatoes and pesto, season with salt and pepper and bring to the boil. Pour into the slow cooker pot, then stir in the stock.

Rinse the brown rice well in a sieve under cold running water, then stir into the slow cooker pot with the wild rice. Arrange the chicken breasts on top of the rice, browned side up, pressing them just below the level of the liquid so that they don't dry out during cooking. Cover with the lid and cook on high for 3–4 hours or until the chicken is cooked and the rice is tender.

Spoon on to serving plates and serve with a rocket salad tossed in an olive oil and lemon dressing

FOR RED PEPPER, LEMON & CHICKEN PILAF, fry 4 boneless, skinless chicken breasts as above and transfer to a plate. In the pan, fry 1 large, roughly chopped onion and 1 cored, deseeded and diced red pepper until the onion is just turning golden. Add a 400 g (13 oz) can chopped tomatoes, 2 tablespoons finely chopped lemon thyme leaves and the grated rind and juice of 1 lemon. Bring to the boil and add to the slow cooker with the hot chicken stock and rice as above with the chicken. Continue as above.

MOROCCAN MEATBALLS

Serves **4**
Preparation time **30 minutes**
Cooking temperature **low**
Cooking time **6–8 hours**

500 g (1 lb) **minced turkey**
100 g (3½ oz) drained **canned green lentils**
1 **egg yolk**
1 tablespoon **olive oil**
1 **onion**, sliced
2 **garlic cloves**, finely chopped
1 teaspoon **ground turmeric**
1 teaspoon **ground coriander**
½ teaspoon **ground cumin**
½ teaspoon **ground cinnamon**
2.5 cm (1 inch) piece of **fresh root ginger**, peeled and finely chopped
400 g (13 oz) can **chopped tomatoes**
150 ml (¼ pint) **chicken stock**
salt and **pepper**

Preheat the slow cooker if necessary. Mix together the minced turkey, green lentils, a little salt and pepper and the egg yolk in a bowl or food processor. Divide into 20 pieces, then shape into small balls with wetted hands.

Heat the oil in a large frying pan, add the meatballs and fry, stirring, until browned but not cooked through. Lift out of the pan with a slotted spoon and put into the slow cooker pot. Add the onion and fry until softened, then stir in the garlic, spices and ginger and cook for 1 minute.

Stir in the tomatoes, stock and a little salt and pepper and bring to the boil, stirring. Pour over the meatballs, cover with the lid and cook on low for 6–8 hours or until cooked through. Stir, then spoon on to couscous-lined plates (*see* below).

FOR LEMON COUSCOUS TO ACCOMPANY THE MEATBALLS, put 200 g (7 oz) couscous into a bowl and pour over 450 ml (¾ pint) boiling water. Add the grated rind and juice of 1 lemon, 2 tablespoons olive oil and some salt and pepper, cover and leave to stand for 5 minutes. Fluff up with a fork and stir in a small bunch of chopped coriander.

FISH & SEAFOOD

FISH PIE

Serves **4–5**
Preparation time **20 minutes**
Cooking temperature **low**
Cooking time **2–3 hours**

1 tablespoon **sunflower oil**
1 **leek**, thinly sliced
50 g (2 oz) **butter**
50 g (2 oz) **plain flour**
450 ml (¾ pint) **UHT milk**
150 ml (¼ pint) **fish stock**
75 g (3 oz) **Cheddar cheese**, grated
1 **bay leaf**
800 g (1 lb 10 oz) mixed **salmon**
   and **smoked** and **unsmoked**
   haddock fillet, skinned and cut
   into large cubes
salt and **pepper**

TOPPING
4 tablespoons chopped **parsley**
800 g (1 lb 10 oz) hot **homemade** or
   shop-bought mashed potato
25 g (1 oz) **butter**
15 g (½ oz) **Cheddar cheese**, grated

Preheat the slow cooker if necessary. Heat the oil in a saucepan, add the leek and fry, stirring, for 4–5 minutes or until softened. Scoop out of the pan with a slotted spoon and transfer to a plate.

Add the butter, flour and milk to the pan and bring to the boil, whisking constantly until thickened and smooth. Mix in the stock, cheese, bay leaf and a little salt and pepper.

Arrange the cubed fish in the slow cooker pot so that it is in an even layer, then pour over the hot sauce. Cover and cook on low for 2–3 hours or until the fish flakes easily when pressed in the centre with a knife.

When almost ready to serve, stir the parsley into the hot mashed potato. Stir the fish, then spoon into individual ovenproof dishes, if liked. Spoon the potato over the top, dot with the butter and sprinkle with the cheese. If not using separate dishes, lift the pot out of the housing using oven gloves and place under a preheated medium grill until golden. Serve with steamed asparagus, if liked.

FOR MIXED FISH & SPINACH GRATIN, wash 400 g (13 oz) baby spinach leaves in cold water, drain and place in a large saucepan. Cover and cook until just wilted. Transfer to a sieve and squeeze out as much water as possible. Spoon into the base of a 5 cm (2 inch) deep ovenproof dish. Make up the fish pie mixture as above and spoon out of the slow cooker pot on to the spinach, then sprinkle with 50 g (2 oz) grated Cheddar cheese and 4 tablespoons fresh breadcrumbs. Grill as above.

TUNA ARRABIATA ♥

Serves **4**
Preparation time **20 minutes**
Cooking temperature **low**
Cooking time **4–5 hours**

1 tablespoon **olive oil**
1 **onion**, chopped
2 **garlic cloves**, finely chopped
1 **red pepper**, cored, deseeded
    and diced
1 teaspoon **smoked paprika**
¼–½ teaspoon **crushed dried
    red chillies**
400 g (13 oz) can
    chopped tomatoes
150 ml (¼ pint) **vegetable** or
    fish stock
200 g (7 oz) can **tuna in
    water**, drained
salt and **pepper**

TO SERVE
375 g (12 oz) **dried spaghetti**
4 tablespoons freshly grated
    Parmesan cheese
small handful of **basil leaves**

Preheat the slow cooker if necessary. Heat the oil in a large frying pan over a medium heat, add the onion and cook, stirring, for 5 minutes or until just browning around the edges. Add the garlic, red pepper, paprika and chillies and cook for 2 minutes.

Add the tomatoes and stock and season to taste. Bring to the boil, then transfer to the slow cooker pot. Break the tuna into large pieces and stir into the tomato mixture. Cover and cook on low for 4–5 hours.

Meanwhile, cook the spaghetti in a saucepan of lightly salted boiling water according to the packet instructions until just tender. Drain and stir into the tomato sauce.

Spoon into 4 shallow bowls and sprinkle with the grated Parmesan and basil leaves.

FOR DOUBLE TOMATO ARRABIATA, follow the recipe above using 75 g (3 oz) sliced, drained sun-dried tomatoes in oil and 100 g (3½ oz) sliced button mushrooms instead of the tuna. Cook and serve as above.

MACARONI WITH SMOKED HADDOCK

Serves **4**
Preparation time **15 minutes**
Cooking temperature **low**
Cooking time **2¼–3¼ hours**

200 g (7 oz) **dried macaroni**
1 tablespoon **olive oil**
1 **onion**, chopped
50 g (2 oz) **butter**
50 g (2 oz) **plain flour**
450 ml (¾ pint) **UHT milk**
450 ml (¾ pint) **fish stock**
175 g (6 oz) **Cheddar cheese**, grated
¼ teaspoon grated **nutmeg**
500 g (1 lb) **smoked haddock fillet**,
    skinned and cut into 2.5 cm
    (1 inch) cubes
200 g (7 oz) can **sweetcorn**, drained
125 g (4 oz) **spinach**, rinsed, drained
    and roughly torn
salt and **pepper**

Preheat the slow cooker if necessary. Tip the macaroni into a bowl, cover with plenty of boiling water and leave to soak for 10 minutes while preparing the rest of the dish.

Heat the oil in a saucepan, add the onion and fry gently, stirring, for 5 minutes or until softened. Add the butter and, when melted, stir in the flour. Gradually mix in the milk and bring to the boil, stirring until smooth. Stir in the stock, 125 g (4 oz) of the cheese, the nutmeg and salt and pepper and bring back to the boil, stirring.

Drain the macaroni and add to the slow cooker pot with the haddock and sweetcorn. Pour over the sauce and gently stir together. Cover with the lid and cook on low for 2–3 hours.

Stir the spinach into the macaroni, replace the lid and cook on low for 15 minutes. Lift the pot out of the housing using oven gloves and stir once more. Sprinkle the remaining cheese over the macaroni, then place under a preheated hot grill until the top is golden. Serve with grilled cherry tomatoes on the vine, if liked.

FOR STILTON MACARONI WITH BACON, soak the macaroni as above. Make up the cheese sauce with the milk, adding vegetable stock in place of fish stock and replacing the Cheddar cheese with Stilton cheese. Omit the fish and cook as above with the sweetcorn. Stir in the spinach and 6 grilled smoked back bacon rashers, diced. Cook for 15 minutes, then finish with a little extra Stilton and brown under the grill as above.

CHERMOULA POACHED SALMON

Serves **4**
Preparation time **15 minutes**
Cooking temperature **low**
Cooking time **1¾–2¼ hours**

6 **spring onions**
25 g (1 oz) **parsley**
25 g (1 oz) **coriander**
grated rind and juice of **1 lemon**
4 tablespoons **olive oil**
½ teaspoon **cumin seeds**,
    roughly crushed
500 g (1 lb) **thick-end salmon**
    fillet no longer than 18 cm
    (7 inches), skinned
250 ml (8 fl oz) **fish stock**
6 tablespoons **mayonnaise**
125 g (4 oz) **mixed salad leaves**
salt and **pepper**

Preheat the slow cooker if necessary. Finely chop the spring onions and herbs with a large knife, or in a food processor if you have one. Mix with the lemon rind and juice, the oil, cumin and a little salt and pepper.

Rinse the salmon with cold water, drain well and put on a long piece of foil the width of the salmon. Press half the herb mixture over both sides of the salmon then use the foil to lower the fish into the slow cooker pot.

Bring the stock to the boil in a small saucepan, pour over the salmon and tuck the ends of the foil down if needed. Cover with the lid and cook on low for 1¾–2¼ hours or until the fish flakes into opaque pieces when pressed in the centre with a knife.

Lift the salmon out of the slow cooker pot using the foil and transfer to a plate. Mix the remaining herb mixture with the mayonnaise. Arrange the salad leaves on 4 plates. Cut the salmon into 4 pieces and place on the salad. Serve with spoonfuls of the herb mayonnaise.

FOR CLASSIC POACHED SALMON, omit the chermoula herb mixture. Rinse the salmon as above, then lower into the slow cooker pot on a piece of foil. Add ½ sliced lemon, ½ sliced onion, 2 tarragon sprigs and a little salt and pepper. Bring 200 ml (7 fl oz) fish stock and 4 tablespoons white wine to the boil in a small saucepan, pour over the fish and cook as above. Drain and serve hot or cold with salad and spoonfuls of plain mayonnaise.

SQUID IN PUTTANESCA SAUCE

Serves **4**
Preparation time **25 minutes**
Cooking temperature **low**
Cooking time **3½–4½ hours**

500 g (1 lb) **prepared squid tubes**
1 tablespoon **olive oil**
1 **onion**, chopped
2 **garlic cloves**, finely chopped
400 g (13 oz) can **chopped tomatoes**
150 ml (¼ pint) **fish stock**
4 teaspoons drained **capers**
50 g (2 oz) **pitted black olives**
2–3 **thyme sprigs**, plus extra leaves
   to garnish (optional)
1 teaspoon **fennel seeds**,
   roughly crushed
1 teaspoon **caster sugar**
salt and pepper
cooked **linguine**, to serve

Preheat the slow cooker if necessary. Take the tentacles out of the squid tubes and rinse inside the tubes with cold water. Put them in a sieve and rinse the outside of the tubes and the tentacles. Drain well, put the tentacles in a small bowl, cover and return to the refrigerator. Thickly slice the squid tubes.

Heat the oil in a large frying pan, add the onion and fry, stirring, for 5 minutes or until golden. Add the garlic and cook for 2 minutes. Stir in the tomatoes, stock, capers, olives, thyme, crushed fennel seeds, sugar and salt and pepper and bring to the boil.

Pour the sauce into the slow cooker pot, add the sliced squid and press the pieces below the surface of the sauce. Cover with the lid and cook on low for 3–4 hours.

Stir the squid mixture and add the tentacles, pressing them below the surface of the sauce. Cook on low for a further 30 minutes. Serve tossed with linguine and garnished with extra thyme leaves, if liked.

FOR SQUID IN RED WINE & TOMATO SAUCE, replace the stock, capers, olives and fennel seeds with 150 ml (¼ pint) red wine. Cook as above, then garnish with chopped parsley and serve with warm crusty bread.

BRAISED TROUT WITH WARM PUY LENTILS ♥

Serves **4**
Preparation time **20 minutes**
Cooking temperature **low**
Cooking time **2½–3 hours**

400 g (13 oz) can **Puy lentils**, drained
2 tablespoons **balsamic vinegar**
4 **spring onions**, chopped
3 **tomatoes**, chopped
4 **thick trout steaks**, 150 g
   (5 oz) each
finely grated rind and juice of
   ½ **lemon**
leaves from 2–3 **thyme sprigs**
large pinch of **crushed dried**
   red chillies
150 ml (¼ pint) hot **fish stock**
salt and **pepper**
50 g (2 oz) **rocket leaves**, to serve

Preheat the slow cooker if necessary. Place the lentils in the slow cooker pot, then stir in the balsamic vinegar, spring onions and tomatoes.

Arrange the trout steaks on top in a single layer, then sprinkle with the lemon rind and juice, thyme leaves and chillies and season to taste. Pour the stock around the trout steaks, then cover with the lid and cook on low for 2½–3 hours or until the trout is cooked through and flakes easily when pressed in the centre with a small knife.

Divide the rocket leaves between 4 serving plates. Arrange the trout and lentils on top and spoon over a little of the stock. Serve immediately.

FOR SMOKED COD & SPINACH SALAD, follow the recipe above, using 100 g (3½ oz) sliced button mushrooms instead of the tomatoes and 4 thick smoked cod loin steaks, 150 g (5 oz) each, instead of the trout. After cooking, stir 50 g (2 oz) baby spinach leaves, rinsed and drained, into the lentil mixture and serve each portion topped with a poached egg.

SALMON IN HOT MISO BROTH

Serves **6**
Preparation time **15 minutes**
Cooking temperature **low** and **high**
Cooking time **1 hour 40 minutes–2 hours 10 minutes**

4 **salmon steaks**, about 125 g (4 oz) each
1 **carrot**, thinly sliced
4 **spring onions**, thinly sliced
4 **cup mushrooms**, about 125 g (4 oz) in total, thinly sliced
1 large **red chilli**, halved, deseeded and finely chopped
2 cm (¾ inch) piece of **fresh root ginger**, peeled and finely chopped
3 tablespoons **miso**
1 tablespoon **dark soy sauce**
2 tablespoons **mirin** (optional)
1.2 litres (2 pints) hot **fish stock**
75 g (3 oz) **mangetout**, thinly sliced
coriander leaves, to garnish

Preheat the slow cooker if necessary. Rinse the salmon in cold water, drain and place in the slow cooker pot. Arrange the carrot, spring onions, mushrooms, chilli and ginger on top of the fish.

Add the miso, soy sauce and mirin, if using, to the hot stock and stir until the miso has dissolved. Pour the stock mixture over the salmon and vegetables. Cover with the lid and cook on low for 1½–2 hours or until the fish is tender and the soup is piping hot.

Lift the fish out with a fish slice and transfer it to a plate. Flake it into chunky pieces, discarding the skin and any bones. Return the fish to the slow cooker pot and add the mangetout. Cook on high for 10 minutes or until the mangetout are just tender, then ladle the soup into bowls and garnish with coriander leaves.

FOR SALMON IN AROMATIC THAI BROTH, follow the recipe as above, adding 3 teaspoons Thai red curry paste, 3 small dried kaffir lime leaves and 2 teaspoons fish sauce instead of the miso and mirin.

TAPENADE-TOPPED COD ♥

Serves **4**
Preparation time **15 minutes**
Cooking temperature **low**
Cooking time **3½–4 hours**

200 g (7 oz) **passata**
200 g (7 oz) **spinach**, rinsed and drained
175 g (6 oz) **tomatoes**, roughly chopped
50 g (2 oz) **chorizo**, skinned and diced
4 **skinless cod steaks**, 150 g (5 oz) each
85 g (3¼ oz) **green olives stuffed with hot pimento**
small handful of **basil leaves**, plus extra to garnish
salt and **pepper**

Preheat the slow cooker if necessary. Spoon the passata over the base of the slow cooker pot, then arrange the spinach, tomatoes and chorizo in an even layer on top. Season to taste and place the fish steaks on top in a single layer, then season again.

Place the olives and basil in a food processor and blitz until finely chopped, or chop with a knife. Spread the mixture over the cod steaks, then cover and cook on low for 3½–4 hours until the fish is bright white and flakes easily when pressed in the centre with a small knife. Serve garnished with extra basil.

FOR HERB-TOPPED COD, mix 15 g (½ oz) finely chopped parsley and 15 g (½ oz) finely chopped basil with ½ teaspoon crushed cumin seeds and the grated rind of 1 lemon. Follow the recipe above, using this herb mixture to spread over the cod steaks before cooking instead of the olives and basil.

MACKEREL WITH HARISSA POTATOES

Serves **4**
Preparation time **20 minutes**
Cooking temperature **low**
Cooking time **5–7 hours**

500 g (1 lb) **new potatoes**, scrubbed and thickly sliced
1 tablespoon **olive oil**
1 **onion**, chopped
½ **red pepper**, cored, deseeded and diced
½ **yellow pepper**, cored, deseeded and diced
1 **garlic clove**, finely chopped
2 teaspoons **harissa**
200 g (7 oz) **tomatoes**, roughly chopped
1 tablespoon **tomato purée**
300 ml (½ pint) **fish stock**
4 small **mackerel**, about 300 g (10 oz), each gutted
   and heads removed
salt and **pepper**

Preheat the slow cooker if necessary. Bring a saucepan of water to the boil, add the potatoes and cook for 4–5 minutes or until almost tender. Drain and reserve.

Heat the oil in a frying pan, add the onion and fry, stirring, for 5 minutes or until softened and just beginning to turn golden. Stir in the peppers and garlic and fry for 2–3 minutes. Mix in the harissa, tomatoes, tomato purée, stock and a little salt and pepper and bring to the boil.

Tip the potatoes into the base of the slow cooker pot. Rinse the fish well, drain and arrange in a single layer on top of the potatoes, then cover with the hot tomato mixture. Cover and cook on low for 5–7 hours or until the potatoes are tender and the fish flakes when pressed in the centre with a small knife.

Spoon into shallow bowls and serve with warmed pitta breads, if liked.

FOR HARISSA-SPICED POTATOES WITH FETA, follow the recipe as above but omit the fish and instead sprinkle the top of the tomato mixture with 125 g (4 oz) crumbled feta cheese and 50 g (2 oz) pitted black olives. Cook as above and sprinkle with torn parsley just before serving.

HOT SOUSED HERRINGS

Serves **4**
Preparation time **15 minutes**
Cooking temperature **high**
Cooking time **1½–2 hours**

1 large **red onion**, thinly sliced
1 large **carrot**, cut into matchsticks
1 large **celery stick**, thinly sliced
6 small **herrings**, gutted, filleted, rinsed and drained
2 **tarragon sprigs**, plus extra to garnish
1 **bay leaf**
150 ml (¼ pint) **cider vinegar**
25 g (1 oz) **caster sugar**
600 ml (1 pint) boiling **water**
½ teaspoon **mixed peppercorns**
salt

Preheat the slow cooker if necessary. Put half the onion, carrot and celery in the base of the slow cooker pot. Arrange the herring fillets on top, then cover with the remaining vegetables.

Add the tarragon, bay leaf, vinegar and sugar, then pour over the measurement boiling water. Add the peppercorns and a little salt. Cover with the lid and cook on high for 1½–2 hours.

Spoon the fish, vegetables and a little of the cooking liquid into shallow bowls, halving the fish fillets if liked. Garnish with tarragon sprigs. Serve with pickled beetroot, dill cucumbers and bread and butter, if liked.

FOR SWEDISH BAKED HERRINGS, make as above, adding 2 dill sprigs instead of the tarragon and increasing the amount of sugar to 50 g (2 oz). Leave to cool once cooked and serve with 8 tablespoons soured cream mixed with 1 teaspoon hot horseradish and accompanied by pickled cucumber salad.

SALMON & ASPARAGUS RISOTTO

Serves **4**
Preparation time **15 minutes**
Cooking temperature **high**
Cooking time **1¾–2 hours**

25 g (1 oz) **butter**
1 tablespoon **olive oil**
1 **onion**, chopped
grated rind of 1 **lemon**
200 g (7 oz) **risotto rice**
150 ml (¼ pint) **dry white wine**
900 ml (1½ pints) **fish** or
   vegetable stock
4 **salmon steaks**, about 150 g
   (5 oz) each
bunch of **asparagus**, trimmed and
   thickly sliced
salt and **pepper**
chopped **chives**, to garnish
125 ml (4 fl oz) **crème fraîche**,
   to serve

Preheat the slow cooker if necessary. Heat the butter and oil in a large frying pan, add the onion and fry for 5 minutes or until softened. Stir in the lemon rind and rice and cook for 1 minute. Mix in the wine, stock and a little salt and pepper and bring to the boil, stirring.

Pour into the slow cooker pot. Arrange the salmon steaks in a single layer on the rice, turning on their sides, if needed, so that they are just below the surface of the stock. Cover with the lid and cook on low for 1¾–2 hours or until the rice is tender and the salmon flakes into opaque pieces when pressed in the centre with a knife.

When almost ready to serve, bring a saucepan of water to the boil, add the asparagus and cook for 5 minutes or until just tender. Spoon the rice into shallow bowls and top with spoonfuls of the crème fraîche, the drained asparagus and salmon steaks, broken into pieces. Sprinkle with chopped chives and a little extra pepper.

FOR SMOKED FISH KEDGEREE, add ½ teaspoon ground turmeric and 1 bay leaf to the fried onion instead of the lemon rind. Add 1 litre (1¾ pints) stock and bring to the boil, then transfer to the slow cooker pot. Replace the salmon with 625 g (1¼ lb) smoked haddock fillet, cut into 2 pieces, then cook as above. Skin and flake the fish. Discard the bay leaf, then return the fish to the pot and stir in 4 tablespoons double cream and 75 g (3 oz) just cooked frozen peas. Spoon into bowls and top with 4 hard-boiled eggs, cut into wedges. Sprinkle with chopped chives and a little extra pepper.

POACHED SALMON WITH BEURRE BLANC

Serves **4**
Preparation time **25 minutes**
Cooking temperature **low**
Cooking time **1¾–2¼ hours**

100 g (3½ oz) **butter**
1 large **onion**, thinly sliced
1 **lemon**, sliced, plus extra to garnish
500 g (1 lb) piece of **thick-end
    salmon fillet**, no longer than
    18 cm (7 inches)
1 **bay leaf**
200 ml (7 fl oz) **dry white wine**
150 ml (¼ pint) **fish stock**
3 tablespoons finely chopped **chives**,
    plus extra to garnish
salt and **pepper**

Preheat the slow cooker if necessary. Brush the inside of the slow cooker pot with a little of the butter. Fold a large piece of foil into 3, then place it in the base of the pot with the ends sticking up to use as a strap. Arrange the onion slices and half the lemon slices over the foil. Place the salmon, flesh side up, on top. Season with salt and pepper, then add the bay leaf and remaining lemon slices.

Pour the wine and stock into a saucepan, bring to the boil, then pour over the salmon. Fold the foil down if necessary to fit the cooker lid, then cook on low for 1¾–2¼ hours until the fish is opaque and flakes easily when pressed in the centre with a knife.

Lift the salmon carefully out of the pot using the foil strap, draining off as much liquid as possible. Transfer to a serving plate, discard the bay leaf and lemon and onion slices and keep warm. Strain the cooking liquid into a saucepan and boil rapidly for 4–5 minutes or until reduced to about 4 tablespoons.

Reduce the heat and gradually whisk in small pieces of the remaining butter, little by little, until the sauce thickens and becomes creamy. (Don't be tempted to hurry making the sauce either by adding the butter in one go or by increasing the heat to the sauce, or you may find that it separates.) Stir in the chopped chives and adjust the seasoning if needed.

Cut the salmon into 4 portions, discard the skin and transfer to individual plates. Spoon a little of the sauce around the fish. Garnish with extra lemon slices and chives.

BAKED SEAFOOD WITH SAFFRON

Serves **4**
Preparation time **15 minutes**
Cooking temperature **low** and **high**
Cooking time **5½–7½ hours**

1 **onion**, finely chopped
1 **red pepper**, cored, deseeded
   and diced
2 **garlic cloves**, finely chopped
400 g (13 oz) can **chopped tomatoes**
150 ml (¼ pint) **dry white wine** or
   fish stock
large pinch of **saffron threads**
2 **thyme sprigs**
1 tablespoon **olive oil**
400 g (13 oz) pack **frozen seafood**
   (prawns, mussels, squid), thawed
300 g (10 oz) **dried tagliatelle**
salt and **pepper**
chopped **parsley**, to serve

Preheat the slow cooker if necessary. Put the onion, red pepper, garlic and tomatoes into the slow cooker pot, then add the wine or stock, saffron, thyme, oil and a little salt and pepper.

Cover with the lid and cook on low for 5–7 hours. Rinse the seafood with cold water, drain and then stir into the slow cooker pot. Replace the lid and cook on high for 30 minutes or until piping hot.

When almost ready to serve, cook the tagliatelle in a large saucepan of lightly salted boiling water according to the packet instructions until just tender. Drain and toss with chopped parsley. Spoon into shallow bowls and top with the seafood sauce.

FOR BAKED SALMON WITH PESTO, omit the seafood and drain a 400 g (13 oz) can red salmon, remove the skin and bones and break the fish into large flakes. Put the onion, red pepper and garlic into the slow cooker pot. Heat the tomatoes and wine or stock in a small saucepan or the microwave, then add to the pot with 2 teaspoons pesto and the oil, omitting the saffron and thyme. Mix in the salmon and continue as above.

SMOKED COD WITH BEAN MASH

Serves **4**
Preparation time **15 minutes**
Cooking temperature **low**
Cooking time **1½–2 hours**

2 x 410 g (13½ oz) cans **cannellini beans**, drained
bunch of **spring onions**, thinly sliced; white and green parts kept separate
400 ml (14 fl oz) boiling **fish stock**
1 teaspoon **wholegrain mustard**
grated rind and juice of 1 **lemon**
4 **smoked cod loins**, about 625 g (1¼ lb) in total
4 tablespoons **crème fraîche**
small bunch of **parsley**, **watercress** or **rocket leaves**, roughly chopped
salt and pepper

Preheat the slow cooker if necessary. Put the drained beans into the slow cooker pot with the white spring onion slices. Mix the fish stock with the mustard, lemon rind and juice and a little salt and pepper, then pour into the pot.

Arrange the fish on top and sprinkle with a little extra pepper. Cover with the lid and cook on low for 1½–2 hours or until the fish flakes easily when pressed in the centre with a knife.

Lift out the fish with a fish slice and transfer to a plate. Pour off nearly all the cooking liquid, then mash the beans roughly. Stir in the crème fraîche, the green spring onion slices and the parsley, watercress or rocket. Taste and adjust the seasoning, if needed. Spoon the mash on to plates and top with the fish.

FOR BAKED SALMON WITH BASIL BEAN MASH, add the beans to the slow cooker pot with the ingredients as above, omitting the mustard. Arrange 4 salmon steaks, about 150 g (5 oz) each, on top, season and cook as above. Mash the beans with the crème fraîche, green spring onion slices and a small bunch of roughly torn basil and serve with the fish as above.

BAKED MACKEREL WITH BEETROOT

Serves **4**
Preparation time **20 minutes**
Cooking temperature **high**
Cooking time **1½–2 hours**

2 tablespoons **olive oil**
1 **onion**, sliced
1 **celery stick**, sliced
1 **carrot**, thinly sliced
2 tablespoons **light muscovado sugar**
4 tablespoons **cider vinegar**
200 ml (7 fl oz) **fish stock**
2 **bay leaves**
4 **cloves**
250 g (8 oz) pack **cooked beetroot
  in natural juice**, drained and sliced
1 **dessert apple**, peeled, cored
  and sliced
4 **mackerel**, about 200 g (7 oz)
  each, gutted, heads removed,
  rinsed and drained
salt and **pepper**

MUSTARD CREAM
2 teaspoons **wholegrain mustard**
6 tablespoons **crème fraîche**
2 tablespoons chopped **chives**, plus
  extra to garnish

Preheat the slow cooker if necessary. Heat the oil in a frying pan, add the onion, celery and carrot and fry for about 5 minutes or until softened.

Add the sugar, vinegar, stock, bay leaves, cloves and a little salt and pepper and bring to the boil. Arrange the beetroot in the base of the slow cooker pot, then top with the apple. Slash the fish 2 or 3 times on each side, then arrange in a single layer on top of the apple.

Pour over the hot stock and vegetables, cover with the lid and cook on high for 1½–2 hours or until the fish flakes easily when pressed in the centre with a knife.

When almost ready to serve, mix together the ingredients for the mustard cream in a small bowl and season to taste. Carefully transfer the fish, vegetables and some of the stock to shallow bowls, then garnish with chives. Serve with spoonfuls of the mustard cream and crusty sliced bread, if liked.

FOR BAKED MACKEREL WITH HOT POTATO SALAD, make up the recipe as above, omitting the beetroot. When the fish is almost ready, cook 400 g (13 oz) scrubbed baby new potatoes in a saucepan of boiling water for 15 minutes or until just tender. Make the mustard cream as above and toss with the hot potatoes. Serve with the drained mackerel and sliced pickled cucumbers.

TROUT SPIRALS WITH LEMON FOAM

Serves **4**
Preparation time **30 minutes**
Cooking temperature **low**
Cooking time **1½–2 hours**

50 g (2 oz) **butter**, at room temperature
grated rind and juice of 1 **lemon**
4 **trout fillets**, skinned, about 650 g (1 lb 5 oz) in total
1 **plaice**, filleted into 4, skinned
200 ml (7 fl oz) boiling **fish stock**
3 **egg yolks**
salt and **pepper**

Preheat the slow cooker if necessary. Beat the butter with the lemon rind and a little salt and pepper.

Lay the trout fillets on a chopping board so that the skinned sides are uppermost. Trim the edges to neaten, if needed, and spread with half the lemon butter. Top with the plaice fillets, skinned side uppermost, and spread with the remaining butter. Roll up each fish stack, starting at the tapered end. Secure each spiral with 2 cocktail sticks at right angles to each other and arrange in the base of the slow cooker pot.

Pour the lemon juice and boiling stock over the fish and add a little salt and pepper. Cover with the lid and cook on low for 1½–2 hours or until the fish flakes easily when pressed in the centre with a knife.

Lift the fish spirals out of the slow cooker pot with a slotted spoon, put on to a serving plate and remove the cocktail sticks. Strain the cooking juices into a bowl. Put the egg yolks in a saucepan and gradually whisk in the strained stock until smooth. Cook over a medium heat, whisking constantly without boiling, for 3–4 minutes or until lightly thickened and foamy. Pour into a jug. Serve the fish with a generous drizzle of the sauce with salad and a separate bowl of tiny new potatoes, if liked.

FOR SALMON STEAKS WITH LEMON & TARRAGON FOAM, put 4 salmon steaks, about 150 g (5 oz) each and spread with the lemon butter, in the base of the slow cooker pot and continue as above. Make up the sauce as above, then whisk in 2 teaspoons chopped tarragon just before serving.

SMOKED MACKEREL KEDGEREE

Serves **4**
Preparation time **15 minutes**
Cooking temperature **low**
Cooking time **3¼–4¼ hours**

1 tablespoon **sunflower oil**
1 **onion**, chopped
1 teaspoon **ground turmeric**
2 tablespoons **mango chutney**
750–900 ml (1¼–1½ pints) **vegetable stock**
1 **bay leaf**
175 g (6 oz) **easy-cook brown long-grain rice**
250 g (8 oz) or 3 **smoked mackerel fillets**, skinned
100 g (3½ oz) **frozen peas**
25 g (1 oz) **watercress** or **rocket leaves**
4 **hard-boiled eggs**, cut into wedges
salt and **pepper**

Preheat the slow cooker if necessary. Heat the oil in a frying pan, add the onion and fry, stirring, for 5 minutes or until softened and just beginning to turn golden.

Stir in the turmeric, chutney, stock, bay leaf and a little salt and pepper and bring to the boil. Pour into the slow cooker pot and add the rice. Add the smoked mackerel to the pot in a single layer. Cover with the lid and cook on low for 3–4 hours or until the rice is tender and has absorbed almost all the stock.

Stir in the peas, breaking up the fish into chunky pieces. Add extra hot stock if needed. Cook, still on low, for 15 minutes more. Stir in the watercress or rocket, spoon on to plates and garnish with the wedges of egg.

FOR SMOKED HADDOCK KEDGEREE WITH CARDAMOM, make up the recipe as above but omit the mango chutney and instead add 4 crushed cardamom pods with their black seeds. Replace the smoked mackerel with 400 g (13 oz) skinned smoked haddock fillet, cut into 2 pieces. Continue as above, adding the peas and egg wedges at the end but omitting the watercress or rocket. Drizzle with 4 tablespoons double cream.

SALMON-WRAPPED COD WITH LEEKS

Serves **4**
Preparation time **30 minutes**
Cooking temperature **low**
Cooking time **1½–2 hours**

2 **cod loins**, about 750 g (1½ lb)
  in total
juice of 1 **lemon**
4 **dill sprigs**, plus extra
  to garnish (optional)
4 slices of **smoked salmon**, about
  175 g (6 oz) in total
1 **leek**, thinly sliced, white and green
  parts kept separate
4 tablespoons **Noilly Prat**
200 ml (7 fl oz) boiling **fish stock**
2 teaspoons drained **capers**
  (optional)
75 g (3 oz) **butter**, diced
2 tablespoons chopped **chives**
  or **parsley**
salt and **pepper**

Preheat the slow cooker if necessary. Cut each cod loin in half to give 4 portions, then drizzle with the lemon juice and sprinkle with salt and pepper. Add a dill sprig to the top of each portion, then wrap with a slice of smoked salmon.

Put the white leek slices into the base of the slow cooker pot and arrange the fish on top in a single layer, tilting them at an angle, if needed, to fit. Add the Noilly Prat and hot stock, then cover and cook on low for 1½–2 hours or until the fish flakes easily when pressed in the centre with a knife.

Lift out the fish with a fish slice and put it on a serving plate, cover with foil and keep hot. Pour the white leeks and cooking juices from the slow cooker pot into a saucepan, add the reserved green leek slices and the capers, if using, and boil rapidly for about 5 minutes or until the liquid is reduced to 4–6 tablespoons. Scoop out and reserve the leeks as soon as the green slices have softened.

Whisk in the butter, a piece at a time until melted, and continue until all the butter has been added and the sauce is smooth and glossy. Return the cooked leeks to the sauce with the chopped herbs and taste and adjust the seasoning. Arrange the fish on plates, then spoon the sauce around. Sprinkle with extra dill and serve with baby new potatoes, if liked.

FOR SMOKED COD WITH BUTTERED LEEKS, make up the recipe as above, with smoked cod loins, omitting the smoked salmon and dill and replacing the Noilly Prat with dry white wine.

THREE-FISH GRATIN ♥

Serves **4**
Preparation time **20 minutes**
Cooking temperature **low**
Cooking time **2–3 hours**

2 tablespoons **cornflour**
400 ml (14 fl oz) **skimmed milk**
50 g (2 oz) **mature Cheddar cheese**, grated
3 tablespoons chopped **parsley**
1 **leek**, thinly sliced
1 **bay leaf**
500 g (1 lb) mixed **skinless fish fillets** (such as salmon, cod and smoked haddock), diced
salt and **pepper**

TOPPING
20 g (¾ oz) fresh breadcrumbs
40 g (1½ oz) **mature Cheddar cheese**, grated

TO SERVE
325 g (11 oz) steamed **peas**
325 g (11 oz) steamed **mangetout**

Preheat the slow cooker if necessary. Place the cornflour in a saucepan with a little of the milk and mix to a smooth paste. Stir in the rest of the milk, then add the cheese, parsley, leek and bay leaf. Season to taste and bring to the boil, stirring until thickened.

Place the fish in the slow cooker pot. Pour over the hot leek sauce, cover and cook on low for 2–3 hours until the fish is cooked through.

Transfer the fish mixture to a shallow ovenproof dish, sprinkle the breadcrumbs and cheese over the top, then place under a preheated hot grill for 4–5 minutes until golden brown. Serve immediately with the steamed peas and mangetout.

FOR FISH PIES, follow the recipe above, omitting the breadcrumb and cheese topping. Cut 625 g (1¼ lb) potatoes into chunks and cook in a saucepan of lightly salted boiling water for 15 minutes or until tender. Drain and mash with 4 tablespoons skimmed milk, then season and stir in 40 g (1½ oz) grated mature Cheddar cheese. Divide the cooked fish mixture between 4 individual pie dishes, spoon over the mash, rough up the top with a fork, then brush with 1 beaten egg. Cook under a preheated medium grill until golden.

SALMON BOURRIDE ♥

Serves **4**
Preparation time **20 minutes**
Cooking temperature **low**
Cooking time **3–3½ hours**

low-calorie cooking oil spray
1 **onion**, chopped
2 **garlic cloves**, finely chopped
½ **red pepper**, cored, deseeded and
   very thinly sliced
½ **orange pepper**, cored, deseeded
   and very thinly sliced
400 g (13 oz) can **chopped tomatoes**
150 ml (¼ pint) **vegetable stock**
1 teaspoon **granular sweetener**
1 teaspoon **cornflour**
400 g (13 oz) can **artichoke
   hearts**, drained
4 **salmon steaks**, 140 g (4½ oz) each
finely grated rind of 1 **lemon**
½ teaspoon **dried
   Mediterranean herbs**
salt and **pepper**
200 g (7 oz) steamed **green beans**,
   to serve

Preheat the slow cooker if necessary. Spray a large frying pan with a little low-calorie cooking oil spray and place over a high heat until hot. Add the onion, garlic and peppers and cook for 4–5 minutes until softened.

Stir in the tomatoes, stock and sweetener. Mix the cornflour to a smooth paste with a little cold water and stir into the pan. Season to taste and bring to the boil, stirring.

Transfer the mixture to the slow cooker pot, stir in the artichoke hearts, then arrange the salmon steaks in a single layer on top, pressing them down into the liquid. Sprinkle the lemon rind and herbs over the salmon and season lightly.

Cover and cook on low for 3–3½ hours until the salmon steaks are cooked and flake easily when pressed in the centre with a small knife. Spoon into shallow bowls and serve with the steamed green beans.

FOR SQUID BOURRIDE, rinse 625 g (1¼ lb) prepared squid tubes and take the tentacles out of the tubes. Slice the squid tubes and drain well. Follow the recipe above, using the sliced squid tubes instead of the salmon and cooking on low for 4–5 hours. Add the squid tentacles and continue cooking for a further 30 minutes until tender, then serve with the steamed green beans.

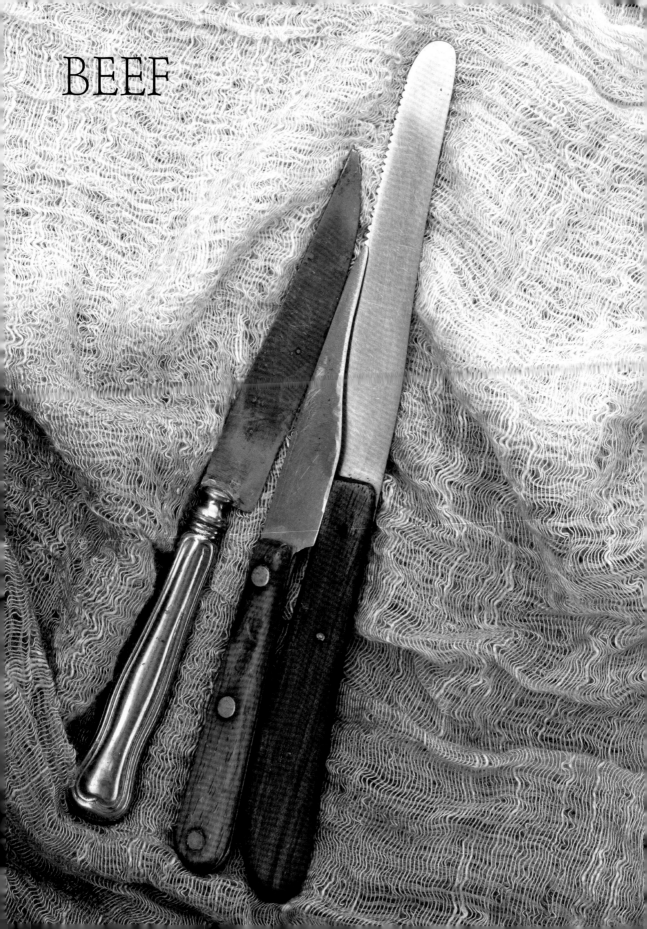

BEEF

JUMBO BURGER WITH TOMATO SAUCE

Serves **4**
Preparation time **25 minutes**
Cooking temperature **high**
Cooking time **3–4 hours**

vegetable oil, for oiling
bunch of **spring onions**, chopped
250 g (8 oz) **lean minced beef**
250 g (8 oz) **lean herby sausages**,
  skins split and removed
4 tablespoons **fresh breadcrumbs**
2 tablespoons **Worcestershire sauce**
400 g (13 oz) can **chopped tomatoes**
125 ml (4 fl oz) **vegetable stock**
1 teaspoon **English mustard**
1 tablespoon **light muscovado sugar**
1 **green** or **red pepper**, cored,
  deseeded and diced
salt and **pepper**

TO SERVE
4 **burger buns**
shredded **lettuce**

Preheat the slow cooker if necessary. Lightly oil the inside of 2 x 350 ml (12 fl oz) soufflé dishes 10 cm (4 inches) in diameter and 6 cm (2½ inches) deep and base-line with circles of nonstick baking paper, checking first that they will fit in the slow cooker pot.

Add half the spring onions, the beef, sausagemeat and breadcrumbs to a bowl or food processor. Add 1 tablespoon of the Worcestershire sauce, season with salt and pepper and mix together. Divide between the 2 dishes and press down well to level off the surface. Cover with foil and put the dishes side by side in the slow cooker pot.

Add the tomatoes, stock, remaining Worcestershire sauce, mustard and sugar to a small saucepan. Season with salt and pepper and bring to the boil. Stir in the remaining spring onions and the green or red pepper and spoon the mixture into the gaps around the dishes.

Cover with the lid and cook on high for 3–4 hours until the burgers are cooked. Test with a skewer to make sure the juices do not run pink. Lift the burger dishes out of the slow cooker with a tea towel, pour the excess fat from the dishes, then turn the burgers out.

Split the burger buns and add shredded lettuce to the bottom halves. Cut the burgers in half horizontally. Place 1 half on each bun, then top with spoonfuls of the tomato sauce and serve the remaining sauce in a small bowl. Accompany with microwave or oven chips, if liked.

FOR TURKEY BURGER & TOMATO SAUCE, omit the minced beef and add 250 g (8 oz) minced turkey leg meat. Make and cook as above.

BEEF BOURGUIGNON ♥

Serves **4**
Preparation time **20 minutes**
Cooking temperature **low**
Cooking time **10–11 hours**

low-calorie cooking oil spray
625 g (1¼ lb) **stewing beef**,
   trimmed of fat and cubed
100 g (3½ oz) **bacon**, diced
300 g (10 oz) small
   shallots, peeled
3 **garlic cloves**, finely chopped
1 tablespoon **plain flour**
150 ml (¼ pint) **red wine**
300 ml (½ pint) **beef stock**
1 tablespoon **tomato purée**
small bunch of **mixed herbs** or
   a **dried bouquet garni**
salt and **pepper**
chopped **parsley**, to garnish

Preheat the slow cooker if necessary. Spray a large frying pan with a little low-calorie cooking oil spray and place over a high heat until hot. Add the beef a few pieces at a time until all the meat is in the pan and cook for 5 minutes, stirring, until browned. Use a slotted spoon to transfer the beef to the slow cooker pot.

Add the bacon and shallots to the frying pan and cook over a medium heat for 2–3 minutes until the bacon is just beginning to brown. Stir in the garlic and flour, then add the wine, stock, tomato purée and herbs. Season to taste and bring to the boil, stirring.

Pour the sauce over the beef, cover and cook on low for 10–11 hours until the beef is tender. Stir the bourguignon, garnish with chopped parsley and serve with rice, if liked.

FOR BEEF GOULASH, follow the recipe above, adding 2 teaspoons mild paprika, 1 teaspoon caraway seeds, ¼ teaspoon ground cinnamon and ¼ teaspoon ground allspice instead of the herbs.

BEEF STEW WITH DUMPLINGS

Serves **4**
Preparation time **35 minutes**
Cooking temperature **low** and **high**
Cooking time **8–10½ hours**

2 tablespoons **olive oil**
750 g (1½ lb) **braising beef**, trimmed
    of fat and cubed
1 large **onion**, chopped
2–3 **garlic cloves**, chopped
2 tablespoons **plain flour**
300 ml (½ pint) **Burgundy red wine**
300 ml (½ pint) **beef stock**
1 tablespoon **tomato purée**
2 **bay leaves**
150 g (5 oz) **baby carrots**, larger
    ones halved
250 g (8 oz) **leeks**, thinly sliced
salt and pepper

HORSERADISH DUMPLINGS
150 g (5 oz) **self-raising flour**, plus
    extra for dusting
75 g (3 oz) **shredded suet**
2 teaspoons **creamed horseradish**
3 tablespoons snipped **chives**
5–7 tablespoons **water**

Preheat the slow cooker if necessary. Heat the oil in a frying pan and add the beef a few pieces at a time until all the meat is in the pan. Fry over a high heat until just beginning to brown, then add the onion and fry, stirring, for 5 minutes.

Stir in the garlic and flour, then gradually mix in the wine and stock. Add the tomato purée and bay leaves and season with salt and pepper. Bring to the boil, then transfer the mixture to the slow cooker pot. Cover with the lid and cook on low for 7–9 hours.

Stir the stew, then add the carrots, replace the lid and cook on high for 30–45 minutes.

Meanwhile, make the dumplings. Mix the flour, suet, horseradish, chives and salt and pepper together in a bowl. Stir in enough of the measurement water to make a soft but not sticky dough. With floured hands, shape into 8 balls.

Stir the leeks into the stew, then add the dumplings, replace the lid and cook, still on high, for another 30–45 minutes or until the dumplings are light and fluffy. Spoon into shallow dishes and serve, remembering to remove the bay leaves.

FOR GUINNESS BEEF STEW WITH MUSTARD DUMPLINGS, make up the stew as above, replacing the red wine with 300 ml (½ pint) Guinness or stout. Top with dumplings made with 3 teaspoons wholegrain mustard instead of the creamed horeradish and chives.

BEEF & ROOT VEGETABLE HOTPOT

Serves 4
Preparation time 25 minutes
Cooking temperature high
Cooking time 7–8 hours

1 tablespoon **sunflower oil**
750 g (1½ lb) **braising beef**, trimmed
   of fat and cubed
1 **onion**, chopped
2 tablespoons **plain flour**
600 ml (1 pint) **beef stock**
2 tablespoons **Worcestershire sauce**
1 tablespoon **tomato purée**
2 teaspoons **English mustard**
3 **rosemary sprigs**
125 g (4 oz) **carrots**, diced
125 g (4 oz) **swede**, diced
125 g (4 oz) **parsnip**, diced
700 g (1 lb 6 oz) **potatoes**,
   thinly sliced
25 g (1 oz) **butter**
salt and **pepper**

Preheat the slow cooker if necessary. Heat the oil in a frying pan, add the beef a few pieces at a time until all the meat is in the pan and fry over a high heat, stirring, until browned. Scoop the beef out of pan with a slotted spoon and transfer to the slow cooker pot.

Add the onion to the pan and fry, stirring, for 5 minutes or until softened and just beginning to turn golden. Stir in the flour, then gradually mix in the stock. Add the Worcestershire sauce, tomato purée, mustard and leaves from 2 sprigs of the rosemary. Season and bring to the boil, stirring.

Add the diced vegetables to the slow cooker pot. Pour the onions and sauce over them, then cover with the potato slices, arranging them so that they overlap and pressing them down into the stock. Sprinkle with the leaves torn from the remaining rosemary sprig and a little salt and pepper.

Cover and cook on high for 7–8 hours until the potatoes are tender. Lift the pot out of the housing using oven gloves, dot the potatoes with the butter and brown under a preheated hot grill, if liked.

FOR CHICKEN & BLACK PUDDING HOTPOT, replace the beef with 625 g (1¼ lb) chicken thighs that have been skinned, boned and diced. Continue as above, adding 100 g (3½ oz) diced, skinned black pudding along with the root vegetables. Cover with the potatoes and cook as above.

STEAK & MUSHROOM PUDDING

Serves **4**
Preparation time **40 minutes**
Cooking temperature **high**
Cooking time **5–6 hours**

25 g (1 oz) **butter**, plus extra
    for greasing
1 tablespoon **sunflower oil**
2 large **onions**, roughly chopped
2 teaspoons **caster sugar**
100 g (3½ oz) **cup mushrooms**, sliced
1 tablespoon **plain** or
    self-raising flour
150 ml (¼ pint) hot **beef stock**
1 teaspoon **Dijon mustard**
1 tablespoon **Worcestershire sauce**
700 g (1 lb 6 oz) **rump steak**, trimmed
    of fat and thinly sliced
salt and **pepper**

PASTRY
300 g (10 oz) **self-raising flour**, plus
    extra for dusting
½ teaspoon **salt**
150 g (5 oz) **shredded suet**
about 200 ml (7 fl oz) **water**

Preheat the slow cooker if necessary. Heat the butter and oil in a frying pan, add the onions and fry for 5 minutes or until softened. Sprinkle the sugar over the onions and fry for 5 more minutes or until browned. Add the mushrooms and fry for 2–3 minutes. Stir in the flour.

Mix the stock, mustard, Worcestershire sauce and salt and pepper in a jug together.

Make the suet pastry. Put the flour, salt and suet in a bowl and mix well. Gradually stir in enough of the measurement water to make a soft but not sticky dough. Knead the dough lightly, then roll out on a floured surface to a round 33 cm (13 inches) in diameter. Cut out a quarter segment and reserve. Press the remaining dough into a 1.5 litre (2½ pint) buttered pudding basin, butting the edges together.

Layer the fried onions, mushrooms and sliced steak in the basin. Pour the stock over the top. Pat the reserved pastry into a round the same size as the top of the basin. Fold the top edges of the pastry in the basin over the filling, brush with a little water and cover with the pastry lid.

Cover the pudding with a large domed circle of buttered foil so that there is room for the pastry to rise. Tie with string. Stand the basin in the slow cooker pot on top of an upturned saucer. Pour boiling water into the pot to come halfway up the sides of the basin. Cover with the lid and cook on high for 5–6 hours.

Remove the basin from the slow cooker using a tea towel and remove the string and foil. The pastry should have risen and feel dry to the touch.

BEEF ADOBO

Serves **4**
Preparation time **25 minutes**
Cooking temperature **low**
Cooking time **8–10 hours**

1 tablespoon **sunflower oil**
750 g (1½ lb) **braising beef**, trimmed
    of fat and cubed
1 large **onion**, sliced
2 **garlic cloves**, finely chopped
2 tablespoons **plain flour**
450 ml (¾ pint) **beef stock**
4 tablespoons **soy sauce**
4 tablespoons **wine vinegar**
1 tablespoon **caster sugar**
2 **bay leaves**
juice of 1 **lime**
salt and **pepper**
boiled **long-grain rice**, to serve

TO GARNISH
1 **carrot**, cut into thin sticks
½ bunch of **spring onions**, cut into
    shreds
coriander leaves

Preheat the slow cooker if necessary. Heat the oil in a large frying pan and add the beef a few pieces at a time until all the meat is in the pan. Fry over a high heat, turning, until evenly browned, lift out of the pan with a slotted spoon and transfer to a plate.

Add the onion to the pan and fry for 5 minutes or until it is just beginning to brown. Mix in the garlic and cook for 2 minutes. Stir in the flour, then gradually mix in the stock. Add the soy sauce, vinegar, sugar, bay leaves and salt and pepper and bring to the boil, stirring.

Transfer the beef to the slow cooker pot, pour over the onion and stock mixture, cover with the lid and cook on low for 8–10 hours.

Stir in lime juice to taste and garnish with the carrot sticks, shredded spring onions and coriander leaves. Serve in shallow bowls lined with rice.

FOR HOISIN BEEF, combine 3 tablespoons each soy sauce and rice or wine vinegar with 2 tablespoons hoisin sauce and 2.5 cm (1 inch) piece of peeled and finely chopped fresh root ginger. Add this mixture to the beef stock with the sugar. Omit the bay leaves. Bring the mixture to the boil, then continue as above, adding the lime juice just before serving.

OLIVE & LEMON MEATBALLS

Serves **4**
Preparation time **30 minutes**
Cooking temperature **low**
Cooking time **6–8 hours**

MEATBALLS
50 g (2 oz) **pitted black
    olives**, chopped
grated rind of ½ **lemon**
500 g (1 lb) **extra-lean minced beef**
1 **egg yolk**
1 tablespoon **olive oil**

SAUCE
1 **onion**, chopped
2 **garlic cloves**, finely chopped
400 g (13 oz) can **chopped tomatoes**
1 teaspoon **caster sugar**
150 ml (¼ pint) **chicken stock**
salt and **pepper**
small **basil leaves**, to garnish
cooked **tagliatelle** tossed with
    chopped **basil** and melted **butter**,
    to serve

Preheat the slow cooker if necessary. Put all the ingredients for the meatballs except for the oil in a bowl and mix with a wooden spoon. Wet your hands and shape the mixture into 20 balls.

Heat the oil in a large frying pan, add the meatballs and cook over a high heat, turning, until browned on all sides. Lift them out of pan with a slotted spoon and transfer to a plate.

Make the sauce. Add the onion to the pan and fry, stirring, for 5 minutes or until lightly browned. Add the garlic, tomatoes, sugar, stock and salt and pepper and bring to the boil, stirring.

Transfer the meatballs to the slow cooker pot, pour over the hot sauce, cover and cook on low for 6–8 hours. Garnish with basil leaves and serve with tagliatelle tossed with chopped basil and melted butter.

FOR HERB & GARLIC MEATBALLS, replace the olives and lemon rind with 2 finely chopped garlic cloves and 2 tablespoons chopped basil leaves. Mix, shape and cook the meatballs with the sauce as above, adding a small handful of basil leaves to the sauce just before serving.

INDIAN SPICED COTTAGE PIE

Serves 4
Preparation time **30 minutes**
Cooking temperature **low**
Cooking time **8–10 hours**

1 tablespoon **sunflower oil**
500 g (1 lb) **lean minced beef**
1 **onion**, chopped
4 tablespoons **korma curry paste**
1 teaspoon **ground turmeric**
2 **carrots**, diced
2 tablespoons **plain flour**
100 g (3½ oz) **dried red lentils**,
   rinsed and drained
50 g (2 oz) **sultanas**
1 tablespoon **tomato purée**
900 ml (1½ pints) **beef stock**
salt and **pepper**

TOPPING
875 g (1¾ lb) **potatoes**, cut
   into chunks
50 g (2 oz) **butter**
3 tablespoons **milk**
1 tablespoon **sunflower oil**
bunch of **spring onions**, chopped
½ teaspoon **ground turmeric**

Preheat the slow cooker if necessary. Heat the oil in a large frying pan, add the mince and onion and cook, stirring and breaking up the meat, until it is evenly browned. Stir in the curry paste and turmeric and cook for 1 minute. Stir in the carrots and flour, then add the lentils, sultanas, tomato purée, stock and salt and pepper. Bring to the boil, stirring, then pour into the slow cooker pot. Cover with the lid and cook on low for 8–10 hours or until the lentils are soft and the beef is tender.

When almost ready to serve, put the potatoes in a saucepan of boiling water and simmer for 15 minutes or until tender. Drain and mash with half the butter, the milk and salt and pepper. Heat the oil in a frying pan, add the spring onions and fry for 2–3 minutes or until softened. Add the turmeric and cook for 1 minute, then mix into the mash.

Stir the beef mixture and lift the pot out of the housing using oven gloves. Transfer to a serving dish, if liked. Spoon the mash on top, dot with remaining butter, then place under a preheated medium grill until golden. Serve with cooked peas, if liked.

FOR TRADITIONAL COTTAGE PIE, fry the beef and onion as above. Omit the curry paste and turmeric. Add the carrots and flour, then replace the lentils and sultanas with a 410 g (13½ oz) can baked beans, 1 tablespoon each tomato purée and Worcestershire sauce, 300 ml (½ pint) beef stock and 1 teaspoon dried mixed herbs. Transfer to the slow cooker pot and continue as above. Top with the mash, omitting the spring onions and turmeric. Sprinkle with 50 g (2 oz) grated Cheddar cheese and place under a preheated hot grill until browned.

STIFADO

Serves **4**
Preparation time **25 minutes, plus
  overnight marinating**
Cooking temperature **high** and **low**
Cooking time **10–11 hours**

200 ml (7 fl oz) **red wine**
1 tablespoon **tomato purée**
2 tablespoons **olive oil**
2–3 **thyme sprigs** or **bay leaves**
4 **cloves**
¼ teaspoon **ground allspice**
300 g (10 oz) **shallots**, halved
  if large
2 **garlic cloves**, finely chopped
750 g (1½ lb) **stewing beef**,
  trimmed of fat and cut
  into large chunks
4 teaspoons **cornflour**
150 ml (¼ pint) cold **water**
½ **beef stock cube**
salt and **pepper**

Mix the wine, tomato purée and oil in a shallow non-metallic dish. Add the herbs, spices and a little salt and pepper and mix together. Mix in the shallots and garlic, then add the beef and toss in the marinade. Cover with clingfilm and marinate in the refrigerator overnight.

Preheat the slow cooker if necessary. Put the cornflour into a saucepan, mix in a little of the measurement water to make a smooth paste, then mix in the remaining water. Drain the marinade from the beef into the pan and crumble in the stock cube. Bring to the boil, stirring.

Tip the beef, shallots and flavourings into the slow cooker pot and pour over the hot stock. Cover with the lid and cook on high for 30 minutes. Reduce the heat and cook on low for 9½–10½ hours, or set to auto for 10–11 hours, until the meat is cooked through and tender. Spoon into bowls and serve with toasted French bread and herb butter, if liked.

FOR LAMB STIFADO, mix together 200 ml (7 fl oz) white wine, 1 tablespoon tomato purée, 2 tablespoons olive oil, 2 bay leaves, 2 teaspoons roughly crushed coriander seeds and ½ sliced lemon, add the shallots and garlic and stir in 750 g (1½ lb) diced lamb shoulder or leg. Marinate in the refrigerator overnight, then continue as above.

TAMARIND BEEF WITH GINGER BEER

Serves 4
Preparation time **20 minutes**
Cooking temperature **low**
Cooking time **8–10 hours**

2 tablespoons **sunflower oil**
750 g (1½ lb) **lean stewing beef**, cubed
1 **onion**, chopped
2 **garlic cloves**, finely chopped
2 tablespoons **plain flour**
330 ml can **ginger beer**
6 teaspoons **tamarind paste**
½ teaspoon **crushed dried red chillies**
1 teaspoon **ground mixed spice**
1 tablespoon **dark muscovado sugar**
salt and **pepper**

Preheat the slow cooker if necessary. Heat the oil in a large frying pan, add the beef a few pieces at a time until all the meat is in the pan, then add the onion and fry over a medium heat, stirring, until the meat is browned.

Stir in the garlic and flour. Gradually mix in the ginger beer, then stir in the tamarind paste, chillies, mixed spice, sugar and a little salt and pepper and bring to the boil, stirring.

Transfer to the slow cooker pot and press the beef below the surface of the liquid. Cover with the lid and cook on low for 8–10 hours or until the meat is cooked through and tender.

Stir the beef, then ladle into bowls, top with Ginger & Coriander Croutes (*see* below) and serve with steamed broccoli, if liked.

FOR GINGER & CORIANDER CROUTES TO ACCOMPANY THE CASSEROLE, beat a 2 cm (¾ inch) piece of peeled and grated fresh root ginger with 2 finely chopped garlic cloves and 50 g (2 oz) butter, stir in ½ mild, deseeded and finely chopped red chilli or a large pinch of crushed dried red chillies, 3 tablespoons chopped coriander leaves and a little salt and pepper. Toast 8 slices of French bread on both sides and spread with the butter while hot. Arrange the croutes on top of the casserole and serve immediately.

RANCHEROS PIE

Serves **4**
Preparation time **25 minutes**
Cooking temperature **low**
Cooking time **7–8 hours**

1 tablespoon **sunflower oil**
500 g (1 lb) **minced beef**
1 **onion**, chopped
2 **garlic cloves**, finely chopped
1 teaspoon **cumin seeds**,
   roughly crushed
¼–½ teaspoon **crushed dried red**
   chillies, plus extra for sprinkling
¼ teaspoon **ground allspice**
2 **oregano sprigs**, roughly chopped
3 tablespoons **sultanas**
400 g (13 oz) can **chopped tomatoes**
250 ml (8 fl oz) **beef stock**
salt and **pepper**

TOPPING
500 g (1 lb) **sweet potatoes**,
   thinly sliced
25 g (1 oz) **butter**

Preheat the slow cooker if necessary. Heat the oil in a frying pan, add the mince and onion and fry, stirring and breaking up the mince with a wooden spoon, until it is evenly browned.

Stir in the garlic, spices, oregano, sultanas, tomatoes and stock. Add a little salt and pepper and bring to the boil, stirring. Spoon into the slow cooker pot, cover with the overlapping slices of sweet potato, dot with the butter and sprinkle with a little crushed dried red chillies and salt and pepper.

Cover with the lid and cook on low for 7–8 hours until the potato topping is tender. Lift the pot out of the housing using oven gloves and brown under a preheated hot grill, if liked.

FOR COWBOY PIE, fry the mince and onion as above, then omit the garlic, spices, oregano, sultanas and tomatoes but add 2 tablespoons Worcestershire sauce, a 410 g (13½ oz) can baked beans, 1 bay leaf and 200 ml (7 fl oz) beef stock. Cook the mince base as above. Top with 750 g (1½ lb) potatoes, cooked and mashed with butter and salt and pepper. Sprinkle with 50 g (2 oz) grated Cheddar cheese and brown under a preheated hot grill.

BEEF & GUINNESS PUFF PIE

Serves **4–5**
Preparation time **50 minutes**
Cooking temperature **low**
Cooking time **8–10 hours**

2 tablespoons **sunflower oil**, plus
   extra for oiling
750 g (1½ lb) **lean stewing
   beef**, cubed
1 **onion**, chopped
2 tablespoons **plain flour**, plus extra
   for dusting
300 ml (½ pint) **Guinness**
150 ml (¼ pint) **beef stock**
2 teaspoons **hot horseradish**
1 tablespoon **tomato purée**
1 **bay leaf**
200 g (7 oz) **cup mushrooms**, sliced
salt and **pepper**

PASTRY
beaten **egg**, to glaze
500 g (1 lb) **puff pastry**, thawed
   if frozen
100 g (3½ oz) **Stilton cheese** (rind
   removed), crumbled

Preheat the slow cooker if necessary. Heat the oil in a large frying pan, add the beef a few pieces at a time until all the meat is in the pan, then add the onion and fry over a medium heat, stirring, until the meat is browned.

Stir in the flour, then gradually mix in the Guinness and the stock. Stir in the horseradish, tomato purée and a little salt and pepper, then add the bay leaf and bring to the boil. Transfer to the slow cooker pot and press the meat below the surface of the liquid. Cover with the lid and cook on low for 8–10 hours or until the meat is cooked through and very tender.

When almost ready to serve, discard the bay leaf and divide the beef mixture between 4 pie dishes, each about 450 ml (¾ pint). Mix in the mushrooms, then brush the top edge of the dishes with a little egg. Cut the pastry into 4 and roll each piece out on a floured surface until a little larger than the dishes, then press on to the dishes. Trim off the excess pastry and crimp the edges. Mark diagonal lines on top and brush with beaten egg. Put on an oiled baking sheet and cook in a preheated oven, 200°C (400°F), Gas Mark 6, for 30 minutes or until golden. Sprinkle with the Stilton and leave to melt for 1–2 minutes. Serve with green beans and curly kale, if liked.

FOR BEERY BEEF HOTPOT, make up the meat base as above, omitting the mushrooms and adding 2 diced carrots. Spoon into the slow cooker pot, then cover with 700 g (1 lb 6 oz) thinly sliced potatoes, pressing them just below the stock. Cook as above. Dot 25 g (1 oz) butter over the potatoes, lift the pot out of the housing using oven gloves and brown under a preheated hot grill.

CHILLIED BEEF WITH CHOCOLATE

Serves **4**
Preparation time **15 minutes**
Cooking temperature **low**
Cooking time **8–10 hours**

1 tablespoon **sunflower oil**
500 g (1 lb) **minced beef**
1 **onion**, chopped
3 **garlic cloves**, finely chopped
1 teaspoon **ground cinnamon**
1 teaspoon **ground cumin**
½–1 teaspoon **smoked** or **hot paprika**,
    plus extra to garnish
¼–½ teaspoon **crushed dried**
    red chillies
1 **bay leaf**
400 g (13 oz) can **chopped tomatoes**
410 g (13½ oz) can **red kidney**
    beans, drained
2 tablespoons **dark muscovado sugar**
300 ml (½ pint) **beef stock**
25 g (1 oz) **plain dark chocolate**
salt and **pepper**

TO SERVE
soured cream
boiled **rice**

Preheat the slow cooker if necessary. Heat the oil in a frying pan, add the mince and onion and fry, stirring and breaking up the mince with a wooden spoon, until it is evenly browned.

Stir in the garlic, ground spices, chillies and bay leaf and cook for 1 minute. Mix in the tomatoes, beans, sugar and stock, then add the chocolate and a little salt and pepper and bring to the boil, stirring.

Pour into the slow cooker pot, cover and cook on low for 8–10 hours or until cooked through. Stir, spoon on to plates and top with a little soured cream, salsa (*see* below), if liked, and extra paprika. Serve with rice.

FOR AVOCADO & RED ONION SALSA TO ACCOMPANY THE CHILLIED BEEF, halve, stone and peel 1 large ripe avocado. Dice the flesh, then toss in the grated rind and juice of 2 limes. Mix with 1 small, finely chopped red onion, 1 chopped tomato and a small bunch of chopped coriander.

BEERY
BARLEY BEEF

BEERY
BEEF CHEEKS

Serves **4**
Preparation time **15 minutes**
Cooking temperature **low**
Cooking time **9–10 hours**

1 tablespoon **sunflower oil**
625 g (1¼ lb) **lean stewing beef**, cubed
1 **onion**, chopped
1 tablespoon **plain flour**
250 g (8 oz) **carrots**, diced
250 g (8 oz) **parsnips** or **potatoes**, diced
300 ml (½ pint) **light ale**
750 ml (1¼ pint) **beef stock**
small bunch of **mixed herbs** or **dried bouquet garni**
100 g (3½ oz) **pearl barley**
salt and **pepper**

Preheat the slow cooker if necessary. Heat the oil in a frying pan, add the beef a few pieces at a time until the meat is all in the pan, then fry over a high heat, stirring, until browned. Remove the beef with a slotted spoon and transfer to the slow cooker pot.

Add the onion to the frying pan and fry, stirring, for 5 minutes or until lightly browned. Mix in the flour, then add the root vegetables and beer and bring to the boil, stirring. Pour into the slow cooker pot.

Add the stock to the frying pan with the herbs and a little salt and pepper, bring to the boil, then pour into the slow cooker pot. Add the pearl barley, cover with the lid and cook on low for 9–10 hours until the beef is tender. Serve with Herb Croutons (*see* below), if liked.

FOR HERB CROUTONS TO ACCOMPANY THE BEEF,
beat 2 tablespoons each chopped parsley and chives, 1 tablespoon chopped tarragon and a little pepper into 75 g (3 oz) soft butter. Thickly slice ½ French stick, toast lightly on both sides, then spread with the herb butter.

Serves **4**
Preparation time **20 minutes**
Cooking temperature **high**
Cooking time **5–6 hours**

1 tablespoon **sunflower oil**
600 g (1 lb 3½ oz) **beef cheeks**, cut into 3.5 cm (1½ inch) thick slices
2 **red onions**, cut into wedges
250 ml (8 fl oz) **brown ale**
150 ml (¼ pint) **beef stock**
1 tablespoon **tomato purée**
2 teaspoons **cornflour**
2 **rosemary sprigs**
2 **bay leaves**
300 g (10 oz) small **Chantenay carrots**, halved lengthways
2 **celery sticks**, thickly sliced
salt and **pepper**

Heat the oil in a large frying pan over a high heat until hot. Add the beef a few pieces at a time until all the meat is in the pan and cook for 5 minutes, stirring, until browned. Use a slotted spoon to transfer the beef to the slow cooker pot, arranging it in a single layer.

Add the onions to the frying pan and cook for 3–4 minutes until softened. Add the brown ale, stock and tomato purée. Mix the cornflour to a smooth paste with a little cold water and stir into the pan with the herbs. Season to taste and bring to the boil, stirring.

Place the carrots and celery on top of the beef, then pour over the hot beer mixture. Cover and cook on high for 5–6 hours until the beef is very tender. Spoon into shallow bowls and serve with sugar snap peas and frozen peas, if liked.

FOR BEERY CHESTNUTS & MUSHROOMS, follow the recipe above, using 500 g (1 lb) whole mixed small mushrooms instead of the beef, and adding 175 g (6 oz) canned chestnuts at the same time as the herbs.

GOURMET BOLOGNESE

Serves **4**
Preparation time **20 minutes**
Cooking temperature **low**
Cooking time **8–10 hours**

1 tablespoon **olive oil**
500 g (1 lb) **lean minced beef**
1 **onion**, chopped
225 g (7½ oz) **chicken livers**, thawed
    if frozen
2 **garlic cloves**, finely chopped
50 g (2 oz) **pancetta** or **smoked back
    bacon rashers**, diced
150 g (5 oz) **cup mushrooms**, sliced
1 tablespoon **plain flour**
150 ml (¼ pint) **red wine**
150 ml (¼ pint) **beef stock**
400 g (13 oz) can **chopped tomatoes**
2 tablespoons **tomato purée**
1 **bouquet garni**
salt and **pepper**
300 g (10 oz) **dried tagliatelle**

TO SERVE
Parmesan cheese shavings
basil leaves

Preheat the slow cooker if necessary. Heat the oil in a frying pan, add the mince and onion and fry, stirring and breaking up the mince with a wooden spoon, until it is evenly browned.

Meanwhile, rinse the chicken livers in a sieve, drain and then chop roughly, discarding any white cores. Add to the frying pan with the garlic, pancetta or bacon and mushrooms and cook for 2–3 minutes or until the chicken livers are browned.

Stir in the flour, then mix in the wine, stock, tomatoes, tomato purée, bouquet garni and seasoning. Bring to the boil, stirring. Spoon into the slow cooker pot, cover with the lid and cook on low for 8–10 hours.

When almost ready to serve, cook the tagliatelle in a large saucepan of lightly salted boiling water according to the packet instructions until just tender. Drain and stir into the Bolognese sauce. Spoon into shallow bowls and sprinkle with Parmesan shavings and some basil leaves.

FOR BUDGET BOLOGNESE, omit the chicken livers and pancetta or bacon and add 1 diced carrot and 1 diced courgette along with the garlic and mushrooms. Replace the wine with extra stock and continue as above.

LAMB

SLOW-COOKED GREEK LAMB ♥

Serves **4**
Preparation time **20 minutes**
Cooking temperature **low** and **high**
Cooking time **9¼–10½ hours**

low-calorie cooking oil spray
4 **lean lamb leg steaks**, about
    125 g (4 oz) each
1 large **onion**, thinly sliced
2 **garlic cloves**, finely chopped
1 **lemon**, diced
250 g (8 oz) **tomatoes**,
    roughly chopped
2 teaspoons **coriander seeds**,
    roughly crushed
1 **bay leaf**
1 teaspoon **granular sweetener**
1 tablespoon **sun-dried tomato paste**
300 ml (½ pint) **lamb stock**
300 g (10 oz) **baby new potatoes**,
    scrubbed and thickly sliced
300 g (10 oz) **courgettes**, diced
salt and **pepper**
2 tablespoons chopped **parsley**,
    to garnish

Preheat the slow cooker if necessary. Spray a large frying pan with a little low-calorie cooking oil spray and place over a high heat until hot. Add the lamb steaks and cook for 4–5 minutes, turning once, until browned on both sides. Transfer to a plate.

Add the onion to the frying pan and cook for 4–5 minutes until softened, then add the garlic, lemon and tomatoes. Add the coriander, bay leaf, sweetener, tomato paste and stock, season to taste and bring to the boil.

Arrange the potatoes over the base of the slow cooker pot, then place the lamb steaks in a single layer on top. Pour over the hot stock mixture, cover and cook on low for 9–10 hours until the lamb and potatoes are tender.

Add the courgettes, cover again and cook on high for 15–30 minutes until tender. Spoon into shallow bowls, sprinkle with the parsley and serve.

FOR SLOW-COOKED LAMB WITH ROSEMARY, follow the recipe above, adding 3 rosemary sprigs instead of the lemon, crushed coriander seeds and bay leaf. Cook as above, adding the courgettes at the end. Serve garnished with the parsley.

POT ROAST LAMB WITH ROSEMARY

Serves **4**
Preparation time **5 minutes**
Cooking temperature **high**
Cooking time **7–8 hours**

½ **lamb shoulder on the bone**,
    about 1–1.2 kg (2–2 lb 7 oz)
3 **rosemary sprigs**
1 **red onion**, cut into wedges
2 tablespoons **redcurrant jelly**
250 ml (8 fl oz) **red wine**
250 ml (8 fl oz) **lamb stock**
salt and **pepper**

Preheat the slow cooker if necessary. Put the lamb into the slow cooker pot, add the rosemary on top and tuck the onion wedges around the sides of the joint.

Spoon the redcurrant jelly into a small saucepan and add the wine, stock and a little salt and pepper. Bring to the boil, stirring so that the jelly melts, then pour over the lamb. Cover with the lid and cook on high for 7–8 hours or until a knife goes into the centre of the lamb easily and the meat is almost falling off the bone.

Lift the joint out of the slow cooker pot and put it on to a serving plate with the onions. Discard the rosemary sprigs and pour the wine and stock mixture into a jug to serve as gravy. Carve the lamb on to plates and serve with steamed green vegetables and baby potatoes or Crushed New Potatoes with Rosemary Cream (*see* below), if liked.

FOR CRUSHED NEW POTATOES WITH ROSEMARY CREAM TO ACCOMPANY THE LAMB, bring a pan of water to the boil, add 500 g (1 lb) scrubbed baby new potatoes and cook for 15 minutes. Add 200 g (7 oz) Tenderstem broccoli, thickly sliced, for the last 5 minutes. Drain and then roughly break up with a fork. Stir in 1 tablespoon finely chopped rosemary, 4 tablespoons crème fraîche and a little salt and pepper. Spoon a mound of potatoes into the centre of 4 serving plates, then top with the carved pot roast lamb and drizzle the gravy around the edges of the mash.

SPICED LAMB WRAPS

Serves **4**
Preparation time **20 minutes**
Cooking temperature **low**
Cooking time **8–9 hours**

1 tablespoon **olive oil**
500 g (1 lb) **minced lamb**
1 **red onion**, finely chopped
2 teaspoons **ground cumin**
1 teaspoon **ground cinnamon**
½ teaspoon **chilli powder**
1 teaspoon **dried oregano**
1 tablespoon **tomato purée**
75 g (3 oz) **bulgar wheat**
600 ml (1 pint) boiling **beef stock**
salt and **pepper**

TO SERVE
8 large soft flour wraps
400 g (13 oz) **hummus**
1 **cos lettuce**, shredded
small handful of **mint**, finely chopped
½ **cucumber**, cut into strips

Preheat the slow cooker if necessary. Heat the oil in a frying pan, add the mince and onion and fry, stirring and breaking up the mince with a wooden spoon, until it is evenly browned.

Stir in the ground spices, oregano and tomato purée, then season with a little salt and pepper.

Spoon the mixture into the slow cooker pot, add the bulgar wheat, then stir in the boiling stock. Cover with the lid and cook on low for 8–9 hours until the lamb is tender.

When ready to serve, warm the wraps in a dry frying pan or in the microwave according to the packet instructions, then spread each one with a little hummus. Stir the mince mixture. Spoon it over the wraps, then top with the lettuce, mint and cucumber. Fold in the top and bottom of each wrap, then roll it up tightly to enclose the filling. Cut the wraps in half and serve immediately.

FOR CHILLI BEEF WRAPS, omit the lamb and fry 500 g (1 lb) minced beef with the onion as above. Stir in the spices, oregano and tomato purée as above, adding ¼–½ teaspoon crushed dried red chillies to taste. Cook and serve as above.

SLOW-COOKED LAMB SHANKS

Serves **4**
Preparation time **20 minutes**
Cooking temperature **high**
Cooking time **5–7 hours**

2 tablespoons **olive oil**
4 **lamb shanks**, about 375 g
   (12 oz) each
625 g (1¼ lb) **new potatoes**,
   scrubbed and thickly sliced
2 **onions**, sliced
3–4 **garlic cloves**, finely chopped
300 ml (½ pint) **white wine**
150 ml (¼ pint) **lamb stock**
1 tablespoon **clear honey**
1 teaspoon **dried oregano**
75 g (3 oz) **preserved lemons**, cut
   into chunks
75 g (3 oz) **green olives** (optional)
salt and **pepper**
chopped **parsley**, to garnish

Preheat the slow cooker if necessary. Heat the oil in a large frying pan, add the lamb and fry, turning, until browned on all sides. Arrange the potatoes in the base of the slow cooker pot, then put the lamb on top.

Add the onions to the pan and fry until softened, then mix in the garlic. Add the wine, stock, honey, oregano and a little salt and pepper and bring to the boil. Pour over the lamb, then add the lemon and olives, if using.

Cover with the lid and cook on high for 5–7 hours or until the potatoes are tender and the lamb is almost falling off the bone. Spoon into shallow bowls and sprinkle with parsley. Serve with a green salad, if liked.

FOR SLOW-COOKED LAMB SHANKS WITH PRUNES, fry the lamb as above and add to the potatoes. Fry the onion and garlic with 3 diced streaky bacon rashers, then mix in 300 ml (½ pint) red wine, 150 ml (¼ pint) lamb stock, 1 tablespoon tomato purée, 75 g (3 oz) ready-to-eat pitted prunes, a small bunch of mixed herbs and salt and pepper. Cover and cook as above.

WARMING LAMB POT ROAST ♥

Serves **4**
Preparation time **20 minutes**
Cooking temperature **high**
Cooking time **5–6 hours**

low-calorie cooking oil spray
875 g (1¾ lb) **leg of lamb on the bone**
1 **leek**, thickly sliced, white and green
    parts kept separate
2 teaspoons **plain flour**
450 ml (¾ pint) **lamb stock**
1 tablespoon **redcurrant jelly**
15 g (½ oz) **mint leaves**, chopped,
    plus extra to garnish
200 g (7 oz) **celeriac**, cut into 2 cm
    (¾ inch) cubes
200 g (7 oz) **swede**, cut into 2 cm
    (¾ inch) cubes
300 g (10 oz) **baby Chantenay**
    carrots, halved lengthways
salt and **pepper**

Preheat the slow cooker if necessary. Spray a large frying pan with a little low-calorie cooking oil spray and place over a high heat until hot. Season the lamb and seal in the hot pan for 5–10 minutes, turning, until browned on all sides. Transfer to the slow cooker pot.

Add the white leek slices to the frying pan with a little extra low-calorie cooking oil spray, cook for 2–3 minutes, then sprinkle in the flour and stir well. Add the stock, redcurrant jelly and mint, then bring to the boil, stirring.

Arrange the celeriac, swede and carrots around the lamb, then pour over the leeks and stock. Cover and cook on high for 5–6 hours until the lamb starts to fall off the bone and the vegetables are tender, adding the reserved green leek slices for the last 15 minutes of cooking.

Serve the lamb in shallow bowls with the hot vegetables and stock, garnished with extra mint. If you prefer a thicker sauce, drain the stock into a small saucepan and boil rapidly to reduce by half.

FOR LAMB POT ROAST WITH FLAGEOLET BEANS, follow the recipe above, adding a 400 g (13 oz) can flageolet beans, drained, 2 rosemary sprigs and 2 finely chopped garlic cloves instead of the mint, swede and celeriac.

LAMB STEAKS WITH CUMBERLAND SAUCE ♥

Serves **4**
Preparation time **20 minutes**
Cooking temperature **low**
Cooking time **8–10 hours**

1 tablespoon **sunflower oil**
800 g (1 lb 9 oz) **lamb rump steaks**, trimmed of fat
1 **onion**, sliced
2 teaspoons **plain flour**
125 ml (4 fl oz) **red wine**
125 ml (4 fl oz) **lamb stock**
finely shredded rind and juice of 1 **orange**
finely shredded rind and juice of 1 **lemon**
2.5 cm (1 inch) piece of **fresh root ginger**, peeled and finely chopped
1 tablespoon **tomato purée**
1 tablespoon **redcurrant jelly**
1 tablespoon **granular sweetener**
salt and **pepper**
750 g (1½ lb) **celeriac**, diced, to serve

Preheat the slow cooker if necessary. Heat the oil in a large frying pan over a high heat until hot. Add the lamb and cook for 2–3 minutes, turning once, until browned on both sides. Use a slotted spoon to transfer the lamb to the slow cooker pot.

Add the onion to the pan and cook, stirring, over a medium heat for 4–5 minutes, until softened. Stir in the flour, then add the wine, stock, half the orange and lemon rind, the orange and lemon juice, ginger, tomato purée, redcurrant jelly and sweetener. Season to taste with salt and pepper and bring to the boil, stirring. Pour the mixture over the lamb, cover and cook on low for 8–10 hours.

When almost ready to serve, cook the celeriac in a saucepan of lightly salted boiling water for 10–15 minutes until tender. Drain and mash with a little of the cooking water until smooth, then season to taste. Serve with the lamb in bowls, garnished with the remaining orange and lemon rind.

FOR LAMB STEAKS WITH CRANBERRY SAUCE, follow the recipe above, using 25 g (1 oz) dried cranberries and 1 tablespoon cranberry sauce instead of the ginger and redcurrant jelly. Cook and serve as above.

LAMB TAGINE WITH FIGS & ALMONDS

Serves **4**
Preparation time **15 minutes**
Cooking temperature **low**
Cooking time **8–10 hours**

1 tablespoon **olive oil**
750 g (1½ lb) **lamb fillet**, diced, or
   ready-diced lamb
1 **onion**, sliced
2 **garlic cloves**, finely chopped
2.5 cm (1 inch) piece of **fresh**
   root ginger, peeled and
   finely chopped
2 tablespoons **plain flour**
600 ml (1 pint) **lamb stock**
1 teaspoon **ground cinnamon**
2 large pinches of **saffron threads**
75 g (3 oz) **dried figs**, stalks
   trimmed and diced
40 g (1½ oz) toasted
   flaked almonds
salt and **pepper**

Preheat the slow cooker if necessary. Heat the oil in a frying pan, add the lamb a few pieces at a time until all the meat is in the pan, then fry over a high heat, stirring until browned. Remove from the pan with a slotted spoon and transfer to the slow cooker pot.

Add the onion and fry, stirring, for 5 minutes or until softened and just beginning to turn golden. Stir in the garlic and ginger, then mix in the flour. Gradually stir in the stock. Add the spices, figs and a little salt and pepper and bring to the boil, stirring.

Spoon into the slow cooker pot, cover and cook on low for 8–10 hours or until the lamb is tender. Stir, then sprinkle with the toasted flaked almonds. Serve with Lemon & Chickpea Couscous (*see* below), if liked.

FOR LEMON & CHICKPEA COUSCOUS TO ACCOMPANY THE TAGINE, put 200 g (7 oz) couscous into a bowl, add the grated rind and juice of 1 lemon, 2 tablespoons olive oil, a 410 g (13½ oz) can chickpeas, drained, and some salt and pepper. Pour over 150 ml (¼ pint) boiling water, then cover the bowl with a plate and leave to stand for 5 minutes. Remove the plate, add 4 tablespoons chopped parsley or coriander and fluff up with a fork.

EASY LAMB & BARLEY RISOTTO

Serves **4**
Preparation time **10 minutes**
Cooking temperature **low**
Cooking time **7–8 hours**

20 g (¾ oz) **mixed dried mushrooms**
1 litre (1¾ pint) boiling
   vegetable stock
4 tablespoons **cream sherry** or **fresh
   orange juice**
1 **onion**, finely chopped
1 teaspoon **ground cumin**
2 **garlic cloves**, finely chopped
40 g (1½ oz) **sultanas**
125 g (4 oz) **pearl barley**
4 **lamb chump chops**, about 150 g
   (5 oz) each
250 g (8 oz) **ready-prepared
   pumpkin** or **butternut squash**, cut
   into 2 cm (¾ inch) dice
salt and **pepper**
chopped **mint** and **parsley**, to garnish

Preheat the slow cooker if necessary. Add the dried mushrooms to the slow cooker pot and pour in the boiling stock, then stir in the sherry or orange juice, onion, cumin, garlic and sultanas. Spoon in the barley and season with salt and pepper.

Arrange the chops on top in a single layer, season, then tuck the pumpkin or squash into the gaps between the chops. Press the chops and squash down lightly into the stock, then cover with the lid and cook on low for 7–8 hours until the lamb and vegetables are tender.

Lift the chops out of the slow cooker, stir the barley, then spoon on to plates, top with the chops, broken into pieces, and sprinkle with the herbs. Serve with spoonfuls of harissa, if liked.

FOR PUMPKIN & BARLEY RISOTTO, omit the lamb and use 400 g (13 oz) ready-prepared, diced pumpkin. Cook as above, then add 125 g (4 oz) spinach, rinsed and drained, to the risotto for the last 15 minutes of cooking. Serve topped with spoonfuls of Greek yogurt, chopped mint and parsley and buttery fried flaked almonds.

POT ROAST LAMB WITH ZA'ATAR RUB

Serves **4**
Preparation time **20 minutes**
Cooking temperature **high**
Cooking time **5–6 hours**

1 tablespoon **extra virgin olive oil**
2 **onions**, thinly sliced
2 **garlic cloves**, finely chopped
250 ml (8 fl oz) **lamb stock**
1 tablespoon **tomato purée**
2 teaspoons **za'atar spice mix**
200 ml (7 fl oz) **dry white wine** or
    extra lamb stock
1 tablespoon **cornflour**
400 g (13 oz) **new potatoes**,
    scrubbed and thickly sliced
½ **boneless lamb shoulder**, about
    750 g (1½ lb)
salt and **pepper**
chopped **parsley** and **mint**, to garnish

TO SERVE
2 **courgettes**, thinly sliced
1 tablespoon **olive oil**
½ teaspoon **za'atar spice mix**
400 g (13 oz) **hummus**

Preheat the slow cooker if necessary. Heat the oil in a large frying pan, add the onions and fry for 5 minutes until softened and just beginning to brown. Stir in the garlic, stock, tomato purée and half the za'atar. Pour in the wine or extra stock, reserving about 2 tablespoons.

Stir the cornflour into the reserved wine or stock until smooth, then add to the frying pan. Bring to the boil, stirring.

Add the potatoes to the base of the slow cooker pot, then pour in the hot stock mixture. Remove the strings from the lamb, open it out flat and rub with the reserved za'atar, then season with salt and pepper. Add to the slow cooker pot and press the meat beneath the liquid. Cover with the lid and cook on high for 5–6 hours or until the lamb is almost falling apart.

When almost ready to serve, toss the sliced courgettes with the oil, za'atar and a little salt and pepper. Cook in a preheated ridged griddle pan until lightly browned and tender. Divide the hummus between 4 serving plates, spread into an even layer and make a thin ridge around the sides to contain the lamb sauce. Break the lamb into pieces, then spoon it on to the hummus with the sauce. Add the courgettes and sprinkle with chopped parsley and mint.

FOR POT ROAST LAMB WITH ROSEMARY, add 200 ml (7 fl oz) red wine in place of the white wine, if using, in the sauce, plus 2 tablespoons redcurrant jelly and 3 rosemary sprigs. Mix the cornflour with the reserved wine or stock as above. Add the potatoes and plain lamb joint to the slow cooker, then pour over the hot stock mixture. Cook as above and serve with mixed steamed vegetables.

LAMB RAGÙ

LAMB SHANKS WITH JUNIPER

Serves **4**
Preparation time **15 minutes**
Cooking temperature **low**
Cooking time **8–9 hours**

650 g (1 lb 5 oz) jar **tomato and pepper ragù sauce**
125 ml (4 fl oz) **red wine** or **lamb stock**
300 g (10 oz) **baby new potatoes**, scrubbed and thickly sliced
600 g (1 lb 3½ oz) **lamb**, diced
1 **red pepper**, cored, deseeded and cut into chunks
1 **yellow pepper**, cored, deseeded and cut into chunks
basil leaves, to garnish

Preheat the slow cooker if necessary. Pour the ragù sauce and wine or stock into a saucepan and bring to the boil. Alternatively, heat the mixture in a microwave.

Place the potato slices on the base of the slow cooker pot, arrange the lamb on top, then add the red and yellow peppers. Pour over the hot sauce, then cover with the lid and cook on low for 8–9 hours until the potatoes and lamb are tender.

Stir the ragù. Serve garnished with basil leaves and accompanied by warm garlic bread, if liked.

FOR BEEF & MUSHROOM RAGÙ, make up the recipe as above adding 600 g (1 lb 3½ oz) diced beef instead of the lamb and 150 g (5 oz) sliced cup mushrooms in place of the yellow pepper.

Serves **4**
Preparation time **15 minutes**
Cooking temperature **high**
Cooking time **5–7 hours**

25 g (1 oz) **butter**
4 **lamb shanks**, about 1.5 kg (3 lb) in total
2 small **red onions**, cut into wedges
2 tablespoons **plain flour**
200 ml (7 fl oz) **red wine**
450 ml (¾ pint) **lamb stock**
2 tablespoons **cranberry sauce** (optional)
1 tablespoon **tomato purée**
2 **bay leaves**
1 teaspoon **juniper berries**, roughly crushed
1 small **cinnamon stick**, halved
pared rind of 1 small **orange**
salt and **pepper**

Preheat the slow cooker if necessary. Heat the butter in a frying pan, add the lamb shanks and fry over a medium heat, turning, until browned all over. Drain and put into the slow cooker pot.

Add the onions to the pan and fry for 4–5 minutes or until just beginning to turn golden. Stir in the flour. Gradually mix in the wine and stock, then add the cranberry sauce, if using, and the remaining ingredients. Bring to the boil, stirring.

Transfer to the slow cooker pot, cover with the lid and cook on high for 5–7 hours or until the lamb is beginning to fall off the bone. If you prefer a thick sauce, pour it into a saucepan and boil rapidly for 5 minutes or until reduced by one-third.

FOR LAMB SHANKS WITH LEMON, fry the lamb shanks as above, then fry 2 sliced white onions. Mix with the flour and add 200 ml (7 fl oz) dry white wine, the lamb stock, 4 teaspoons roughly crushed coriander seeds, the bay leaves, the pared rind of 1 lemon and 2 teaspoons clear honey. Season and bring to the boil, pour over the lamb and cook as above.

MINTED LAMB WITH COUSCOUS

Serves **4**
Preparation time **25 minutes**
Cooking temperature **high**
Cooking time **7–8 hours**

1 tablespoon **olive oil**
½ **shoulder of lamb**, about
    900 g–1 kg (1 lb 14 oz–2 lb)
1 **onion**, sliced
2 **garlic cloves**, finely chopped
2 tablespoons **plain flour**
3 tablespoons **mint jelly**
150 ml (¼ pint) **red wine**
300 ml (½ pint) **lamb stock**
salt and **pepper**

HERBY COUSCOUS
200 g (7 oz) **couscous**
150 g (5 oz) **cooked beetroot**,
    peeled and diced
400 ml (14 fl oz) boiling **water**
grated rind and juice of 1 **lemon**
2 tablespoons **olive oil**
small bunch of **parsley**,
    finely chopped
small bunch of **mint**, finely chopped

Preheat the slow cooker if necessary. Heat the oil in a frying pan, add the lamb and fry on both sides until browned. Lift out with 2 slotted spoons and transfer to the slow cooker pot. Fry the onion, stirring, for 5 minutes or until softened and just turning golden.

Stir in the garlic, then the flour. Add the mint jelly and wine and mix until smooth. Pour in the stock, season and bring to the boil, stirring. Pour the sauce over the lamb, cover with the lid and cook on high for 7–8 hours or until the lamb is almost falling off the bone.

When almost ready to serve, put the couscous and beetroot into a bowl, pour over the boiling water, then add the lemon rind and juice, oil and some seasoning. Cover with a plate and leave to soak for 5 minutes.

Add the herbs to the couscous and fluff up with a fork, then spoon on to plates. Lift the lamb on to a serving plate and carve into rough pieces, discarding the bone. Divide between the plates and serve the sauce separately in a jug to pour over as needed.

FOR CORIANDER & HONEY-BRAISED LAMB, fry the onion and garlic as above. Add 1 tablespoon roughly crushed coriander seeds with the flour. Stir in 1 tablespoon set honey instead of the mint jelly and 150 ml (¼ pint) dry white wine instead of red. Add the lamb stock, 1 bay leaf and seasoning. Bring to the boil, then add to the browned lamb in the slow cooker pot. Cover and cook as above. Serve with rice and green beans.

PORK

PRUNE STUFFED PORK TENDERLOIN

Serves **4**
Preparation time **40 minutes**
Cooking temperature **high**
Cooking time **3½–4 hours**

2 **pork tenderloins**, just under
　　400 g (13 oz) each
1 slice of **bread**, crusts removed
1 small **onion**, quartered
2 **garlic cloves**, halved
3.5 cm (1½ inch) piece of **fresh root
　　ginger**, peeled and sliced
¼ teaspoon **ground allspice**
10 **ready-to-eat pitted prunes**
4 **smoked streaky bacon rashers**
1 tablespoon **olive oil**
12 **shallots**, halved if large
2 tablespoons **cornflour**
200 ml (7 fl oz) **red wine**
300 ml (½ pint) **chicken stock**
1 tablespoon **tomato purée**
salt and **pepper**

Preheat the slow cooker if necessary. Trim the thinnest end off each pork tenderloin so that each is 23 cm (9 inches) long, reserving the trimmings. Make a slit along the length of each and open out flat.

Put the pork trimmings into a food processor with the bread, onion, garlic, ginger, allspice and salt and pepper and mix until finely chopped. Spoon half the mixture along the length of 1 piece of pork, press the prunes on top, then cover with the rest of the stuffing and the remaining tenderloin. Season, then wrap the bacon around the pork and tie in place with string.

Heat the oil in a large frying pan, add the pork and shallots and fry, turning the pork, until golden all over. Transfer to the slow cooker pot. Make a smooth paste with the cornflour and a little cold water, then add to the pan with the remaining ingredients. Bring to the boil, stirring until thickened, then pour over the pork.

Cover with the lid and cook on high for 3½–4 hours or until the pork is cooked through and tender. Transfer the pork to a serving plate. Serve cut into thick slices, with the shallots and sauce, accompanied with steamed asparagus and creamy potato dauphinoise, if liked.

FOR APRICOT & PISTACHIO STUFFED PORK TENDERLOIN, slit the tenderloins as above. Replace the prunes with 25 g (1 oz) roughly chopped pistachio nuts, the grated rind of ½ orange and 75 g (3 oz) chopped ready-to-eat dried apricots and add to the pork trimmings mixture, then continue as above. To make the sauce, replace the red wine with 200 ml (7 fl oz) dry cider.

ORIENTAL PORK WITH PAK CHOI ♥

Serves **4**
Preparation time **20 minutes**
Cooking temperature **low** and **high**
Cooking time **6¼–7¼ hours**

4 **pork medallions**, 350 g (11½ oz)
   in total
1 **red onion**, thinly sliced
2.5 cm (1 inch) piece of **fresh root**
   ginger, peeled and thinly sliced
1 **garlic clove**, thinly sliced
small handful of **coriander leaves**
¼ teaspoon **crushed dried**
   red chillies
2 small **star anise**
1 teaspoon **Thai fish sauce**
2 teaspoons **tomato purée**
4 teaspoons **dark soy sauce**
350 ml (12 fl oz) hot **chicken stock**
200 g (7 oz) **pak choi**,
   thickly sliced
100 g (3½ oz) **asparagus tips**
250 g (8 oz) **dried egg noodles**

Preheat the slow cooker if necessary. Place the pork medallions in the slow cooker pot in a single layer and scatter with the onion, ginger and garlic. Sprinkle half the coriander leaves on top.

Stir the chillies, star anise, fish sauce, tomato purée and soy sauce into the hot chicken stock, then pour over the pork. Cover and cook on low for 6–7 hours until the pork is tender.

Add the pak choi and asparagus to the pot, cover and cook on high for 15 minutes until the vegetables are just tender and still bright green.

Meanwhile, cook the egg noodles according to the packet instructions.

Drain and divide between 4 bowls, top with the pork and vegetables, then spoon over the broth and serve garnished with the remaining coriander.

FOR ORIENTAL PORK WITH MIXED VEGETABLES, follow the recipe above, adding 300 g (10 oz) ready-prepared mixed stir fry vegetables instead of the pak choi and asparagus.

SHAKSHUKA ♥

Serves **4**
Preparation time **20 minutes**
Cooking temperature **high**
Cooking time **3¼–4¼ hours**

low-calorie cooking oil spray
2 **red onions**, roughly chopped
75 g (3 oz) **chorizo**, skinned
   and diced
625 g (1¼ lb) **tomatoes**, chopped
½ teaspoon crushed **dried
   red chillies**
1 tablespoon **tomato purée**
2 teaspoons **granular sweetener**
2 teaspoons **paprika**
1 teaspoon **dried oregano**
4 **eggs**
salt and **pepper**

TO SERVE
chopped **parsley**
4 small slices of **wholemeal
   bread**, toasted

Preheat the slow cooker if necessary. Spray a large frying pan with a little low-calorie cooking oil spray and place over a medium heat until hot. Add the onions and chorizo and cook for 5 minutes, stirring, until the onions have softened.

Add the chopped tomatoes, chillies, tomato purée, sweetener, paprika and oregano and season to taste. Transfer the mixture to the slow cooker pot, cover and cook on high for 3–4 hours until the tomatoes have softened and the sauce is thick.

Make 4 indents in the tomato mixture with the back of a dessert spoon, then break an egg into each one. Cover again and cook, still on high, for 15 minutes or until the eggs are set to your liking. Sprinkle with a little chopped parsley, then spoon on to plates and serve with toast.

FOR MIXED VEGETABLE SHAKSHUKA, follow the recipe above, omitting the chorizo and using just 1 chopped red onion. Add 1 cored, deseeded and diced red pepper, 1 large diced courgette and 2 finely chopped garlic cloves to the frying pan with the onion and continue as above.

PULLED PORK ♥

Serves **4**
Preparation time **15 minutes**
Cooking temperature **high**
Cooking time **5–6 hours**

700 g (1 lb 6 oz) **boneless pork
  shoulder joint**, trimmed of fat
1 tablespoon **treacle**
½ teaspoon **ground allspice**
½ teaspoon **ground ginger**
½ teaspoon **ground cumin**
½ teaspoon **crushed dried
  red chillies**
¼ teaspoon **salt**
leaves from 2–3 **thyme sprigs**
1 **onion**, sliced
200 ml (7 fl oz) hot **chicken stock**
pepper

TO SERVE
4 **hamburger buns**, split
4 **lettuce leaves**, shredded
3 **tomatoes**, thinly sliced
1 **dill cucumber**, drained and sliced

Preheat the slow cooker if necessary. Remove the strings, unroll the pork joint and make a cut through the middle to reduce the thickness by half. Place in the slow cooker pot and spread with the treacle.

Mix the ground spices, chillies, salt and thyme leaves together and season with pepper. Rub over the pork joint, then tuck the onion slices around it. Pour the hot stock over the onions, then cover with the lid and cook on high for 5–6 hours or until the pork is very tender.

Place the pork on a chopping board and pull into shreds using 2 forks. Top the bottom halves of the buns with the lettuce, tomato and dill cucumber, then pile the hot pork on top. Add a few of the onion slices to each bun and drizzle with the cooking juices. Replace the tops of the buns and serve.

FOR HERBY PULLED PORK, follow the recipe above to prepare the pork and spread it with the treacle. Mix the crushed dried red chillies, salt and thyme leaves with 2 finely chopped sage sprigs and rub over the treacle-spread pork. Add the onion and stock and continue as above.

CIDERED PORK WITH SAGE DUMPLINGS

Serves **4**
Preparation time **25 minutes**
Cooking temperature **low**
Cooking time **9–11 hours**

1 tablespoon **sunflower oil**
750 g (1½ lb) **pork shoulder steaks**, trimmed of fat and cubed
1 **leek**, thinly sliced, the white and green parts kept separate
2 tablespoons **plain flour**
300 ml (½ pint) **dry cider**
300 ml (½ pint) **chicken stock**
200 g (7 oz) **carrot**, diced
1 **dessert apple**, cored and diced
2–3 **sage sprigs**
salt and **pepper**

DUMPLINGS
150 g (5 oz) **self-raising flour**, plus extra for dusting
75 g (3 oz) **shredded vegetable suet**
1 tablespoon chopped **sage**
2 tablespoons chopped **parsley**
5–7 tablespoons **water**

Preheat the slow cooker if necessary. Heat the oil in a frying pan, add the pork a few pieces at a time until all the meat is in the pan, then fry over a high heat until lightly browned. Lift out of the pan with a slotted spoon and transfer to the slow cooker pot.

Add the white leek slices to the pan and fry for 2–3 minutes or until softened. Stir in the flour, then gradually mix in the cider and stock. Add the carrot, apple, sage and some salt and pepper. Bring to the boil, stirring. Pour the mixture into the slow cooker pot, cover with the lid and cook on low for 8–10 hours or until the pork is tender.

Make the dumplings. Put the flour, suet, herbs and a little salt and pepper into a bowl and mix together, then gradually stir in enough of the measurement water to make a soft but not sticky dough. Cut into 12 pieces and roll into balls with floured hands. Stir the green leek slices into the pork casserole and arrange the dumplings on the top. Cover and cook, still on low, for 1 hour until they are well risen. Spoon into shallow bowls to serve.

FOR BEERY PORK WITH ROSEMARY DUMPLINGS, make up the casserole as above, adding 300 ml (½ pint) blonde beer or lager instead of the cider and 300 g (10 oz) mixed diced parsnip, carrot and swede instead of the carrot and apple. Flavour with 2 rosemary sprigs instead of the sage and add 1 tablespoon chopped rosemary instead of sage to the dumplings.

BAKED HAM IN COLA

Serves **4**
Preparation time **20 minutes, plus overnight soaking**
Cooking temperature **high**
Cooking time **6–7 hours**

1.25 kg (2½ lb) **boneless smoked gammon joint**, soaked overnight in cold water
5 **cloves**
1 **onion**, cut into 8 wedges
2 **carrots**, thickly sliced
410 g (13½ oz) can **black beans** or **red kidney beans**, drained
2 **bay leaves**
900 ml (1½ pints) **cola**
1 tablespoon **dark muscovado sugar**
1 tablespoon **tomato purée**
2 teaspoons **English mustard**

Preheat the slow cooker if necessary. Drain the gammon joint and put it into the slow cooker pot. Press the cloves into 5 of the onion wedges and add with the remaining onion wedges and carrot slices to the gammon. Tip in the drained beans and add the bay leaves.

Pour the cola into a saucepan, add the sugar, tomato purée and mustard and bring to the boil, stirring. Pour over the gammon, cover with the lid and cook on high for 6–7 hours or until the gammon is tender.

Strain the cooking liquid into a saucepan and boil rapidly for 10 minutes to reduce by half. Keep the gammon and vegetables hot in the turned-off slow cooker with the lid on.

Slice the gammon thinly and arrange on plates with the vegetables, beans and a drizzle of sauce. Serve with baked potatoes and broccoli, if liked.

FOR BAKED HAM WITH PARSLEY SAUCE, soak the gammon as above and cook in the slow cooker pot with the cloves, onion, carrots, bay leaves and 900 ml (1½ pints) boiling water instead of the cola. Omit the beans and remaining ingredients. Melt 25 g (1 oz) butter in a saucepan for the parsley sauce. Stir in 25 g (1 oz) plain flour, cook for 1 minute, then mix in 300 ml (½ pint) milk. Bring to the boil, stirring, until thickened and smooth. Stir in 1 teaspoon English mustard, 3 tablespoons chopped parsley and salt and pepper. Serve with the sliced gammon and drained onion and carrots.

SAUSAGES WITH ONION GRAVY

Serves **4**
Preparation time **15 minutes**
Cooking temperature **low**
Cooking time **6–8 hours**

1 tablespoon **sunflower oil**
8 **'gourmet' flavoured sausages**, such
    as Sicilian or Toulouse
2 **red onions**, halved and thinly sliced
2 teaspoons **light muscovado sugar**
2 tablespoons **plain flour**
450 ml (¾ pint) **beef stock**
1 tablespoon **sun-dried tomato paste**
    or **tomato purée**
1 **bay leaf**
salt and **pepper**

TO SERVE
4 large **ready-made**
    Yorkshire puddings
steamed **carrots**
steamed **broccoli**

Preheat the slow cooker if necessary. Heat the oil in a frying pan, add the sausages and fry over a high heat for 5 minutes, turning, until browned on all sides but not cooked through. Drain and transfer to the slow cooker pot.

Add the onions to the frying pan and fry over a medium heat for 5 minutes or until softened. Add the sugar and fry, stirring, for 5 more minutes or until the onion slices are caramelized around the edges.

Stir in the flour, then gradually mix in the stock. Add the tomato purée, the bay leaf and some salt and pepper and bring to the boil, stirring. Pour over the sausages. Cover with the lid and cook on low for 6–8 hours or until the sausages are tender.

Serve spooned into the Yorkshire puddings, reheated according to the pack instructions, accompanied by steamed carrots and broccoli.

FOR SAUSAGES WITH BEERY ONION GRAVY, fry 8 large traditional herb sausages instead of the 'gourmet' ones until browned. Drain, then fry 2 sliced white onions until softened, and omit the sugar. Stir in the plain flour, then mix in 150 ml (¼ pint) stout or brown ale and reduce the beef stock to 300 ml (½ pint). Replace the tomato purée with 1 tablespoon wholegrain mustard and 2 tablespoons Worcestershire sauce. Season and bring to the boil. Cook in the slow cooker for 6–8 hours.

MAPLE-GLAZED RIBS

Serves **4**
Preparation time **25 minutes**
Cooking temperature **high**
Cooking time **5–7 hours**

1.25 kg (2½ lb) **pork ribs**, rinsed
  and drained
1 **onion**, quartered
1 **carrot**, thickly sliced
2 **bay leaves**
2 tablespoons **malt vinegar**
1 teaspoon **black peppercorns**
½ teaspoon **salt**
1 litre (1¾ pints) boiling **water**

GLAZE
2 teaspoons **English mustard**
1 teaspoon **ground allspice**
2 tablespoons **tomato purée**
2 tablespoons **brown sugar**
125 ml (4 fl oz) **maple syrup**

COLESLAW
2 **carrots**, grated
¼ **red cabbage**, shredded
3 **spring onions**, sliced
100 g (3½ oz) **sweetcorn**, thawed
  if frozen
2 tablespoons **mayonnaise**
2 tablespoons **natural yogurt**

Preheat the slow cooker if necessary. Put the pork ribs, onion, carrot, bay leaves, vinegar, peppercorns, salt and measurement boiling water into the slow cooker pot, cover with the lid and cook on high for 5–7 hours or until the ribs are tender.

Lift the ribs out of the slow cooker using a slotted spoon and transfer to a foil-lined grill pan. Mix together the ingredients for the glaze with 150 ml (¼ pint) hot stock from the slow cooker pot. Spoon over the ribs, then cook under a preheated hot grill for 10–15 minutes, turning once or twice, until browned and sticky.

Meanwhile, mix the ingredients for the coleslaw together and spoon into 4 small bowls. Place these on serving plates, then pile the ribs on to the plates to serve.

FOR CHINESE RIBS, cook the pork ribs in the slow cooker as above. Drain and transfer to a foil-lined grill pan, then glaze with a mixture of 2 tablespoons each tomato purée and soy sauce, 4 tablespoons hoisin sauce, 2 tablespoons light muscovado sugar, the juice of 1 orange and 150 ml (¼ pint) stock from the slow cooker pot. Grill for 10–15 minutes as above.

HONEY-GLAZED GAMMON

Serves **4**
Preparation time **20 minutes, plus overnight soaking**
Cooking temperature **high**
Cooking time **5–7 hours**

1 kg (2 lb) **boneless smoked gammon joint**, soaked overnight in cold water
1 **onion**, cut into wedges
300 g (10 oz) **carrots**, halved lengthways and cut into 2.5 cm (1 inch) chunks
500 g (1 lb) **baking potatoes**, scrubbed and quartered
2 **bay leaves**
6 **cloves**
½ teaspoon **black peppercorns**
900 ml (1½ pints) boiling water

GLAZE
2 tablespoons **clear honey**
2 teaspoons **English mustard**

Preheat the slow cooker if necessary. Put the gammon joint into the slow cooker pot. Tuck the vegetables around the sides, then add the bay leaves, cloves and peppercorns. Pour over the measurement boiling water to just cover the gammon.

Cover with the lid and cook on high for 5–7 hours or until the gammon and vegetables are cooked through and tender. Lift the gammon out of the slow cooker pot and transfer to the base of a grill pan. Cut away the rind and discard.

Mix the honey and mustard together for the glaze, spoon over the top and sides of the joint, then add 3 ladlefuls of stock from the slow cooker pot to the base of the grill pan. Cook under a preheated medium grill until the gammon is golden brown. Carve into slices and serve with the sauce from the grill pan and drained vegetables from the slow cooker pot. Accompany with steamed green beans, if liked.

FOR GLAZED GAMMON WITH PEASE PUDDING, soak 200 g (7 oz) dried yellow split peas in cold water overnight while soaking the gammon in a separate bowl of cold water. Next day, drain the peas, add to a saucepan with 1.2 litres (2 pints) water, bring to the boil and boil rapidly for 10 minutes. Add the gammon joint, onion, carrots, bay leaves, cloves and peppercorns to the slow cooker pot, omitting the potatoes. Pour in the hot peas and their water, then continue as above. When the glazed gammon is grilled, drain off most of the stock from the peas and carrots, then mash and stir in 25 g (1 oz) butter and a little salt, if needed. Serve the pease pudding with the sliced gammon.

BACON & LEEK SUET PUDDING

Serves **4**
Preparation time **30 minutes**
Cooking temperature **high**
Cooking time **4–5 hours**

25 g (1 oz) **butter**
2 **smoked gammon steaks**, about
    450 g (14½ oz) in total, trimmed of
    fat and rind and diced
250 g (8 oz) **leeks**, sliced
300 g (10 oz) **self-raising flour**, plus
    extra for dusting
150 g (5 oz) **shredded**
    vegetable suet
3 teaspoons **mustard powder**
200–250 ml (7–8 fl oz) **water**
salt and **pepper**

PARSLEY SAUCE
25 g (1 oz) **butter**
25 g (1 oz) **plain flour**
300 ml (½ pint) **milk**
20 g (¾ oz) **parsley**, finely chopped

Preheat the slow cooker if necessary. Heat the butter in a frying pan, add the gammon and leeks and fry, stirring, for 4–5 minutes or until the leeks have just softened. Season with pepper only. Leave to cool slightly.

Put the flour, ½ teaspoon salt, a large pinch of pepper, the suet and mustard powder in a bowl and mix well. Gradually stir in enough of the measurement water to make a soft but not sticky dough. Knead lightly, then roll out on a large piece of floured nonstick baking paper to a rectangle 23 x 30 cm (9 x 12 inches). Turn the paper so that the shorter edges are facing you.

Spoon the gammon mixture over the pastry, leaving 2 cm (¾ inch) around the edges. Roll up, starting at the shorter edge, using the paper to help. Wrap in the paper, then in a sheet of foil. Twist the ends together tightly, leaving some space for the pudding to rise.

Transfer the pudding to the slow cooker pot and raise off the base slightly by standing it on 2 ramekin dishes. Pour boiling water into the pot to come a little up the sides of the pudding, being careful that the water cannot seep through any joins. Cover with the lid and cook on high for 4–5 hours or until the pudding is well risen.

When almost ready to serve, melt the butter for the sauce in a saucepan. Stir in the flour, then gradually mix in the milk and bring to the boil, stirring until smooth. Cook for 1–2 minutes, then stir in the parsley and season. Lift the pudding out of the slow cooker pot using a tea towel, unwrap and cut into slices. Arrange on serving plates and spoon over a little sauce. Serve with sugar snap peas, if liked.

BALSAMIC BRAISED PORK CHOPS

Serves **4**
Preparation time **15 minutes**
Cooking temperature **high** and **low**
Cooking time **7–8 hours**

4 **spare rib pork chops**, about 750 g
   (1½ lb) in total
3 tablespoons **apple balsamic** or
   plain balsamic vinegar
2 tablespoons **light muscovado sugar**
2 **onions**, thinly sliced
2 **dessert apples**, peeled, cored
   and quartered
2 tablespoons **cornflour**
3 teaspoons **English mustard**
200 ml (7 fl oz) boiling **chicken stock**
chopped **chives**, to garnish (optional)

Preheat the slow cooker if necessary. Put the pork chops into the base of the slow cooker pot and spoon over the vinegar and sugar. Sprinkle the onions on top, then add the apples.

Put the cornflour and mustard in a small bowl and mix with a little cold water to make a smooth paste, then gradually stir in the boiling stock until smooth. Pour over the pork. Cover and cook on high for 30 minutes. Reduce the heat and cook on low for 6½–7½ hours, or set to auto for 7–8 hours, until the pork is cooked through and tender.

Transfer the pork to serving plates, stir the sauce and spoon over the chops. Sprinkle with chopped chives and serve with mashed potato and Brussels sprouts, if liked.

FOR CIDER-BRAISED PORK, prepare the pork chops as above, omitting the vinegar. Bring 200 ml (7 fl oz) dry cider to the boil in a saucepan. Make up the cornflour paste as above, then gradually stir in the boiling cider instead of the stock. Pour over the chops and continue as above.

PORK WITH BLACK BEAN SAUCE

Serves **4**

Preparation time **20 minutes, plus overnight marinating**

Cooking temperature **high** and **low**

Cooking time **8–10 hours**

4 **spare rib pork steaks**, about 175 g (6 oz) each

2 tablespoons **cornflour**

4 tablespoons **soy sauce**

3.5 cm (1½ inch) piece of **fresh root ginger**, peeled and finely chopped

2 **garlic cloves**, finely chopped

100 g (3½ oz) **black bean sauce**

300 ml (½ pint) boiling **chicken stock**

pepper

TO SERVE

1 tablespoon **sunflower oil**

300 g (10 oz) **ready-prepared mixed stir-fry vegetables**

cooked **rice**

Put the pork steaks into a shallow non-metallic dish. Put the cornflour and soy sauce in a small bowl and mix to a smooth paste, then add the ginger, garlic, black bean sauce and a little pepper. Pour over the pork, cover with clingfilm and marinate in the refrigerator overnight.

Preheat the slow cooker if necessary. Put the pork and marinade into the slow cooker pot. Pour over the boiling stock, cover with the lid and cook on high for 30 minutes. Reduce the heat and cook on low for 7½–9½ hours, or set to auto for 8–10 hours, until the pork is cooked through and tender.

When almost ready to serve, heat the oil in a large frying pan, add the mixed vegetables and stir-fry for 2–3 minutes or until just tender. Spoon the pork on to plates lined with rice and top with the vegetables.

FOR SWEET & SOUR PORK, omit the black bean sauce from the marinade and add the marinated pork to the slow cooker pot with a bunch of sliced spring onions, 1 cored, deseeded and sliced red pepper and 100 g (3½ oz) sliced mushrooms. Replace the chicken stock with a 425 g (14 oz) jar sweet and sour sauce. Bring the sauce to the boil in a saucepan or the microwave, then pour into the slow cooker pot. Continue as above.

ASIAN GLAZED RIBS

Serves **4**

Preparation time **25 minutes, plus overnight marinating**

Cooking temperature **high** and **low**

Cooking time **8–10 hours**

1 **onion**, quartered

5 cm (2 inch) piece of **fresh root ginger**, peeled and sliced

2 tablespoons **rice** or **white wine vinegar**

4 **star anise**

1 **cinnamon stick**, halved

1.25 kg (2½ lb) **pork ribs**

1 litre (1¾ pints) boiling **water**

2 **English breakfast teabags**

GLAZE

4 tablespoons **clear honey**

4 tablespoons **soy sauce**

Put the onion, ginger, vinegar, star anise and cinnamon into a bowl and cover with clingfilm. Chill in the refrigerator overnight.

Preheat the slow cooker if necessary. Pour the measurement boiling water over the teabags and leave to brew for 2–3 minutes, then squeeze out the bags and discard. Rinse the ribs, drain and put into the slow cooker pot with the spiced onion mixture and the hot tea.

Cover with the lid and cook on high for 30 minutes. Reduce the heat and cook on low for 7½–9½ hours, or set to auto for 8–10 hours, until the meat is almost falling off the bones.

Lift the ribs out of the slow cooker pot and transfer to a foil-lined grill pan. Put 6 tablespoons of stock from the pot into a bowl and mix in the honey and soy sauce. Spoon over the ribs, then cook under a preheated hot grill for 10–15 minutes, turning several times and spooning soy mixture over, until browned and glazed. Serve with Pickled Cucumber (*see* below) and rice, if liked.

FOR PICKLED CUCUMBER TO ACCOMPANY THE RIBS, mix together ¼–½ mild red chilli, deseeded and finely chopped, 3 tablespoons chopped coriander, 1 tablespoon rice or white wine vinegar, 1 teaspoon fish sauce and ½ teaspoon caster sugar in a salad bowl. Very thinly slice ½ cucumber, add to the dressing and toss together gently. This dish can be made, covered with clingfilm and kept in the refrigerator overnight.

STICKY
JERK RIBS ♥

PORK, ORANGE
& STAR ANISE

Serves **4**
Preparation time **20 minutes**
Cooking temperature **high**
Cooking time **5–6 hours**

1.25 kg (2½ lb) **lean pork ribs**
1 **onion**, cut into wedges
1 large **carrot**, sliced
3 **bay leaves**
2 tablespoons **malt vinegar**
low-calorie cooking oil spray
salt and **pepper**

JERK GLAZE
8 tablespoons **passata**
3 tablespoons **soy sauce**
½ teaspoon **ground cinnamon**
½ teaspoon **ground allspice**
¼ teaspoon **chilli powder**
1 tablespoon **dark muscovado sugar**
grated rind and juice of ½ **orange**
4 **spring onions**, finely chopped

Preheat the slow cooker if necessary. Place the pork ribs, onion and carrot in the slow cooker pot and add the bay leaves and vinegar. Season generously, then pour over enough boiling water to cover the ribs, making sure the level is at least 2.5 cm (1 inch) from the top of the pot. Cover and cook on high for 5–6 hours until the meat is starting to fall away from the bones. Transfer the ribs to a foil-lined grill pan or baking sheet.

Mix together the glaze ingredients, then brush all over the ribs. Spray with a little low-calorie cooking oil spray and cook under a preheated hot grill, with the ribs about 5 cm (2 inches) away from the heat, for about 10 minutes, turning from time to time and brushing with the pan juices, until a deep brown. Serve with salad, if liked.

FOR STICKY HOISIN RIBS, follow the recipe above to cook the ribs in the slow cooker. Make a glaze by mixing together 3 tablespoons hoisin sauce, 8 tablespoons passata, ¼ teaspoon chilli powder, the grated rind and juice of ½ orange and 4 finely chopped spring onions. Brush over the ribs and grill as above.

Serves **4**
Preparation time **20 minutes**
Cooking temperature **low**
Cooking time **8–10 hours**

1 tablespoon **sunflower oil**
4 **pork shoulder steaks** or **boneless spare rib chops**,
    about 700 g (1 lb 6 oz) in total, each cut into 3
1 **onion**, chopped
2 tablespoons **plain flour**
450 ml (¾ pint) **chicken stock**
grated rind and juice of 1 **orange**
3 tablespoons **plum sauce**
2 tablespoons **soy sauce**
3–4 **star anise**
1 **fresh** or **dried red chilli**, halved (optional)
salt and **pepper**
grated rind of 1 **orange**
mashed potato mixed with **steamed green
    vegetables**, to serve

Preheat the slow cooker if necessary. Heat the oil in a large frying pan, add the pieces of pork and fry over a high heat until browned on both sides. Lift the pork out of the pan with a slotted spoon and transfer to a plate.

Add the onion to the pan and fry, stirring, for 5 minutes or until lightly browned. Stir in the flour, then mix in the stock, orange rind and juice, plum sauce, soy sauce, star anise and chilli, if using. Season with salt and pepper and bring to the boil, stirring.

Transfer the pork to the slow cooker pot and pour the sauce over it. Cover and cook on low for 8–10 hours. Sprinkle with grated orange rind and serve with mashed potato mixed with steamed green vegetables.

FOR PORK, ORANGE & BAY LEAVES, prepare the dish as above, but replace the plum sauce, soy sauce, star anise and red chilli with 2 bay leaves, 2 teaspoons light muscovado sugar and 1 tablespoon balsamic vinegar.

TIPSY MUSTARD PORK ♥

Serves **4**
Preparation time **20 minutes**
Cooking temperature **high**
Cooking time **4–5 hours**

low-calorie cooking oil spray
4 **pork loin chops on the bone**, 225 g
  (7½ oz) each, trimmed of fat
1 **onion**, chopped
1 tablespoon **plain flour**
2 teaspoons **wholegrain mustard**
1 teaspoon **ground turmeric**
150 ml (¼ pint) **dry cider**
300 ml (½ pint) **chicken stock**
500 g (1 lb) **swede**, cut into 2.5 cm
  (1 inch) pieces
250 g (8 oz) **potatoes**, cut into
  2.5 cm (1 inch) pieces
1 **dessert apple**, cored and
  thickly sliced
salt and **pepper**
200 g (7 oz) **sugar snap peas**,
  steamed, to serve

Preheat the slow cooker if necessary. Spray a large frying pan with a little low-calorie cooking oil spray and place over a high heat until hot. Add the chops in a single layer and cook for 5 minutes, turning once, until browned on both sides, then transfer to a plate.

Add a little extra low-calorie cooking oil spray to the pan if necessary, then add the onion and cook over a medium heat for 4–5 minutes until softened. Stir in the flour, then add the mustard, turmeric, cider and stock. Season to taste and bring to the boil, stirring.

Place the swede and potatoes in the slow cooker pot. Arrange the chops in a single layer on top, then add the apple slices. Pour over the hot stock mixture, cover and cook on high for 4–5 hours until the pork is very tender.

Transfer the pork to a plate. Divide the vegetables between 4 shallow dishes, top with the chops and drizzle with the sauce. Serve with the steamed sugar snap peas.

FOR MUSTARD CHICKEN WITH CELERIAC, follow the recipe above, browning 4 skinless chicken leg joints in the frying pan instead of the pork chops. Continue, replacing the swede with 500 g (1 lb) diced celeriac. Cook on low for 8–10 hours until the chicken is cooked through with no hint of pink juices and the celeriac is tender.

VEGETARIAN

HOPPIN' JOHN RICE ♥

Serves **4**

Preparation time **15 minutes, plus soaking**

Cooking temperature **high**

Cooking time **1½–2 hours**

200 g (7 oz) **white basmati rice**, soaked in cold water for 10 minutes

4 **spring onions**, chopped

1 **red pepper**, cored, deseeded and diced

150 g (5 oz) peeled and deseeded **pumpkin** or **butternut squash**, cut into 1 cm (½ inch) dice

2 **tomatoes**, diced

400 g (13 oz) can **black eye beans**, drained

leaves from 2 **thyme sprigs**

½–1 **red chilli**, deseeded

½ teaspoon **ground allspice**

½ teaspoon **salt**

750 ml (1¼ pints) boiling **water**

15 g (½ oz) **coriander**, finely chopped

pepper

Preheat the slow cooker if necessary. Drain the soaked rice in a sieve and rinse under cold running water. Drain again and place in the slow cooker pot with the spring onions, red pepper, pumpkin or butternut squash, tomatoes, beans, thyme and chilli, to taste.

Stir the allspice and salt into the measurement boiling water and pour over the rice. Season generously with pepper. Cover and cook on high for 1½–2 hours until the rice is tender and has absorbed the water, stirring once during cooking and adding a little more hot water if the rice is too dry. Add the coriander and fluff up the rice with a fork before serving.

FOR PUMPKIN RICE, place the soaked and rinsed rice in the slow cooker pot with the spring onions, 375 g (12 oz) peeled, deseeded and diced pumpkin, 2 chopped garlic cloves, leaves from 2 thyme sprigs, a 2.5 cm (1 inch) piece of fresh root ginger, peeled and grated, and ½–1 red chilli. Pour over 750 ml (1¼ pints) boiling water, season generously and cook as above. Stir in the chopped coriander just before serving.

BARLEY RISOTTO WITH BLUE CHEESE

Serves **4**
Preparation time **20 minutes**
Cooking temperature **low**
Cooking time **6¼–8¼ hours**

175 g (6 oz) **pearl barley**
1 **onion**, finely chopped
2 **garlic cloves**, finely chopped
500 g (1 lb) **butternut squash**,
   peeled, deseeded and cut into
   2 cm (¾ inch) pieces
1 litre (1¾ pints) boiling
   vegetable stock
125 g (4 oz) **baby spinach**, rinsed
   and well drained

BLUE CHEESE BUTTER
100 g (3½ oz) **butter**, at
   room temperature
100 g (3½ oz) **blue cheese**
   (rind removed)
1 **garlic clove**, finely chopped
¼ teaspoon **crushed dried
   red chillies**
salt and **pepper**

Preheat the slow cooker if necessary. Put the pearl barley, onion, garlic and butternut squash into the slow cooker pot. Add the boiling stock and a little salt and pepper. Cover with the lid and cook on low for 6–8 hours or until the barley and squash are tender.

Meanwhile, make the blue cheese butter. Put the butter on a plate, crumble the cheese on top, add the garlic and chillies and mash together with a fork. Spoon the butter into a line on a piece of nonstick baking paper, then wrap it in paper and roll it backwards and forwards to make a neat sausage shape. Chill in the refrigerator until required.

When almost ready to serve, stir the risotto, slice half the blue cheese butter and add to the slow cooker pot. Mix together until just beginning to melt, then add the spinach. Replace the lid and cook, still on low, for 15 minutes or until the spinach has just wilted. Ladle into shallow bowls and top with slices of the remaining butter.

FOR BARLEY RISOTTO WITH GARLIC & CORIANDER CREAM, make up the risotto as above, replacing the squash with 500 g (1 lb) sweet potato, cut into 2 cm (¾ inch) pieces, and adding 150 g (5 oz) sliced cup mushrooms with the stock. Cook as above, omitting the spinach and blue cheese butter. Mix together 200 g (7 oz) crème fraîche, 1 finely chopped garlic clove, 3 tablespoons finely chopped coriander and 3 chopped spring onions. Ladle the risotto into bowls and top with spoonfuls of the cream.

GREEN BEAN RISOTTO WITH PESTO

Serves **4**
Preparation time **20 minutes**
Cooking temperature **low**
Cooking time **2 hours 5 minutes–
  2½ hours**

25 g (1 oz) **butter**
1 tablespoon **olive oil**
1 **onion**, chopped
2 **garlic cloves**, chopped
250 g (8 oz) **risotto rice**
1.2 litres (2 pints) hot
  vegetable stock
2 teaspoons **pesto**
125 g (4 oz) **extra-fine frozen
  green beans**
125 g (4 oz) **frozen peas**
salt and **pepper**

TO GARNISH
vegetarian hard cheese shavings
basil leaves

Preheat the slow cooker if necessary. Heat the butter and oil in a saucepan, add the onion and fry, stirring, for 5 minutes or until softened and just beginning to brown.

Stir in the garlic and rice and cook for 1 minute. Add all but 150 ml (¼ pint) of the stock, season with salt and pepper, then bring to the boil. Transfer to the slow cooker pot, cover with the lid and cook on low for 1¾–2 hours.

Stir in the pesto and the remaining stock if more liquid is needed. Place the frozen vegetables on top of the rice, replace the lid and cook for another 20–30 minutes or until the vegetables are hot. Serve, garnished with vegetarian hard cheese shavings and basil leaves.

FOR GREEN BEAN RISOTTO WITH SAGE, make up the risotto as above, replacing the pesto with 2 sage sprigs. Replace the basil leaves with some tiny sage leaves.

DUM ALOO

Serves **4**
Preparation time **15 minutes**
Cooking temperature **high**
Cooking time **6¼–7¼ hours**

2 tablespoons **sunflower oil**
1 large **onion**, sliced
1 teaspoon **cumin seeds**, crushed
4 **cardamom pods**, crushed
1 teaspoon **black onion
    seeds** (optional)
1 teaspoon **ground turmeric**
½ teaspoon **ground cinnamon**
2.5 cm (1 inch) piece of **fresh root
    ginger**, peeled and finely chopped
400 g (13 oz) can **chopped tomatoes**
300 ml (½ pint) **vegetable stock**
1 teaspoon **caster sugar**
750 g (1½ lb) **baby new
    potatoes**, scrubbed
100 g (3½ oz) **baby leaf spinach**,
    rinsed and drained
salt and **pepper**
torn **coriander leaves**, to garnish

Preheat the slow cooker if necessary. Heat the oil in a large frying pan, add the onion and fry, stirring, for 5 minutes or until lightly browned.

Mix in the crushed cumin seeds and cardamom pods with their black seeds, onion seeds, if using, ground spices and ginger. Cook for 1 minute, then mix in the tomatoes, stock and sugar and season with salt and pepper. Bring to the boil, stirring.

Cut the potatoes into thick slices or halves (if they are small) so that all the pieces are of a similar size. Transfer to the slow cooker pot and pour the sauce over the top. Cover and cook on high for 6–7 hours or until the potatoes are tender.

Add the spinach and cook on high for 15 minutes until it is just wilted. Stir the curry and serve sprinkled with torn coriander leaves and accompanied by warmed naan bread, a lentil dahl and boiled rice, if liked.

FOR DUM ALOO WITH SAFFRON & CHICKPEAS, add 2 large pinches of saffron threads instead of the turmeric and mix into the pan when you add the tomatoes. Reduce the amount of potatoes to 500 g (1 lb). Drain a 400 g (13 oz) can chickpeas and stir into the mixture. Pour over the hot sauce and cook as above.

MOROCCAN SEVEN-VEGETABLE STEW

Serves **4**
Preparation time **25 minutes**
Cooking temperature **low** and **high**
Cooking time **6¼ hours–8 hours
20 minutes**

2 tablespoons **olive oil**
1 large **onion**, chopped
2 **carrots**, diced
300 g (10 oz) **swede**, diced
1 **red pepper**, cored, deseeded
and chopped
3 **garlic cloves**, finely chopped
200 g (7 oz) **frozen broad beans**
400 g (13 oz) can **chopped tomatoes**
3 teaspoons **harissa**
1 teaspoon **ground turmeric**
2 cm (¾ inch) piece of **fresh root
ginger**, peeled and finely chopped
250 ml (8 fl oz) **vegetable stock**
125 g (4 oz) **okra**, thickly sliced
salt and **pepper**
torn **mint leaves**, to garnish
prepared **couscous**, flavoured with
olive oil, **lemon juice** and **sultanas**,
to serve

Preheat the slow cooker if necessary. Heat the oil in a large frying pan, add the onion and fry, stirring, for 5 minutes or until lightly browned.

Add the carrots and swede to the pan with the red pepper, garlic, beans and tomatoes. Mix in the harissa, turmeric and ginger, then pour on the stock and season with salt and pepper. Bring to the boil, stirring.

Spoon the mixture into the slow cooker pot and press the vegetables beneath the surface of the stock. Cover and cook on low for 6–8 hours or until the root vegetables are tender.

Stir in the okra, cover and cook on high for 15–20 minutes or until the okra are tender but still bright green. Garnish with torn mint leaves and serve with couscous flavoured with olive oil, lemon juice and sultanas.

RATATOUILLE WITH RICOTTA DUMPLINGS

Serves **4**
Preparation time **25 minutes**
Cooking temperature **high**
Cooking time **3¼–4 hours
    20 minutes**

3 tablespoons **olive oil**
1 **onion**, chopped
1 **aubergine**, sliced
2 **courgettes**, about 375 g (12 oz)
    in total, sliced
1 **red pepper**, cored, deseeded
    and cubed
1 **yellow pepper**, cored, deseeded
    and cubed
2 **garlic cloves**, finely chopped
1 tablespoon **plain flour**
400 g (13 oz) can **chopped tomatoes**
300 ml (½ pint) **vegetable stock**
2–3 **rosemary sprigs**
salt and **pepper**

DUMPLINGS
100 g (3½ oz) **plain flour**, plus extra
    for dusting
75 g (3 oz) **ricotta cheese**
grated rind of ½ **lemon**
1 **egg**, beaten

Preheat the slow cooker if necessary. Heat the oil in a frying pan, add the onion and aubergine and fry, stirring, for 5 minutes or until softened and just beginning to turn golden.

Stir in the courgettes, peppers and garlic and fry for 3–4 minutes. Mix in the flour, then the tomatoes, stock, rosemary and a little salt and pepper. Bring to the boil, then spoon into the slow cooker pot. Cover and cook on high for 3–4 hours until the vegetables are tender.

When almost ready to serve, make the dumplings. Put the flour, ricotta, lemon rind and a little salt and pepper into a bowl. Add the egg and mix to a soft but not sticky dough. Cut into 12 pieces and roll each piece into a ball with floured hands.

Stir the ratatouille and arrange the dumplings on the top. Replace the lid and cook for 15–20 minutes or until light and firm to the touch. Spoon into bowls and eat with a spoon and fork.

PUMPKIN & CHEESE GNOCCHI

SPANISH POTATOES

Serves **4**
Preparation time **20 minutes**
Cooking temperature **low**
Cooking time **6–8 hours**

1 tablespoon **olive oil**
25 g (1 oz) **butter**
1 **onion**, thinly sliced
2 **garlic cloves**, finely chopped
2 tablespoons **plain flour**
150 ml (¼ pint) **dry white wine**
300 ml (½ pint) **vegetable stock**
2–3 **sage sprigs**, plus extra leaves to garnish (optional)
400 g (13 oz) peeled and deseeded **pumpkin** or
    butternut squash, diced
500 g (1 lb) **gnocchi**, chilled
125 ml (4 fl oz) **double cream**
freshly grated **vegetarian hard cheese**
salt and **pepper**

Preheat the slow cooker if necessary. Heat the oil and butter in a frying pan, add the onion and fry, stirring, for 5 minutes or until just beginning to turn golden.

Stir in the garlic and cook for 2 minutes, then stir in the flour. Gradually mix in the wine and stock and heat, stirring, until smooth. Add the sage and season well.

Add the pumpkin or squash to the slow cooker pot, pour over the hot sauce, then press the pumpkin or squash beneath the surface of the liquid. Cover with the lid and cook on low for 6–8 hours or until the pumpkin or squash is tender.

When almost ready to serve, bring a large saucepan of water to the boil, add the gnocchi, bring the water back to the boil and cook for 2–3 minutes or until the gnocchi float to the surface and are piping hot. Tip into a colander to drain.

Stir the cream, then the gnocchi into the slow cooker pot and mix together lightly. Spoon into shallow bowls and serve topped with freshly grated vegetarian hard cheese and a few extra sage leaves, if liked.

Serves **4**
Preparation time **15 minutes**
Cooking temperature **high**
Cooking time **4–5 hours**

2 tablespoons **olive oil**
1 large **red onion**, thinly sliced
2 **garlic cloves**, finely chopped
1 teaspoon **smoked paprika**
¼–½ teaspoon **crushed dried red chillies**, to taste
1 **red pepper**, cored, deseeded and diced
1 **yellow pepper**, cored, deseeded and diced
400 g (13 oz) can **chopped tomatoes**
300 ml (½ pint) **vegetable stock**
2–3 **thyme sprigs**
50 g (2 oz) **pitted dry olives**
625 g (1¼ lb) **baking potatoes**, cut into 2.5 cm
    (1 inch) chunks
salt and **pepper**

Preheat the slow cooker if necessary. Heat the oil in a frying pan, add the onion and fry, stirring, for 5 minutes or until just beginning to turn golden.

Stir in the garlic, paprika, chillies and peppers and cook for 2 minutes. Mix in the tomatoes, stock, thyme, olives and some salt and pepper, then bring to the boil.

Add the potatoes to the slow cooker pot, pour over the hot tomato mixture, cover with the lid and cook on high for 4–5 hours or until the potatoes are tender. Serve with warm crusty bread and a dressed green salad, if liked.

FOR SPANISH SWEET POTATOES, make up the recipe as above, using sweet potatoes instead of baking potatoes and omitting the olives. Cook on high for 3–4 hours and serve in bowls topped with spoonfuls of Greek yogurt and torn coriander leaves.

SWEET POTATO & EGG CURRY

Serves **4**
Preparation time **15 minutes**
Cooking temperature **low**
Cooking time **6¼–8¼ hours**

1 tablespoon **sunflower oil**
1 **onion**, chopped
1 teaspoon **cumin seeds**,
   roughly crushed
1 teaspoon **ground coriander**
1 teaspoon **ground turmeric**
1 teaspoon **garam masala**
½ teaspoon **crushed dried
   red chillies**
300 g (10 oz) **sweet potatoes**, diced
2 **garlic cloves**, finely chopped
400 g (13 oz) can **chopped tomatoes**
410 g (13½ oz) can **lentils**, drained
300 ml (½ pint) **vegetable stock**
1 teaspoon **caster sugar**
6 **eggs**
150 g (5 oz) **frozen peas**
150 ml (¼ pint) **double cream**
small bunch of **coriander**, torn
   into pieces
salt and **pepper**

Preheat the slow cooker if necessary. Heat the oil in a frying pan, add the onion and fry, stirring, for 5 minutes or until softened and just beginning to turn golden.

Stir in the spices, sweet potatoes and garlic and fry for 2 minutes. Add the tomatoes, lentils, stock and sugar and season with a little salt and pepper. Bring to the boil, stirring. Spoon into the slow cooker pot, cover with the lid and cook on low for 6–8 hours.

When almost ready to serve, put the eggs in a small saucepan, cover with cold water and bring to the boil, then simmer for 8 minutes. Drain, crack the shells and cool under cold running water. Peel and halve, then add to the slow cooker pot with the peas, cream and half the coriander. Cover and cook on low for 15 minutes.

Spoon into bowls, garnish with the remaining coriander and serve with rice or warmed naan bread, if liked.

FOR SWEET POTATO & PANEER CURRY, make up the curry as above, adding 400 g (13 oz) diced paneer (Indian cheese) instead of the boiled eggs, reducing the peas to 100 g (3½ oz) and adding 100 g (3½ oz) baby corn cobs, halved if large.

MIXED MUSHROOM & LENTIL BRAISE

Serves **4**
Preparation time **25 minutes**
Cooking temperature **low**
Cooking time **6–8 hours**

2 tablespoons **olive oil**, plus extra
    to serve
1 large **onion**, chopped
3 **garlic cloves**, chopped
400 g (13 oz) can **chopped tomatoes**
300 ml (½ pint) **vegetable stock**
150 ml (¼ pint) **red wine**
    or extra **stock**
1 tablespoon **tomato purée**
2 teaspoons **caster sugar**
125 g (4 oz) **dried Puy lentils**
375 g (12 oz) **cup mushrooms**, halved
    or quartered
125 g (4 oz) **shiitake mushrooms**,
    halved if large
4 large **field mushrooms**, about
    250 g (8 oz) in total
salt and **pepper**

TO SERVE
rocket leaves
vegetarian hard cheese shavings
fried rounds of **polenta**

Preheat the slow cooker if necessary. Heat the oil in a large frying pan, add the onion and fry, stirring, for 5 minutes or until lightly browned. Mix in the garlic, tomatoes, stock, wine or extra stock, tomato purée and sugar and season with salt and pepper. Add the Puy lentils and bring to the boil.

Put the mushrooms in the slow cooker pot and pour over the lentil mixture, then cover and cook on low for 6–8 hours, stirring once if possible.

Serve with rocket leaves tossed with vegetarian hard cheese shavings and a drizzle of olive oil and fried rounds of polenta.

FOR MIXED MUSHROOM & LENTIL CHEESY BAKE, make and cook the mushroom and lentil mixture as above. Mix together 3 eggs, 250 ml (8 fl oz) natural yogurt, 75 g (3 oz) grated feta cheese and a pinch of grated nutmeg. Press the cooked mushroom mixture into an even layer, then spoon the yogurt mix on top. Arrange 2 sliced tomatoes on top and cook on high for 45 minutes, 1½ hours until the topping is set. Lift the pot out of the housing using oven gloves and brown under a preheated hot grill, if liked.

BEETROOT & MASCARPONE RISOTTO

Serves **4**
Preparation time **20 minutes**
Cooking temperature **low**
Cooking time **1¾–2 hours**

25 g (1 oz) **butter**
1 tablespoon **olive oil**
1 **red onion**, chopped
1 **garlic clove**, finely chopped
250 g (8 oz) pack **cooked beetroot in natural juice**, drained and diced
250 g (8 oz) **risotto rice**
150 ml (¼ pint) **red wine**
1 litre (1¾ pints) **vegetable stock**
2 **thyme sprigs**
salt and **pepper**

TO SERVE
150 g (5 oz) **mascarpone cheese**
4 teaspoons chopped **thyme leaves**
vegetarian hard cheese shavings

Preheat the slow cooker if necessary. Heat the butter and oil in a large frying pan, add the onion and fry, stirring, for 5 minutes or until softened.

Stir in the garlic, beetroot and rice and cook for 1 minute, then mix in the wine and stock. Add the thyme and a little salt and pepper and bring to the boil, stirring.

Pour the mixture into the slow cooker pot. Cover with the lid and cook on low for 1¾–2 hours or until the rice is tender and almost all the stock has been absorbed.

Spoon into bowls and top with spoonfuls of the mascarpone mixed with the thyme, a little pepper and a generous sprinkling of vegetarian hard cheese shavings.

FOR MUSHROOM & THYME RISOTTO, soak 15 g (½ oz) dried porcini mushrooms in 150 ml (¼ pint) boiling water for 15 minutes. Fry the onion in butter and oil as above, then add the garlic, 250 g (8 oz) mixed sliced mushrooms and an extra 25 g (1 oz) butter and fry briefly. Omit the beetroot. Add the rice and cook for 1 minute, then add the soaked mushrooms and their soaking liquid, the red wine, stock, thyme and salt and pepper and bring to the boil. Continue as above.

AUBERGINES WITH BAKED EGGS

Serves **4**
Preparation time **20 minutes**
Cooking temperature **high**
Cooking time **2¾–3 hours**
    20 minutes

4 tablespoons **olive oil**
1 **onion**, chopped
2 **aubergines**, cubed
2 **garlic cloves**, finely chopped
500 g (1 lb) **tomatoes**, cut into
    large chunks
½ teaspoon **smoked paprika**
½ teaspoon **ground cumin**
½ teaspoon **ground coriander**
100 g (3½ oz) **quinoa**
300 ml (½ pint) **vegetable stock**
125 g (4 oz) **frozen peas** (optional)
4 **eggs**
salt and **pepper**
chopped **mint**, to garnish

Preheat the slow cooker if necessary. Heat the oil in a large frying pan, add the onion and aubergines and fry, stirring, until the aubergines are golden.

Stir in the garlic, tomatoes and spices and cook for 1 minute. Mix in the quinoa and stock, add a little salt and pepper and bring to the boil. Transfer the mixture to the slow cooker pot. Cover with the lid and cook on high for 2½–3 hours.

Stir in the frozen peas, if using, and add a little boiling water if the quinoa has begun to stick around the edges of the pot. Make 4 indents with the back of a dessert spoon, then break and drop an egg into each one. Cover and cook for 15–20 minutes or until the egg whites are set and the yolks still soft.

Spoon on to plates, sprinkle the eggs with a little extra salt and pepper and garnish with chopped mint. Serve with toasted pitta breads, cut into strips, if liked.

FOR AUBERGINE RATATOUILLE WITH BAKED EGGS, omit the ground spices and quinoa and make up the recipe as above, adding 1 diced courgette and 1 cored, deseeded and diced orange pepper with the garlic, tomatoes and smoked paprika. Add 200 ml (7 fl oz) vegetable stock, season with salt and pepper and continue as above, omitting the peas. Serve sprinkled with torn basil leaves, spooned over toasted rustic-style bread.

SOYA SAUSAGES WITH ONION GRAVY ♥

Serves **4**
Preparation time **20 minutes**
Cooking temperature **high**
Cooking time **4–5 hours**

low-calorie cooking oil spray
2 x 240 g (7½ oz) packs of
    soya sausages
300 g (10 oz) **onions**, thinly sliced
2 teaspoons **dark muscovado sugar**
350 ml (12 fl oz) **vegetable stock**
1 tablespoon **tomato purée**
2 teaspoons **wholegrain mustard**
2 teaspoons **cornflour**
675 g (1 lb 6 oz) **celeriac**, cubed just
    before cooking
salt and **pepper**
chopped **parsley**, to garnish (optional)

TO SERVE
360 g (11¾ oz) **fine green
    beans**, steamed

Preheat the slow cooker if necessary. Spray a large frying pan with a little low-calorie cooking oil spray and place over a high heat until hot. Add the sausages and cook for 2–3 minutes until browned all over. Transfer to the slow cooker pot in a single layer.

Add a little extra low-calorie cooking oil spray to the frying pan, add the onions and cook over a medium heat for 5 minutes until just beginning to soften. Add the sugar and continue to cook for 5 minutes until deep brown, being careful not to burn the onions.

Stir in the stock, tomato purée and mustard. Mix the cornflour to a smooth paste with a little cold water and stir into the pan. Season to taste and bring to the boil, stirring. Pour over the sausages, cover and cook on high for 4–5 hours until the sausages are cooked through.

When almost ready to serve, cook the celeriac in a saucepan of lightly salted boiling water for 15–20 minutes until tender. Drain and mash with 3–4 tablespoons of the cooking water and season to taste. Divide the mash between 4 serving plates and top with the sausages and onion gravy. Sprinkle with a little chopped parsley, if liked, and serve with the steamed green beans.

CHILLI, MUSHROOM & TOMATO RAGÙ ♥

Serves **4**
Preparation time **20 minutes**
Cooking temperature **low**
Cooking time **7–8 hours**

1 tablespoon **olive oil**
1 **red onion**, roughly chopped
2 **garlic cloves**, finely chopped
1 teaspoon **paprika**
½ teaspoon **crushed dried
    red chillies**
1 teaspoon **dried
    Mediterranean herbs**
400 g (13 oz) **passata**
2 teaspoons **granular sweetener**
300 g (10 oz) small
    button mushrooms
300 g (10 oz) **cherry tomatoes**
salt and **pepper**

TO SERVE
200 g (7 oz) **dried penne pasta**
large pinch of **crushed dried
    red chillies** (optional)
handful of **rocket leaves**

Preheat the slow cooker if necessary. Heat the oil in a large frying pan over a medium heat until hot, add the onion and cook for 4–5 minutes, stirring until just beginning to soften. Add the garlic, paprika and chillies, then the dried herbs, passata and sweetener. Season to taste and bring to the boil.

Place the mushrooms and cherry tomatoes in the slow cooker pot, pour over the hot passata mixture and stir well. Cover and cook on low for 7–8 hours.

When almost ready to serve, cook the pasta in a saucepan of lightly salted boiling water according to the packet instructions until just tender. Drain and stir into the ragù, then spoon into shallow bowls, sprinkle with the chillies, if liked, and top with the rocket. Serve immediately.

FOR COURGETTE & TOMATO ARRABIATA, follow the recipe above, using 200 g (7 oz) diced courgette and 1 cored, deseeded and diced red pepper instead of the mushrooms.

LENTIL TAGINE WITH POMEGRANATE ♥

Serves **4**
Preparation time **15 minutes**
Cooking temperature **high**
Cooking time **4–5 hours**

1 tablespoon **olive oil**
1 **onion**, chopped
5 cm (2 inch) piece of **fresh root ginger**, peeled and finely chopped
3 **garlic cloves**, finely chopped
2 teaspoons **cumin seed**s, crushed
1 teaspoon **coriander seeds**, crushed
200 g (7 oz) **dried Puy lentils**
2 **celery sticks**, sliced
250 g (8 oz) **cherry tomatoes**, halved
450 ml (¾ pint) hot **vegetable stock**
juice of 1 **lemon**
15 g (½ oz) **flat leaf parsley**, roughly chopped
15 g (½ oz) **mint**, roughly chopped
salt and **pepper**

TO SERVE
125 ml (4 fl oz) **0% fat Greek yogurt**
1 tablespoon **harissa**
seeds from ½ **pomegranate**

Preheat the slow cooker if necessary. Heat the oil in a large frying pan over a medium heat, add the onion and cook for 4–5 minutes until just beginning to soften. Stir in the ginger, garlic and crushed cumin and coriander seeds.

Place the lentils in a sieve and rinse under cold running water. Drain and transfer to the slow cooker pot. Spoon the onion mixture on top, then add the celery and tomatoes. Pour over the hot stock, season to taste, cover and cook on high for 4–5 hours until the lentils are tender.

Stir in the lemon juice and herbs and spoon into bowls. Top with the yogurt and harissa, then scatter with the pomegranate seeds and serve.

FOR CHICKPEA & LENTIL TAGINE, follow the recipe above, adding ½ teaspoon chilli powder with the other spices and using 100 g (3½ oz) dried Puy lentils and a 400 g (13 oz) can chickpeas, drained, instead of the 200 g (7 oz) lentils. Omit the mint and pomegranate, but stir in 25 g (1 oz) roughly chopped parsley and serve topped with the yogurt and harissa.

MUSHROOM & WALNUT COBBLER

Serves **4**
Preparation time **30 minutes**
Cooking temperature **low** and **high**
Cooking time **6¾–8¾ hours**

2 tablespoons **olive oil**
1 **onion**, chopped
2 **garlic cloves**, chopped
250 g (8 oz) **flat mushrooms**, peeled
  and quartered
250 g (8 oz) **cup chestnut
  mushrooms**, quartered
1 tablespoon **plain flour**
200 ml (7 fl oz) **red wine**
400 g (13 oz) can **chopped tomatoes**
150 ml (¼ pint) **vegetable stock**
1 tablespoon **redcurrant jelly**
2–3 **thyme sprigs**
salt and **pepper**

WALNUT TOPPING
200 g (7 oz) **self-raising flour**, plus
  extra for dusting
50 g (2 oz) **butter**, diced
50 g (2 oz) **walnut pieces**, chopped
75 g (3 oz) **Cheddar cheese**, grated
1 **egg**, beaten
4–5 tablespoons **milk**

Preheat the slow cooker if necessary. Heat the oil in a frying pan, add the onion, garlic and mushrooms and fry, stirring, for 5 minutes or until just turning golden.

Stir in the flour, then mix in the wine, tomatoes and stock. Add the redcurrant jelly, thyme and salt and pepper and bring to the boil. Pour into the slow cooker pot, cover with the lid and cook on low for 6–8 hours.

When almost ready to serve, make the topping. Put the flour and butter in a bowl, then rub in the butter with your fingertips until fine breadcrumbs form. Stir in the walnuts, cheese and salt and pepper. Add half the egg, then mix in enough milk to make a soft dough.

Knead lightly, then roll out the dough on a lightly floured surface until 2 cm (¾ inch) thick. Stamp out 8 rounds with a 6 cm (2½ inch) plain biscuit cutter, re-rolling the trimmings as needed. Stir the mushroom casserole, then arrange the scones, slightly overlapping, around the edge of the dish. Cover and cook on high for 45 minutes or until well risen. Lift the pot out of the housing using oven gloves, brush the tops of the scones with the remaining egg and brown under a preheated medium grill, if liked.

FOR CHEAT'S MUSHROOM PIE, make up the mushroom casserole as above, but omit the stock and scone topping. Unroll 1 pastry sheet from a 425 g (14 oz) pack of 2 and trim the edges to make an oval shape. Transfer to an oiled baking sheet, brush with beaten egg and bake in a preheated oven, 200°C (400°F), Gas Mark 6, for 15–20 minutes or until golden. Cut into wedge shapes and serve on top of the casserole.

TARKA DAHL

NUT & APRICOT PILAF

Serves **4**
Preparation time **15 minutes**
Cooking temperature **high**
Cooking time **3–4 hours**

250 g (8 oz) **dried red lentils**
1 **onion**, finely chopped
½ teaspoon **ground turmeric**
½ teaspoon **cumin seeds**, roughly crushed
2 cm (¾ inch) piece of **fresh root ginger**,
    peeled and finely chopped
200 g (7 oz) **canned chopped tomatoes**
600 ml (1 pint) boiling **vegetable stock**
150 ml (¼ pint) **natural yogurt**
salt and **pepper**
torn **coriander leaves**, to garnish

TARKA
1 tablespoon **sunflower oil**
2 teaspoons **black mustard seeds**
½ teaspoon **cumin seeds**, roughly crushed
pinch of **ground turmeric**
2 **garlic cloves**, finely chopped

Preheat the slow cooker if necessary. Rinse the lentils well with cold running water, drain and put into the slow cooker pot with the onion, spices, ginger, tomatoes and boiling stock.

Stir in a little salt and pepper, cover with the lid and cook on high for 3–4 hours or until the lentils are soft and tender.

When almost ready to serve, make the tarka. Heat the oil in a small frying pan, add the remaining tarka ingredients and fry, stirring, for 2 minutes. Roughly mash the lentil mixture, then spoon into bowls, add spoonfuls of yogurt and drizzle with the tarka. Sprinkle with coriander leaves and serve with warmed naan bread, if liked.

FOR TARKA DAHL WITH SPINACH, cook the lentils in the same way as above, adding 125 g (4 oz) rinsed, drained and roughly shredded spinach leaves for the last 15 minutes. Fry the tarka spices as above, adding ¼ teaspoon crushed dried red chillies, if liked.

Serves **4**
Preparation time **25 minutes**
Cooking temperature **low**
Cooking time **3–3½ hours**

1 tablespoon **olive oil**
1 large **onion**, chopped
75 g (3 oz) mixed **pistachios, walnuts and hazelnuts**,
    plus extra, lightly toasted, to garnish
25 g (1 oz) **sunflower seeds**
200 g (7 oz) **easy-cook long-grain brown rice**
1 litre (1¾ pints) **vegetable stock**
75 g (3 oz) **ready-to-eat dried apricots**, chopped
25 g (1 oz) **currants**
1 **cinnamon stick**, halved
6 **cloves**
3 **bay leaves**
1 tablespoon **tomato purée**
salt and **pepper**

Preheat the slow cooker if necessary. Heat the oil in a frying pan, add the onion and fry, stirring, for 5 minutes or until lightly browned.

Add the nuts and seeds and fry until lightly browned. Stir in the rice and stock, followed by the dried fruit, spices, bay leaves and tomato purée, then season with salt and pepper to taste. Bring to the boil, stirring.

Transfer the mixture to the slow cooker pot. Cover with the lid and cook on low for 3–3½ hours or until the rice is tender and the stock has been absorbed. Discard the cinnamon, cloves and bay leaves before serving, garnished with extra, toasted nuts.

FOR AUBERGINE & APRICOT PILAF, heat 3 tablespoons olive oil, add the onion and 1 sliced aubergine and fry until lightly browned. Continue as above, replacing the hazelnuts with almonds and adding the sunflower seeds, the rice, stock and just 50 g (2 oz) of the apricots plus 50 g (2 oz) chopped pitted dates. Add the remaining ingredients and continue as above.

VEGETABLE GOULASH

Serves **4**
Preparation time **20 minutes**
Cooking temperature **high**
Cooking time **4–5 hours**

1 tablespoon **sunflower oil**
1 **onion**, chopped
250 g (8 oz) **swede**, diced
250 g (8 oz) **carrots**, diced
250 g (8 oz) **potatoes**, diced
1 **red pepper**, cored, deseeded and diced
2 **celery sticks**, sliced
150 g (5 oz) **cup mushrooms**, halved
1 teaspoon **smoked paprika**, plus extra
    to garnish (optional)
¼ teaspoon **crushed dried red chillies**
1 teaspoon **caraway seeds**
1 tablespoon **plain flour**
400 g (13 oz) can **chopped tomatoes**
300 ml (½ pint) **vegetable stock**
2 **bay leaves**
salt and **pepper**

TO SERVE
150 ml (¼ pint) **soured cream**
boiled **rice**

Preheat the slow cooker if necessary. Heat the oil in a large frying pan, add the onion and fry, stirring, until softened. Add the vegetables and fry for 1–2 minutes, then stir in the paprika, chillies and caraway seeds and cook for 1 minute.

Stir in the flour, then mix in the canned tomatoes and stock, add the bay leaves and a little salt and pepper and bring to the boil. Transfer to the slow cooker pot and press the vegetables below the surface of the liquid. Cover with the lid and cook on high for 4–5 hours or until the root vegetables are tender.

Stir the goulash and discard the bay leaves. Spoon on to plates and top with spoonfuls of the soured cream and a sprinkling of extra paprika, if liked. Serve with boiled rice.

MUSHROOM & TOMATO RIGATONI ♥

Serves **4**
Preparation time **20 minutes**
Cooking temperature **low**
Cooking time **2½–3 hours**

250 g (8 oz) **dried rigatoni** or **pasta quills**
3 tablespoons **olive oil**
1 **onion**, sliced
2–3 **garlic cloves**, finely chopped
250 g (8 oz) **closed-cap mushrooms**, sliced
250 g (8 oz) **portabello mushrooms**, sliced
250 g (8 oz) **tomatoes**, cut into chunks
400 g (13 oz) can **chopped tomatoes**
200 ml (7 fl oz) **vegetable stock**
1 tablespoon **tomato purée**
3 **rosemary sprigs**
salt and **pepper**

Preheat the slow cooker if necessary. Place the pasta in a large bowl, cover with boiling water and leave to soak for 10 minutes.

Meanwhile, heat 1 tablespoon of the oil in a large frying pan over a medium heat, add the onion and cook for 5 minutes until softened. Stir in the remaining oil, the garlic and mushrooms and cook, stirring, until the mushrooms are just beginning to brown.

Stir in the fresh and canned tomatoes, stock and tomato purée. Add the rosemary, season to taste and bring to the boil.

Drain the pasta and put it in the slow cooker pot. Pour over the hot mushroom mixture and spread into an even layer. Cover and cook on low for 2½–3 hours or until the pasta is just tender. Spoon into bowls and sprinkle with freshly grated vegetarian hard cheese, if liked.

FOR MUSHROOM PASTICHIO, follow the recipe above, using 250 g (8 oz) dried macaroni instead of the rigatoni. Mix 3 eggs with 250 ml (8 fl oz) natural yogurt, 75 g (3 oz) grated feta cheese and a pinch of grated nutmeg. Spoon the mixture over the top of the mushroom and pasta mixture for the last hour of cooking until set. Place under a preheated hot grill to brown the top before serving.

SPICY FLAVOURS

EASY CAULIFLOWER DAHL ♥

Serves **4**
Preparation time **15 minutes**
Cooking temperature **high**
Cooking time **3–4 hours**

200 g (7 oz) **dried red lentils**, rinsed
  and drained
750 ml (1¼ pints) hot **water**
2 teaspoons **medium curry powder**
½ teaspoon **salt**
pepper

SPICED CAULIFLOWER
400 g (13 oz) **cauliflower**, trimmed
  and cut into small florets
6 tablespoons **water**
1 **onion**, thinly sliced
low-calorie cooking oil spray
1 teaspoon **cumin seeds**,
  roughly crushed
1 teaspoon **ground turmeric**
1 teaspoon **garam masala**

Preheat the slow cooker if necessary. Place the lentils, measurement hot water, curry powder and salt in the slow cooker pot, then season with pepper. Cover and cook on high for 3–4 hours or until the lentils are soft.

Meanwhile, place the cauliflower in a large frying pan with the measurement water, cover and cook over a medium heat for 5 minutes until the cauliflower is almost tender. Drain off any excess water, then add the onion and a little low-calorie cooking oil spray, increase the heat and cook for 2–3 minutes, stirring.

Sprinkle the cumin, turmeric and garam masala over the cauliflower and cook, stirring, for 4–5 minutes until the cauliflower is golden brown. Season to taste. Stir the lentil dahl, spoon into shallow bowls and top with the spiced cauliflower.

FOR EASY AUBERGINE & MUSHROOM DAHL, follow the recipe above to cook the lentil dahl. Spray a large frying pan with a little low-calorie cooking oil spray, add 1 large diced aubergine and 100 g (3½ oz) sliced button mushrooms and cook over a medium heat for 2–3 minutes until beginning to soften. Add a little more low-calorie cooking oil spray, then the cumin, turmeric and garam masala as above and continue to cook until the aubergine is soft. Spoon the spiced vegetables over the dahl and sprinkle with chopped coriander.

INDIAN BLACK PEPPER CHICKEN ♥

Serves **4**
Preparation time **20 minutes**
Cooking temperature **low** and **high**
Cooking time **7¼–8½ hours**

1 large **onion**, quartered
3 **garlic cloves**, halved
3.5 cm (1½ inch) piece of **fresh root ginger**, peeled and sliced
15 g (½ oz) fresh **coriander**
8 small **skinless chicken drumsticks**, 875 g (1¾ lb) in total
low-calorie cooking oil spray
5 cm (2 inch) **cinnamon stick**
1 teaspoon **ground cumin**
1 teaspoon **ground turmeric**
2 teaspoons **black peppercorns**, roughly crushed
juice of ½ **lemon**
350 ml (12 fl oz) **chicken stock**
150 g (5 oz) **baby spinach**, rinsed and drained
salt

Preheat the slow cooker if necessary. Place the onion, garlic, ginger and coriander in a food processor and blitz until very finely chopped.

Slash each chicken drumstick 2 or 3 times with a sharp knife. Spray a large frying pan with a little low-calorie cooking oil spray and place over a high heat until hot. Add the chicken and cook for 4–5 minutes, turning, until browned all over. Transfer the drumsticks to the slow cooker pot, packing them in tightly together.

Add the chopped onion mixture to the frying pan and cook for 2 minutes until just softened. Stir in the cinnamon, cumin, turmeric and crushed peppercorns, then add the lemon juice and stock. Season to taste and bring to the boil, stirring.

Pour the hot stock over the chicken, cover and cook on low for 7–8 hours until the chicken is cooked through and beginning to shrink on the bones. Stir the sauce, add the spinach, cover with the lid again and cook on high for 15–30 minutes until the spinach has wilted. Spoon into shallow bowls and serve.

FOR INDIAN CHICKEN & CHICKPEA CURRY, follow the recipe above, using just 4 chicken drumsticks and adding ¼ teaspoon chilli powder instead of the crushed black peppercorns. Place the browned drumsticks in the slow cooker pot with a 400 g (13 oz) can chickpeas, drained, then pour over the hot stock and cook as above.

SMOKY SWEET POTATO & QUORN CHILLI ♥

Serves **4**
Preparation time **20 minutes**
Cooking temperature **low**
Cooking time **7–8 hours**

1–2 small **dried smoked
    chipotle chillies**
4 tablespoons boiling **water**
low-calorie cooking oil spray
1 **onion**, chopped
2 **garlic cloves**, finely chopped
1 teaspoon **ground cumin**
1 teaspoon **paprika**
2 x 400 g (13 oz) cans
    chopped tomatoes
400 g (13 oz) can **red kidney beans**,
    rinsed and drained
1 tablespoon **Worcestershire
    sauce** (optional)
350 g (11½ oz) **Quorn mince**
300 g (10 oz) **sweet potato**, cut into
    2.5 cm (1 inch) cubes
salt and **pepper**

SALSA
½ **red onion**, finely chopped
3 tablespoons chopped **coriander**
2 **tomatoes**, halved, deseeded
    and diced

Preheat the slow cooker if necessary. Place the dried chillies in a small bowl, pour over the boiling water and leave to stand for 10 minutes.

Meanwhile, spray a large frying pan with a little low-calorie cooking oil spray and place over a medium heat until hot. Add the onion and fry for 4–5 minutes until softened, then add the garlic, cumin and paprika. Stir in the tomatoes, kidney beans and Worcestershire sauce, if using, then the soya mince and sweet potato. Season to taste.

Drain the chillies, reserving the soaking water, then finely chop. Stir into the soya mince mixture with the soaking water. Bring to the boil, stirring, then transfer to the slow cooker pot. Cover and cook on low for 7–8 hours until the sweet potato is tender. Mix the salsa ingredients together, then sprinkle over the chilli to serve.

FOR SWEET POTATO & SOYA MINCE CURRY, follow the recipe above, omitting the chipotle chillies. Add 1 teaspoon ground turmeric, 1 teaspoon garam masala and ½ teaspoon crushed dried red chillies with the cumin and paprika, and a 100 g (3½ oz) can lentils, drained, when adding the soya mince. Cook as above, then stir in 100 g (3½ oz) frozen peas and 4 tablespoons chopped coriander, cover the pot again and cook on high for 15 minutes.

COCONUT, PUMPKIN & CHICKPEA CURRY ♥

Serves **4**
Preparation time **25 minutes**
Cooking temperature **low**
Cooking time **6–8 hours**

2 **onions**
2 **garlic cloves**, halved
4 cm (1½ inch) piece of **fresh root
    ginger**, peeled and sliced
1 **red chilli**, quartered and deseeded
low-calorie cooking oil spray
1½ tablespoons **medium
    curry powder**
1 teaspoon **fennel seeds**,
    roughly crushed
200 ml (7 fl oz) **full-fat coconut milk**
300 ml (½ pint) **vegetable stock**
2 teaspoons **granular sweetener**
650 g (1 lb 5 oz) peeled and
    deseeded **pumpkin**, cut into
    3.5 cm (1½ inch) chunks
400 g (13 oz) can **chickpeas**, drained
1 teaspoon **black mustard seeds**
15 g (½ oz) **coriander**, roughly torn
juice of 1 **lime**
salt and **pepper**

Preheat the slow cooker if necessary. Quarter 1 of the onions and place with the garlic, ginger and chilli in a food processor and blitz until very finely chopped. Alternatively, chop the ingredients finely with a knife. Spray a large frying pan with a little low-calorie cooking oil spray and place over a high heat until hot. Add the onion paste and cook for 2 minutes, then stir in the curry powder and fennel seeds.

Add the coconut milk, stock and sweetener, then season to taste. Bring to the boil, stirring. Place the pumpkin and chickpeas in the slow cooker pot and pour the coconut mixture on top. Cover and cook on low for 6–8 hours until the pumpkin is tender.

When almost ready to serve, make a crispy onion topping. Slice the remaining onion. Heat a little low-calorie cooking oil spray in a clean frying pan and cook the onion over a medium heat for 5 minutes until softened. Stir in the mustard seeds and cook for a few minutes more until the onion is golden and crispy.

Stir the coriander and lime juice into the curry, spoon into bowls and served topped with the crispy onions.

FOR CREAMY COCONUT, AUBERGINE & CHICKPEA CURRY, follow the recipe above, using 625 g (1¼ lb) aubergines, trimmed and diced, instead of the pumpkin.

RED COOKED CHINESE DUCK

Serves **4**
Preparation time **20 minutes**
Cooking temperature **high**
Cooking time **5–6 hours**

4 **duck legs**, about 200 g (7 oz) each
1 **onion**, sliced
2 tablespoons **plain flour**
450 ml (¾ pint) **chicken stock**
2 tablespoons **soy sauce**
1 tablespoon **red wine vinegar**
1 tablespoon **clear honey**
2 teaspoons **tomato purée**
2 teaspoons **fish sauce**
½ teaspoon **crushed dried red chillies**
½ teaspoon **ground allspice**
4 **star anise**
375 g (12 oz) **red plums**, stoned and quartered

Preheat the slow cooker if necessary. Dry-fry the duck legs in a frying pan over a low heat at first until the fat begins to run, then increase the heat and brown on both sides. Lift out of the pan with a slotted spoon and transfer to the slow cooker pot.

Pour off all but 1 tablespoon of the duck fat from the pan, then add the onion and fry, stirring, for 5 minutes or until just turning golden. Stir in the flour, then gradually mix in the stock. Add the remaining ingredients, except for the plums, and bring to the boil, stirring.

Pour the sauce over the duck, add the plums and press the duck beneath the surface of the liquid. Cover with the lid and cook on high for 5–6 hours or until the duck is almost falling off the bones. Serve with rice or with Gingered Noodles (*see* below), if liked.

FOR GINGERED NOODLES TO ACCOMPANY THE DUCK, heat 1 tablespoon sesame oil in a wok, add a 2.5 cm (1 inch) piece of peeled and finely chopped fresh root ginger, 200 g (7 oz) finely shredded pak choi, 50 g (2 oz) halved mangetout and 3 packs, 150 g (5 oz) each, of thick-cut, straight-to-wok noodles. Stir-fry for 3–4 minutes or until the pak choi has just wilted and the noodles are hot.

KEEMA MUTTER

Serves **4**
Preparation time 10 minutes
Cooking temperature **high** and **low**
Cooking time **8–10 hours**

500 g (1 lb) **lean minced beef**
1 **onion**, finely chopped
400 g (13 oz) can **chopped tomatoes**
3 tablespoons **mild curry paste**
2 teaspoons **cumin seeds**
2–3 **green bird's eye chillies**,
   deseeded and sliced, plus extra
   to garnish
2.5 cm (1 inch) piece of **fresh root
   ginger**, peeled and finely chopped
2 **garlic cloves**, finely chopped
50 g (2 oz) **creamed
   coconut**, crumbled
125 ml (4 fl oz) boiling **beef stock**
150 g (5 oz) **frozen peas**
chopped **coriander**, to garnish

Preheat the slow cooker if necessary. Put the beef, onion and tomatoes into the slow cooker pot, then stir in the curry paste, cumin seeds, chillies, ginger and garlic. Sprinkle the coconut over the top, then stir in the boiling stock.

Cover with the lid and cook on high for 30 minutes. Reduce the heat and cook on low for 7–9 hours, or set to auto for 7½–9½ hours. Stir the minced beef well to break up into small pieces, then mix in the peas and cook on high for 30 minutes or until cooked through.

When almost ready to serve, sprinkle with the chopped coriander and extra sliced chillies. Serve with warmed chapattis and a tomato and red onion salad, if liked.

FOR KEEMA ALOO, make up the recipe as above, replacing the minced beef with 500 g (1 lb) minced lamb. Stir in 200 g (7 oz) potatoes, cut into small dice, after adding the garlic. At the end of cooking, replace the peas with 125 g (4 oz) rinsed and drained, torn spinach. Serve sprinkled with 4 finely sliced spring onions and a little chopped coriander.

SPICY TURKEY TORTILLAS ♥

Serves **4**
Preparation time **30 minutes**
Cooking temperature **low**
Cooking time **8–10 hours**

low-calorie cooking oil spray
400 g (13 oz) **minced turkey breast**
1 **onion**, chopped
2 **garlic cloves**, finely chopped
1 teaspoon **crushed dried red chillies**
1 teaspoon **cumin seeds**, crushed
1 teaspoon **mild paprika**
400 g (13 oz) can **chopped tomatoes**
200 g (7 oz) can **red kidney
    beans**, drained
150 ml (¼ pint) **chicken stock**
1 tablespoon **tomato purée**
1 **red pepper**, cored, deseeded
    and diced

TO SERVE
4 x 20 cm (8 inch) **soft tortilla wraps**,
    40 g (1½ oz) each
50 g (2 oz) **salad leaves**
4 tablespoons **0% fat Greek yogurt**
40 g (1½ oz) **reduced-fat Cheddar
    cheese**, grated
torn **coriander leaves**

Preheat the slow cooker if necessary. Spray a large frying pan with a little low-calorie cooking oil spray and place over a high heat until hot. Add the minced turkey and onion and fry for 4–5 minutes, stirring and breaking up the mince with a wooden spoon, until it is just beginning to brown.

Stir in the garlic, chillies, cumin and paprika, then add the tomatoes, kidney beans, stock and tomato purée. Add the red pepper, season to taste and bring to the boil. Transfer to the slow cooker pot, cover and cook on low for 8–10 hours until the turkey is cooked through.

Warm the tortillas in a hot dry frying pan for 1–2 minutes each side, then place on 4 serving plates. Spoon the spicy turkey on top, then divide the salad leaves between each and add a spoonful of yogurt, a little Cheddar and some torn coriander leaves. Serve immediately.

FOR SPICY TURKEY THATCH, follow the recipe above to make and cook the spicy turkey mixture. Cut 750 g (1½ lb) potatoes into chunks and cook in a saucepan of boiling water for 15 minutes or until soft. Drain and mash with 4 tablespoons vegetable stock, then season to taste. Place the turkey mixture in a shallow heatproof dish and spoon the mashed potato on top. Rough up the top with a fork, then brush with ½ beaten egg. Brown under a preheated hot grill before serving.

THAI FISH CURRY ♥

Serves 4
Preparation time **15 minutes**
Cooking temperature **low**
Cooking time **2–3 hours**

1 **onion**, quartered
15 g (½ oz) **coriander leaves** and
    stems, plus extra to garnish
2.5 cm (1 inch) piece of **fresh root
    ginger**, peeled and sliced
1 **lemon grass stalk**, thickly sliced,
    or 1 teaspoon **lemon grass paste**
200 ml (7 fl oz) **light coconut milk**
200 ml (7 fl oz) **fish stock**
1 teaspoon **Thai fish sauce**
1 tablespoon **Thai red curry paste**
4 **salmon steaks**, 500 g (1 lb) in total
low calorie cooking oil spray
400 g (13 oz) **ready-prepared mixed
    stir-fry vegetables**
grated rind and juice of 1 **lime**

Preheat the slow cooker if necessary. Place the onion, coriander, ginger and lemon grass in a food processor and blitz until finely chopped. Transfer to a medium saucepan and stir in the coconut milk, stock, fish sauce and curry paste. This mixture can be chilled until ready to use.

Arrange the salmon steaks in the base of the slow cooker pot. Bring the coconut mixture to the boil, stirring, then pour over the salmon. Cover and cook on low for 2–3 hours until the salmon flakes easily when pressed in the centre with a small knife.

When almost ready to serve, spray a large frying pan with a little low-calorie cooking oil spray and place over a high heat until hot. Add the vegetables and cook for 2–3 minutes until piping hot.

Break the salmon into large flakes and stir the lime rind and juice into the curry. Spoon into bowls and top with the vegetables and a little extra coriander.

FOR THAI VEGETABLE CURRY, follow the recipe above to make the sauce, using 200 ml (7 fl oz) vegetable stock instead of the fish stock, and omitting the fish sauce if serving the curry to vegetarians. Place a 200 g (7 oz) can bamboo shoots in the slow cooker pot with 175 g (6 oz) baby corn cobs, 150 g (5 oz) whole cherry tomatoes and 1 diced courgette. Pour over the sauce, cook and serve with stir-fried vegetables as above.

TANDOORI CHICKEN ♥

Serves **4**
Preparation time **20 minutes, plus**
  overnight marinating
Cooking temperature **high**
Cooking time **3–4 hours**

150 ml (¼ pint) **0% fat Greek yogurt**
3.5 cm (1½ inch) piece of **fresh root**
  ginger, peeled and grated
3 tablespoons chopped
  coriander leaves
3 teaspoons **medium-hot**
  curry powder
½ teaspoon **ground turmeric**
1 teaspoon **paprika**
625 g (1¼ lb) **boneless, skinless**
  chicken thighs, cut into chunks
juice of ½ **lemon**
low-calorie cooking oil spray
salt and **pepper**

TO SERVE
50 g (2 oz) **mixed green salad leaves**
¼ **cucumber**, diced
small handful of **coriander leaves**
juice of ½ **lemon**

Place the yogurt in a bowl and stir in the ginger, coriander, curry powder, turmeric and paprika. Toss the chicken with the lemon juice, season lightly and stir into the yogurt mixture until evenly coated. Cover with clingfilm and marinate in the refrigerator overnight.

Preheat the slow cooker if necessary. Stir the chicken mixture, then transfer to the slow cooker pot in an even layer. Cover and cook on high for 3–4 hours or until the chicken is tender and cooked through. (The yogurt will separate during cooking, but this will not affect the taste.)

Spray a large frying pan with a little low-calorie cooking oil spray and place over a high heat until hot. Transfer the chicken to the frying pan a few pieces at a time until all the chicken is in the pan and cook for 2–3 minutes, turning once, until golden on both sides. This step can be omitted if you are short of time.

Toss the salad leaves, cucumber and coriander leaves with the lemon juice arrange on serving plates and top with the chicken.

FOR GARLICKY TANDOORI CHICKEN, add 3 finely chopped garlic cloves to the yogurt and spice mixture and continue as above.

TOMATO & SQUASH CURRY

Serves **4**
Preparation time **20 minutes**
Cooking temperature **low**
Cooking time **5–6 hours**

25 g (1 oz) **butter**
1 **onion**, chopped
½ **butternut squash**, about 400 g
   (13 oz), peeled, deseeded
   and diced
2 **garlic cloves**, finely chopped
3.5 cm (1½ inch) piece of **fresh root**
   ginger, peeled and finely chopped
½–1 **mild red chilli**, to taste,
   deseeded and finely chopped
4 tablespoons **korma curry paste**
150 ml (¼ pint) **vegetable stock**
8 **plum tomatoes**, about 625 g (1¼ lb)
   in total, halved
50 g (2 oz) **creamed**
   coconut, crumbled
salt and **pepper**
roughly chopped **coriander**,
   to garnish

Preheat the slow cooker if necessary. Heat the butter in a large frying pan, add the onion and fry until softened.

Stir in the butternut squash, garlic, ginger and chilli and cook for 2–3 minutes. Mix in the curry paste and cook for 1 minute to release the curry flavour. Stir in the stock and bring to the boil.

Transfer the mixture to the slow cooker pot. Arrange the tomatoes, cut side uppermost, in a single layer on top of the squash, then sprinkle with the coconut and a little salt and pepper. Cover with the lid and cook on low for 5–6 hours or until the squash is tender and the tomatoes are soft but still holding their shape.

Spoon into bowls, sprinkle with roughly chopped coriander and serve with plain or Quick Pilau Rice (*see* below) and warmed naan bread, if liked.

FOR QUICK PILAU RICE TO ACCOMPANY THE CURRY, rinse 225 g (7½ oz) basmati rice until clear under running water, then drain. Heat 15 g (½ oz) butter and 1 tablespoon sunflower oil in a large frying pan, add 1 chopped onion and fry until softened. Stir in 1 dried red chilli, 1 cinnamon stick, halved, 1 teaspoon cumin seeds, 1 bay leaf, 6 crushed cardamom pods, ½ teaspoon ground turmeric and some salt. Pour on 475 ml (16 fl oz) boiling water, cover with a lid and simmer gently for 10 minutes. Take off the heat and leave for 5–8 minutes – don't be tempted to lift the lid until ready to serve – then fluff up with a fork and spoon on to plates.

FRAGRANT SPICED CHICKEN WITH CHILLI

Serves **4–5**
Preparation time **15 minutes**
Cooking temperature **high**
Cooking time **5¼–6¼ hours**

1.5 kg (3 lb) **oven-ready chicken**
1 **onion**, chopped
200 g (7 oz) **carrots**, sliced
7 cm (3 inch) piece of **fresh root
    ginger**, peeled and sliced
2 **garlic cloves**, sliced
1 large **mild red chilli**, halved
3 large **star anise**
4 tablespoons **soy sauce**
4 tablespoons **rice vinegar**
1 tablespoon **light muscovado sugar**
900 ml (1½ pints) boiling **water**
small bunch of **coriander**
200 g (7 oz) **dried egg noodles**
75 g (3 oz) **mangetout**, thickly sliced
2 **pak choi**, about 150 g (5 oz),
    thickly sliced
salt and **pepper**

Preheat the slow cooker if necessary. Put the chicken, breast side down, into the slow cooker pot. Add the onion, carrots, ginger, garlic, chilli and star anise and spoon over the soy sauce, vinegar and sugar.

Pour over the measurement boiling water. Cut the coriander leaves from the stems, then add the stems to the pot, reserving the leaves. Season, cover and cook on high for 5–6 hours or until the juices run clear when the thickest parts of the leg and breast are pierced with a sharp knife.

When almost ready to serve, cook the noodles according to packet instructions. Lift the chicken out of the slow cooker pot, put on to a plate, cover with foil and keep hot. Add the mangetout and pak choi to the slow cooker pot, replace the lid and cook, still on high, for about 10 minutes or until just wilted.

Carve the chicken into bite-sized pieces. Drain the noodles and divide between 4 bowls. Top with the chicken and the reserved coriander leaves, chopped, then ladle over the hot broth.

FOR ITALIAN SPICED CHICKEN WITH PESTO, put the chicken into the pot with the onion, carrots and garlic only and add 1 sliced fennel bulb and 1 sliced lemon. Continue as above, replacing the coriander with basil. When the chicken is removed, add the mangetout, 3 chopped tomatoes, 150 g (5 oz) chopped purple sprouting broccoli and 2 tablespoons pesto, cover and cook for 5–10 minutes. Omit the pak choi. Cook a 250 g (8 oz) pack fresh tagliatelle in a large saucepan of lightly salted boiling water according to the packet instructions until just tender. Drain and continue as above.

LAMB ROGAN JOSH ♥

Serves **4**
Preparation time **15 minutes**
Cooking temperature **low**
Cooking time **8–10 hours**

25 g (1 oz) **butter**
750 g (1½ lb) **lamb fillet**, sliced
2 **onions**, chopped
3 **garlic cloves**, finely chopped
2.5 cm (1 inch) piece of **fresh root
    ginger**, peeled and finely chopped
1 teaspoon **ground turmeric**
2 teaspoons **ground coriander**
2 teaspoons **cumin seeds**,
    roughly crushed
2 teaspoons **garam masala**
½ teaspoon **crushed dried
    red chillies**
2 tablespoons **plain flour**
400 g (13 oz) can **chopped tomatoes**
300 ml (½ pint) **lamb stock**
4 tablespoons **double cream**

TO GARNISH
small bunch of **coriander**, leaves torn
shredded **red onion**

Preheat the slow cooker if necessary. Heat the butter in a frying pan, add the lamb a few pieces at a time until all the meat is in the pan, then fry, stirring, over a high heat until browned. Lift out of the pan with a slotted spoon and add to the slow cooker pot.

Add the onions to the pan and fry, stirring, for 5 minutes or until softened and just beginning to turn golden. Stir in the garlic, ginger, spices and chillies and cook for 1 minute. Mix in the flour, then add the tomatoes and stock. Bring to the boil, stirring.

Pour the tomato mixture over the lamb, cover with the lid and cook on low for 8–10 hours or until the lamb is tender. Stir in the cream, garnish with coriander leaves and serve with Pilau Rice (*see* below) and naan bread, if liked.

FOR PILAU RICE TO ACCOMPANY THE CURRY, rinse 225 g (7½ oz) basmati rice in a sieve several times, drain then cook in cold water for 15 minutes. Heat 15 g (½ oz) butter in a saucepan, add 1 finely chopped onion and fry for 3 minutes. Add 5 lightly crushed cardamom pods, 5 cloves, ½ cinnamon stick, ½ teaspoon ground turmeric and ½ teaspoon salt. Cook for 1 minute. Drain the rice, add to the pan and cook for 1 minute. Pour in 475 ml (16 fl oz) boiling water, bring back to the boil, cover tightly and simmer gently for 10 minutes. Turn off the heat but do not remove the lid. Leave to stand for 8–10 minutes. Fluff up with a fork and serve.

NEW ORLEANS CHICKEN GUMBO

Serves **4**
Preparation time **20 minutes**
Cooking temperature **low** and **high**
Cooking time **8¼–10¼ hours**

2 tablespoons **olive oil**
500 g (1 lb) **boneless, skinless chicken thighs**, cubed
75 g (3 oz) **ready-diced chorizo**
75 g (3 oz) **smoked streaky bacon rashers**, diced
1 **onion**, sliced
2 **garlic cloves**, chopped
2 tablespoons **plain flour**
600 ml (1 pint) **chicken stock**
2 **bay leaves**
2 **thyme sprigs**
¼–½ teaspoon **cayenne pepper**, to taste
3 **celery sticks**, sliced
½ each of 3 different **coloured peppers**, cored, deseeded and sliced
125 g (4 oz) **okra**, thickly sliced (optional)
salt
chopped **parsley**, to garnish
boiled **rice**, to serve

Preheat the slow cooker if necessary. Heat the oil in a large frying pan, add the chicken a few pieces at time until all the pieces are in the pan, then add the chorizo and bacon and fry, stirring, until the chicken is golden. Lift out of the pan with a slotted spoon and transfer to the slow cooker.

Add the onion to the frying pan and fry until softened. Mix in the garlic, then stir in the flour. Gradually mix in the stock and add the herbs and a little salt and cayenne to taste. Bring to the boil, stirring.

Mix the celery and different coloured peppers into the chicken, then pour over the hot onion mixture. Cover with the lid and cook on low for 8–10 hours or until the chicken is cooked through.

Stir the okra into the chicken gumbo, if using. Replace the lid and cook on high for 15 minutes or until the okra has just softened. Stir once more, then sprinkle with chopped parsley. Ladle into shallow rice-lined bowls and serve with a soup spoon and fork.

FOR CRAB GUMBO SOUP, omit the chicken and make up the gumbo as above, replacing the chicken stock with 600 ml (1 pint) fish stock and adding 2 sliced carrots, 2 diced sweet potatoes and 1 diced courgette to the slow cooker pot with the celery and peppers. Add 200 g (7 oz) large cooked peeled king prawns, thawed if frozen, rinsed with cold water and drained, and a 200 g (7 oz) drained can white crab meat to the pot with the okra, if using, and cook on high for 20–30 minutes or until the fish is piping hot. Serve with rice.

CAULIFLOWER & SPINACH BALTI

Serves **4**
Preparation time **10 minutes**
Cooking temperature **low**
Cooking time **5¼–6¼ hours**

1 tablespoon **sunflower oil**
1 **onion**, chopped
540 g (1 lb 3 oz) can **balti curry sauce**
1 large **cauliflower**, trimmed and cut into large pieces,
   about 750 g (1½ lb) prepared weight
410 g (13½ oz) can **green lentils**, drained
150 g (5 oz) **spinach**, rinsed, drained and torn into pieces

Preheat the slow cooker if necessary. Heat the oil in
a large frying pan, add the onion and fry, stirring, for
5 minutes or until softened. Add the curry sauce and
bring to the boil.

Put the cauliflower and lentils into the slow cooker pot,
then pour over the hot sauce. Cover and cook on low
for 5–6 hours or until the cauliflower is tender.

Stir the cauliflower and lentil mixture and sprinkle the
spinach on top. Replace the lid and cook, still on low,
for 10–15 minutes or until the spinach has just wilted.
Spoon into bowls and serve with warmed naan bread,
if liked.

FOR MUSHROOM & SWEET POTATO BALTI, make up
the sauce as above. Replace the cauliflower with 375 g
(12 oz) quartered cup mushrooms and 375 g (12 oz)
diced sweet potatoes and put into the slow cooker pot
with the lentils. Pour over the sauce, cover with the
lid and cook on low for 6–7 hours or until the sweet
potatoes are tender. Add the spinach and cook and
serve as above.

CHICKEN & SWEET POTATO BALTI

Serves **4**
Preparation time **15 minutes**
Cooking temperature **high** and **low**
Cooking time **6–7 hours**

6 boneless, skinless **chicken thighs**, about 500 g
   (1 lb) in total, cubed
1 **onion**, sliced
375 g (12 oz) **sweet potatoes**, cut into 2 cm
   (¾ inch) cubes
2 **garlic cloves**, finely chopped
425 g (14 oz) jar **balti curry sauce**
roughly chopped **coriander**, to garnish (optional)

Preheat the slow cooker if necessary. Arrange the
chicken, onion and sweet potatoes in the base of the
slow cooker pot in an even layer. Sprinkle with the
chopped garlic.

Bring the curry sauce just to the boil in a small
saucepan or the microwave. Pour into the slow cooker
pot in an even layer. Cover with the lid and cook on
high for 30 minutes. Reduce the heat and cook on low
for 5½–6½ hours, or set to auto for 6–7 hours, until the
chicken is cooked through and the sauce piping hot.

Stir well, then sprinkle with roughly chopped coriander,
if liked. Spoon into bowls and serve with warmed naan
bread, if liked.

FOR HARISSA BAKED CHICKEN WITH SWEET POTATO,
prepare the chicken and vegetables as above. Replace
the balti curry sauce with a 400 g (13 oz) can chopped
tomatoes and 2 teaspoons harissa. Continue as above.

SPICED DATE & CHICKPEA PILAF

Serves **4**
Preparation time **15 minutes**
Cooking temperature **low**
Cooking time **3–4 hours**

1 tablespoon **olive oil**
1 **onion**, chopped
1–2 **garlic cloves**, finely chopped
3.5 cm (1½ inch) piece of **fresh root ginger**, peeled and finely chopped
1 teaspoon **ground turmeric**
1 teaspoon **ground cumin**, plus extra to garnish
1 teaspoon **ground coriander**
200 g (7 oz) **easy-cook brown long-grain rice**
400 g (13 oz) can **chickpeas**, drained
75 g (3 oz) **ready-chopped pitted dates**
1 litre (1¾ pints) **vegetable stock**
salt and **pepper**

ONION GARNISH
1 tablespoon **olive oil**
1 **onion**, thinly sliced
150 ml (¼ pint) **Greek yogurt**
chopped **coriander**

Preheat the slow cooker if necessary. Heat the oil in a large frying pan, add the onion and fry, stirring, for 5 minutes or until softened and just beginning to turn golden.

Stir in the garlic, ginger and ground spices and cook for 1 minute. Add the rice, chickpeas, dates, stock and a little salt and pepper and bring to the boil, stirring. Pour into the slow cooker pot, cover with the lid and cook on low for 3–4 hours or until the rice is tender and almost all the stock has been absorbed.

When almost ready to serve, make the onion garnish. Heat the oil in a frying pan, add the sliced onion and fry over a medium heat, stirring, until crisp and golden. Stir the pilaf, spoon into bowls and top with a spoonful of the yogurt, a little extra cumin, the onions and a little chopped coriander.

FOR CHICKEN & ALMOND PILAF, add 500 g (1 lb) diced boneless, skinless chicken thighs to the frying pan with the onion. Continue as above, omitting the dates. To serve, replace the onion garnish with 40 g (1½ oz) flaked almonds, fried in the oil until golden, and a little chopped mint, if liked.

MEDITERRANEAN

VEGETABLE MOUSSAKA ♥

Serves **4**
Preparation time **25 minutes**
Cooking temperature **low**
Cooking time **6¾–9¼ hours**

low-calorie cooking oil spray
1 **onion**, roughly chopped
1 large **aubergine**, sliced
2 **garlic cloves**, finely chopped
1 **red pepper**, cored, deseeded and
   cut into chunks
1 **yellow pepper**, cored, deseeded
   and cut into chunks
2 large **courgettes**, thickly sliced
500 g (1 lb) **passata**
150 ml (¼ pint) **vegetable stock**
75 g (3 oz) **dried Puy lentils**, rinsed
   and drained
leaves from 3 **rosemary
   sprigs**, chopped
1 teaspoon **granular sweetener**
salt and **pepper**

TOPPING
250 ml (8 fl oz) **0% fat Greek yogurt**
3 **eggs**
25 g (1 oz) **Parmesan cheese**,
   freshly grated

Preheat the slow cooker if necessary. Spray a large frying pan with a little low-calorie cooking oil spray and place over a high heat until hot. Add the onion and aubergine and fry for 4–5 minutes, stirring, until just beginning to brown. Add the garlic, peppers and courgettes and cook for 2 minutes more, then add the passata, stock and lentils.

Add the rosemary and sweetener and season to taste. Bring to the boil, stirring, then transfer to the slow cooker pot. Cover and cook on low for 6–8 hours until the lentils are tender.

Mix the yogurt, eggs and a little pepper together in a bowl until smooth. Stir the vegetable mixture, then smooth the surface with the back of a spoon. Pour the yogurt mixture over the top in an even layer and sprinkle with the Parmesan. Cover and continue cooking for 45 minutes–1¼ hours until the custard has set.

Lift the pot out of the housing using oven gloves, then place under a preheated hot grill for 4–5 minutes until the top is golden. Serve with a green salad, if liked.

FOR PENNE WITH MEDITERRANEAN VEGETABLES, make and cook the vegetable and lentil mixture as above. Cook 90 g (3¼ oz) dried wholewheat penne in a saucepan of lightly salted boiling water according to the packet instructions until just tender. Drain and stir into the cooked vegetables, spoon into shallow dishes and sprinkle with 25 g (1 oz) freshly grated Parmesan cheese.

TOMATO BRAISED SQUID WITH CHORIZO

Serves **4**
Preparation time **20 minutes**
Cooking temperature **low**
Cooking time **3½–5½ hours**

625 g (1¼ lb) **prepared squid
   tubes**, chilled
1 **onion**, thinly sliced
125 g (4 oz) **ready-diced chorizo**
125 g (4 oz) **cup mushrooms**, sliced
1 **red pepper**, cored, deseeded
   and sliced
2 **garlic cloves**, finely chopped
leaves from 2–3 **rosemary sprigs**
1 tablespoon **tomato purée**
1 teaspoon **caster sugar**
400 g (13 oz) can
   chopped tomatoes
100 ml (3½ fl oz) **red wine**
1 tablespoon **cornflour**
salt and **pepper**
chopped **parsley**, to garnish

Preheat the slow cooker if necessary. Rinse the squid inside and out, pulling out the tentacles and reserving. Drain and slice the tubes. Put the tentacles in a bowl, cover with clingfilm and chill in the refrigerator until required.

Put the onion, chorizo, mushrooms and red pepper into the slow cooker pot. Add the garlic, rosemary, tomato purée and sugar, then stir in the sliced squid.

Pour the tomatoes and wine into a saucepan and bring to the boil or heat in the microwave. Add a little salt and pepper, then pour into the slow cooker pot and stir well. Cover with the lid and cook on low for 3–5 hours or until the squid is tender.

Put the cornflour in a small bowl with a little cold water and mix to a smooth paste. Stir into the slow cooker pot, add the squid tentacles, then replace the lid and cook, still on low, for 30 minutes. Spoon into bowls and sprinkle with chopped parsley. Serve with thickly sliced bread or rice, if liked.

FOR TOMATO-BRAISED SQUID WITH RED ONION, replace the onion, mushrooms and chorizo with 2 large thinly sliced red onions and put in the slow cooker pot with the red pepper, garlic, tomato purée and sugar, adding 2 bay leaves instead of the rosemary. Add the squid and continue as above.

MOUSSAKA

Serves **4**
Preparation time **30 minutes**
Cooking temperature **low**
Cooking time **8¾–11¼ hours**

4 tablespoons **olive oil**
1 large **aubergine**, thinly sliced
500 g (1 lb) **minced lamb**
1 **onion**, chopped
2 **garlic cloves**, finely chopped
1 tablespoon **plain flour**
400 g (13 oz) can **chopped tomatoes**
200 ml (7 fl oz) **lamb stock**
1 teaspoon **ground cinnamon**
¼ teaspoon grated **nutmeg**
1 tablespoon **tomato purée**
salt and **pepper**

TOPPING
3 **eggs**
250 ml (8 fl oz) **natural yogurt**
75 g (3 oz) **feta cheese**, grated
pinch of grated **nutmeg**

Preheat the slow cooker if necessary. Heat half the oil in a frying pan and fry the aubergine slices in batches, adding more oil as needed until they have all been fried and are softened and lightly browned on both sides. Drain and transfer to a plate.

Add the minced lamb and onion to the frying pan and dry-fry, stirring and breaking up the lamb with a wooden spoon, until evenly browned. Stir in the garlic and flour, then mix in the tomatoes, stock, spices, tomato purée and a little salt and pepper. Bring to the boil, stirring.

Spoon the lamb mixture into the slow cooker pot and arrange the aubergine slices on top, overlapping. Cover with the lid and cook on low for 8–10 hours.

Make the custard topping. Mix together the eggs, yogurt, feta and nutmeg and spoon over the top of the aubergine. Replace the lid and cook, still on low, for ¾–1¼ hours or until set. Lift the pot out of the housing using oven gloves and brown under a preheated hot grill. Serve with salad, if liked.

FOR GREEK SHEPHERD'S PIE, prepare the mince, top with the fried aubergine slices and cook as above. Omit the custard topping and instead cut 750 g (1½ lb) potatoes into chunks and cook in a saucepan of boiling water for 15 minutes or until soft. Drain and mash with 3 tablespoons Greek yogurt and some salt and pepper. Lift the pot out of the housing using oven gloves, spoon the mash over the aubergine, dot with 25 g (1 oz) butter and brown under a preheated hot grill.

SLOW-BRAISED PORK WITH RATATOUILLE

Serves **4**
Preparation time **20 minutes**
Cooking temperature **high**
Cooking time **7–9 hours**

1 tablespoon **olive oil**
1 **onion**, chopped
1 **red pepper**, cored, deseeded and
    cut into chunks
1 **yellow pepper**, cored, deseeded
    and cut into chunks
375 g (12 oz) **courgettes**, cut
    into chunks
2 **garlic cloves**, finely chopped
400 g (13 oz) can **chopped tomatoes**
150 ml (¼ pint) **red wine** or
    chicken stock
1 tablespoon **cornflour**
leaves from 2–3 **rosemary sprigs**
875 g (1¾ lb) piece of **thick-end belly
    pork**, rind and any string removed
salt and **pepper**
mashed potato, to serve

Preheat the slow cooker if necessary. Heat the oil in a frying pan, add the onion and fry, stirring, for 5 minutes or until just beginning to turn golden.

Add the peppers, courgettes and garlic and fry for 2 minutes, then mix in the tomatoes and the wine or stock. Mix the cornflour to a smooth paste with a little cold water, then stir into the pan with the rosemary leaves and some seasoning. Bring to the boil, stirring.

Tip half the mixture into the slow cooker pot, add the unrolled belly pork and cover with the rest of the vegetable mixture. Cover with the lid and cook on high for 7–9 hours or until the pork is almost falling apart. If you like your sauces thick, ladle it out of the pot into a saucepan and boil for 5 minutes to reduce down. Cut the pork into 4 pieces, then spoon into shallow dishes and serve with mashed potato and the tomato sauce.

FOR BRAISED CHICKEN WITH RATATOUILLE, fry 4 chicken thigh and leg joints in 1 tablespoon olive oil until browned on both sides. Drain and transfer to the slow cooker pot. Make up the ratatouille as above, spoon it over the chicken and cook on high for 5–6 hours or until the chicken is tender and cooked through.

SAUSAGE TAGLIATELLE

Serves **4**
Preparation time **25 minutes**
Cooking temperature **low**
Cooking time **8–10 hours**

1 tablespoon **sunflower oil**
8 **chilli** or **spicy sausages**
1 **onion**, chopped
150 g (5 oz) **cup mushrooms**, sliced
2 **garlic cloves**, finely chopped
400 g (13 oz) can **chopped tomatoes**
150 ml (¼ pint) **beef stock**
250 g (8 oz) **dried tagliatelle**
salt and **pepper**

TO SERVE
torn **basil leaves**
freshly grated **Parmesan**
cheese (optional)

Preheat the slow cooker if necessary. Heat the oil in a large frying pan, add the sausages and fry, turning until browned but not cooked through. Transfer to the slow cooker pot with tongs.

Drain off the excess fat from the pan to leave 2 teaspoons, then add the onion and fry until softened. Mix in the mushrooms and garlic and fry for 1–2 minutes.

Stir in the chopped tomatoes, stock and a little salt and pepper and bring to the boil, stirring. Pour the mixture over the sausages, cover with the lid and cook on low for 8–10 hours or until cooked through.

When almost ready to serve, cook the tagliatelle in a large saucepan of lightly salted boiling water according to the packet instructions until just tender, then drain. Lift the sausages out of the slow cooker pot and slice thickly, then return to the pot with the pasta and mix together. Sprinkle with torn basil leaves and serve with freshly grated Parmesan and a green salad, if liked.

FOR CHICKEN & CHORIZO TAGLIATELLE, omit the sausages and fry 500 g (1 lb) diced boneless chicken thighs in 1 tablespoon olive oil until golden. Drain and transfer to the slow cooker pot. Continue as above, adding 100 g (3½ oz) diced chorizo sausage to the frying pan with the onions and replacing the beef stock with 150 ml (¼ pint) chicken stock.

HOT SPANISH BEANS

Serves **4**
Preparation time **10 minutes**
Cooking temperature **high**
Cooking time **4–5 hours**

125 g (4 oz) **chorizo**, sliced
1 **red onion**, chopped
2 x 400 g (13 oz) cans **haricot beans**, drained
375 g (12 oz) **cherry tomatoes**
2 **garlic cloves**, finely chopped
leaves from 2–3 **rosemary sprigs**
350 g (11½ oz) pack **frankfurters**, chilled, drained and thickly sliced
100 g (3½ oz) **marinated mixed olives** (optional)
200 ml (7 fl oz) boiling **vegetable stock**
1 tablespoon **tomato purée**
salt and **pepper**

Preheat the slow cooker if necessary. Put the chorizo, onion and haricot beans into the slow cooker pot, add the tomatoes, garlic and rosemary and mix together. Arrange the frankfurters and olives, if using, on the top.

Mix the boiling stock with the tomato purée and a little salt and pepper, then pour into the slow cooker pot. Cover with the lid and cook on high for 4–5 hours. Stir the beans, then spoon into bowls. Serve with hot peppered foccacia or garlic bread and a green leafy salad, if liked.

FOR MUSTARD BEANS, put the onion, beans, tomatoes and garlic in the slow cooker pot, omitting the chorizo, rosemary and olives. Add 1 cored, deseeded and diced red pepper. Mix the stock with 2 tablespoons each tomato purée and Worcestershire sauce, 1 tablespoon Dijon mustard, ½ teaspoon smoked paprika and salt and pepper. Pour over the beans and add the frankfurters. Continue as above.

CHICKEN AVGOLEMONO

Serves **4**
Preparation time **30 minutes**
Cooking temperature **high** and **low**
Cooking time **6–8 hours**

8 **boneless, skinless chicken thighs**,
    about 700 g (1 lb 6 oz) in total,
    each cut into 3 or 4 pieces
1 **onion**, thinly sliced
2–3 **oregano** or **basil sprigs**
450 ml (¾ pint) boiling **chicken stock**
grated rind and juice of 1 **lemon**
300 g (10 oz) **dried macaroni** or **orzo**
2 **eggs**
2 **egg yolks**
4 tablespoons chopped **parsley**, plus
    extra to garnish (optional)
salt and **pepper**
lemon rind curls, to garnish (optional)

Preheat the slow cooker if necessary. Put the chicken, onion and herbs into the slow cooker pot. Mix the boiling stock, lemon rind and juice and salt and pepper together, then pour over the chicken.

Cover with the lid and cook on high for 30 minutes. Reduce the heat and cook on low for 5½–7½ hours, or set to auto for 6–8 hours, until the chicken is cooked through and tender. When almost ready to serve, cook the pasta in a large saucepan of lightly salted boiling water according to the packet instructions until just tender, then drain.

Meanwhile, drain the stock from the slow cooker pot into a second large saucepan and boil for 5 minutes until reduced by one-third or to about 200 ml (7 fl oz). Whisk the whole eggs and egg yolks in a bowl, then gradually whisk in 2 ladlefuls of the stock until smooth. Pour into the reduced stock, then whisk over a gentle heat until thickened slightly. Stir in the parsley.

Pour the sauce over the chicken. Spoon the pasta into bowls and top with the chicken. Sprinkle with lemon rind curls and extra chopped parsley, if liked.

FOR SALMON AVGOLEMONO, lower a 500 g (1 lb) thick piece of salmon fillet into the slow cooker pot over a double-thickness strip of foil, add 6 thinly sliced spring onions and the oregano or basil. Pour over 350 ml (12 fl oz) boiling fish stock mixed with the lemon rind and juice as above and salt and pepper. Cover and cook on low for 2½–3 hours or until the fish flakes easily when pressed in the centre with a knife. Cook the pasta and make the sauce as above. Lift the salmon out with the foil, skin and flake into large chunks, then toss with the sauce and pasta.

FEIJOADA HAM ♥

Serves **4**
Preparation time **20 minutes**
Cooking temperature **high**
Cooking time **5–6 hours**

1 **onion**, chopped
2 **celery sticks**, thickly sliced
150 g (5 oz) **carrots**, diced
375 g (12 oz) can **black
    beans**, drained
1 **red chilli**, halved and deseeded
2 **thyme sprigs**
pared rind of 1 **orange**
500 g (1 lb) **unsmoked gammon
    joint**, trimmed of fat
1 teaspoon **mild paprika**
½ teaspoon **ground allspice**
450 ml (¾ pint) hot **vegetable stock**
salt and **pepper**
4 tablespoons chopped **parsley**,
    to garnish
boiled **rice**, to serve (optional)

Preheat the slow cooker if necessary. Place the onion, celery and carrot in the slow cooker pot, then add the beans, chilli, thyme and orange rind. Nestle the gammon joint in the centre.

Stir the paprika and allspice into the hot stock, then season to taste and pour over the gammon joint. Spoon some of the orange rind and thyme on top of the joint, cover and cook on high for 5–6 hours until the gammon is very tender.

When almost ready to serve, cook the rice in a saucepan of lightly salted boiling water according to the packet instructions until tender.

Cut the gammon into pieces, then spoon into shallow bowls with the beans, vegetables and sauce. Sprinkle with the parsley and serve with rice, if liked.

FOR FEIJOADA CHICKEN, substitute a 1.35 kg (2 lb 10 oz) oven-ready chicken for the gammon joint and follow the recipe above. Cook on high for 5–6 hours or until the chicken is thoroughly cooked and the meat juices run clear when the thickest parts of the leg and breast are pierced with a sharp knife.

RIOJA-BRAISED LAMB WITH OLIVES

Serves **4**
Preparation time **20 minutes**
Cooking temperature **high**
Cooking time **5–6 hours**

2 tablespoons **olive oil**
4 **lamb shanks**, 1.5 kg (3 lb) in total
2 **red onions**, cut into wedges
4 large **garlic cloves**, halved
300 ml (½ pint) **Rioja red wine** or
   lamb stock
400 g (13 oz) can
   chopped tomatoes
1 tablespoon **redcurrant jelly**
3 **rosemary sprigs**
150 g (5 oz) **mixed pitted olives**
salt and **pepper**

Preheat the slow cooker if necessary. Heat 1 tablespoon of the oil in a large frying pan, season the lamb shanks, then add them to the pan and brown on all sides. Lift them out of the pan and put them in the slow cooker pot with the meatiest parts downwards.

Add the remaining oil and onion wedges to the pan and fry for 3–4 minutes until just beginning to colour. Add the garlic, wine or stock, tomatoes, redcurrant jelly and rosemary. Season with salt and pepper and bring to the boil, stirring.

Scatter the olives over the lamb, then pour over the hot onion mixture. Cover with the lid and cook on high for 5–6 hours until the lamb is very tender.

When ready to serve, pour the liquid out of the slow cooker into a saucepan and boil for 10 minutes until reduced by half. Put the lamb into shallow bowls lined with some runny polenta flavoured with butter and Parmesan cheese or mashed potato, if liked, spoon over the onions and olives, then serve with the Rioja sauce.

FOR RIOJA-BRAISED CHICKEN WITH OLIVES, substitute a 1.5 kg (3 lb) oven-ready chicken for the lamb shanks and cook as above, with the chicken cooked breast-side down in the liquid, until the chicken is cooked through and the juices run clear when the thickest parts of the leg and breast are pierced with a sharp knife.

BALSAMIC TOMATOES WITH SPAGHETTI

Serves **4**
Preparation time **10 minutes**
Cooking temperature **high**
Cooking time **3–4 hours**

1 tablespoon **olive oil**, for oiling
750 g (1½ lb) **plum tomatoes**, halved
4 tablespoons **white wine**
4 teaspoons **good-quality**
    balsamic vinegar
375 g (12 oz) **dried spaghetti**
salt and **pepper**
basil leaves, to garnish
Parmesan cheese shavings, to serve

Preheat the slow cooker if necessary. Brush the oil over the base of the slow cooker pot, add the tomatoes, cut side down, drizzle over the wine and vinegar and add a little salt and pepper. Cover with the lid and cook on high for 3–4 hours or until the tomatoes are tender.

When almost ready to serve, cook the spaghetti in a large saucepan of lightly salted boiling water according to the packet instructions until just tender. Drain and mix into the sauce. Spoon the pasta into bowls and sprinkle with basil leaves and Parmesan shavings.

FOR PESTO BAKED TOMATOES, oil the base of the slow cooker pot as above, sprinkling with 2 finely chopped garlic cloves before adding the tomatoes. Drizzle with the wine and 1 tablespoon pesto, omitting the vinegar. Cook and serve as above.

PHEASANT WITH PANCETTA

Serves **4**
Preparation time **35 minutes**
Cooking temperature **low**
Cooking time **2½–3 hours**

4 **pheasant breasts**, about 600 g
    (1 lb 3 oz) in total
small bunch of **sage**
100 g (3½ oz) **smoked**
    pancetta, sliced
25 g (1 oz) **butter**
200 g (7 oz) **shallots**, halved if large
2 tablespoons **plain flour**
150 ml (¼ pint) **dry cider**
150 ml (¼ pint) **chicken stock**
1 teaspoon **Dijon mustard**
1 **dessert apple**, cored and sliced
240 g (7¾ oz) can **whole peeled**
    chestnuts, drained
salt and **pepper**
steamed **baby carrots**, to serve

Preheat the slow cooker if necessary. Rinse the pheasant breasts with cold water, pat dry with kitchen paper and season well with salt and pepper. Top each pheasant breast with a few sage leaves, then wrap in pancetta slices until completely covered. Tie at intervals with fine string to keep the pancetta in place.

Heat the butter in a frying pan, add the shallots and fry for 4–5 minutes or until browned. Stir in the flour, then add the cider, stock and mustard. Add the apple and chestnuts and a little extra salt and pepper. Bring to the boil, stirring.

Arrange the pheasant breasts in the slow cooker pot. Pour the hot onion mixture over the top, cover with the lid and cook on low for 2½–3 hours or until the pheasant is tender and cooked through to the centre. Spoon on to plates, remove the string from the pheasant and serve with baby carrots.

FOR PHEASANT WITH BACON & RED WINE, lay 4 smoked streaky bacon rashers on a chopping board and stretch with the flat of a cook's knife until half as long again. Add a sage leaf to each pheasant breast, then wrap each one with a stretched bacon rasher. Fry as above with the shallots until the bacon is browned. Stir in the flour, then add 150 ml (½ pint) red wine in place of the cider, stock and mustard. Omit the apple and instead add 8 halved ready-to-eat pitted prunes and the chestnuts. Cook as above.

PEASANT PAELLA ♥

Serves **4**
Preparation time **20 minutes**
Cooking temperature **high**
Cooking time **4¾–6 hours**

low-calorie cooking oil spray
500 g (1 lb) **boneless, skinless
 chicken thighs,** cubed
1 **onion**, chopped
60 g (2¼ oz) **chorizo**, sliced
2 **garlic cloves**, finely chopped
1 **red pepper**, cored, deseeded
 and diced
1 **orange pepper**, cored, deseeded
 and diced
2 **celery sticks**, diced
2 pinches of **saffron threads**
½ teaspoon **dried
 Mediterranean herbs**
750 ml (1¼ pints) hot **chicken stock**
175 g (6 oz) **easy-cook brown
 long-grain rice**
125 g (4 oz) **frozen peas**
salt and **pepper**
2 tablespoons chopped **parsley**,
 to garnish

Preheat the slow cooker if necessary. Spray a large frying pan with a little low-calorie cooking oil spray and place over a high heat until hot. Add the chicken a few pieces at a time until all the chicken is in the pan and cook for 5 minutes, stirring, until browned. Use a slotted spoon to transfer the chicken to the slow cooker pot.

Add the onion, chorizo and garlic to the pan and cook for 3–4 minutes, stirring, until the onion is beginning to colour. Add the peppers and celery, stir well, then transfer to the slow cooker pot. Mix the saffron and dried herbs with the hot stock, season to taste, then pour into the slow cooker pot and stir well. Cover and cook on high for 3–4 hours.

Place the rice in a sieve and rinse under cold running water, then drain and stir into the chicken mixture. Cover again and cook, still on high, for 1½–1¾ hours until the rice is tender. Stir in the peas and continue cooking for 15 minutes. Serve garnished with the chopped parsley.

FOR SEAFOOD PAELLA, follow the recipe above to cook the paella, omitting the chicken. Thaw a 400 g (13 oz) packet of frozen mixed seafood and pat dry on kitchen paper. Spray a large frying pan with a little low-calorie cooking oil spray and place over a high heat until hot. Add the seafood and fry for 4–5 minutes until piping hot. Stir into the finished paella and garnish with the parsley.

PORK PUTTANESCA ♥

Serves **4**
Preparation time **20 minutes**
Cooking temperature **high**
Cooking time **7–8 hours**

low-calorie cooking oil spray
625 g (1¼ lb) **lean pork**, diced
1 **onion**, chopped
2 **garlic cloves**, finely chopped
400 g (13 oz) can **chopped tomatoes**
4 teaspoons **sherry vinegar**
15 g (½ oz) **basil**, roughly torn, plus
    extra to garnish
1 tablespoon drained **capers in
    brine**, chopped
50 g (2 oz) **pitted olives**, chopped
salt and **pepper**
chopped **parsley**, to garnish
175 g (6 oz) **dried spaghetti**, boiled,
    to serve

Preheat the slow cooker if necessary. Spray a large frying pan with a little low-calorie cooking oil spray and place over a high heat until hot. Add the pork a few pieces at a time until all the meat is in the pan and cook for 5 minutes, stirring, until browned. Use a slotted spoon to transfer the pork to a plate.

Add a little more low-calorie cooking oil spray to the frying pan if necessary, then add the onion and cook for 4–5 minutes, stirring, until just beginning to brown. Add the garlic, tomatoes, vinegar and basil and bring to the boil, stirring.

Mix the capers and olives together and add half to the sauce, reserving the rest for garnish.

Transfer the pork to the slow cooker pot, then pour over the sauce. Cover and cook on high for 7–8 hours until the pork is tender. Stir, then sprinkle with the reserved capers and olives, some extra basil and a little chopped parsley. Serve with the cooked spaghetti.

FOR PORK OSSO BUCCO, follow the recipe above, using 2 tablespoons chopped parsley mixed with the grated rind of 1 lemon and 2 finely chopped garlic cloves instead of the capers and olives. Serve with 225 g (7½ oz) rice, boiled with a few saffron threads.

SKINNY SPAGHETTI BOLOGNESE ♥

Serves **4**
Preparation time **20 minutes**
Cooking temperature **low**
Cooking time **8–10 hours**

low-calorie cooking oil spray
500 g (1 lb) **extra-lean minced beef**
1 **onion**, finely chopped
2 **garlic cloves**, finely chopped
1 **carrot**, coarsely grated
2 **courgettes**, coarsely grated
150 g (5 oz) **button mushrooms**, sliced
500 g (1 lb) **passata**
150 ml (¼ pint) **beef stock**
1 teaspoon **dried oregano**
salt and **pepper**

TO SERVE
300 g (10 oz) **dried spaghetti**
handful of **oregano** or **basil leaves**

Spray a large frying pan with low-calorie cooking oil spray and place over a high heat until hot. Add the minced beef and onion and cook for 5 minutes, stirring and breaking up the mince with a wooden spoon, until evenly browned. Stir in the garlic, carrot, courgettes and mushrooms. Add the passata, stock and oregano, then season to taste. Bring to the boil, stirring. Transfer to the slow cooker pot, cover and cook on low for 8–10 hours.

Cook the spaghetti in a large saucepan of lightly salted boiling water according to the packet instructions until just tender. Drain well, toss with the Bolognese sauce and serve sprinkled with the oregano or basil leaves.

FOR ITALIAN SHEPHERD'S PIE, make the Bolognese sauce as above. Cook 500 g (1 lb) potatoes and 500 g (1 lb) swede, cut into chunks, in a saucepan of lightly salted boiling water for 15–20 minutes until tender. Drain and mash with 4 tablespoons vegetable stock (or 4 tablespoons cooking water). Beat 1 egg and stir half into the mash, then season to taste. Lift the pot out of the housing using oven gloves. Spoon the mash over the Bolognese sauce and rough up the top with a fork. Brush with the remaining beaten egg and brown under a preheated hot grill before serving.

AUBERGINE PARMIGIANA ♥

Serves **4**
Preparation time **20 minutes**
Cooking temperature **high**
Cooking time **4–5 hours**

1 tablespoon **olive oil**
1 **onion**, chopped
2 **garlic cloves**, finely chopped
400 g (13 oz) **tomatoes**, diced
400 g (13 oz) can **chopped tomatoes**
small handful of **basil**, torn, plus extra to garnish
2 teaspoons **granular sweetener**
2 teaspoons **cornflour**
2 large **aubergines**, sliced
75 g (3 oz) **mature Cheddar cheese**, grated
salt and **pepper**
2 tablespoons freshly grated **Parmesan cheese**,
  to garnish

Preheat the slow cooker if necessary. Heat the oil in a large frying pan over a medium heat, add the onion and cook for 4–5 minutes until just beginning to soften. Add the garlic, fresh tomatoes, canned tomatoes, basil and sweetener. Mix the cornflour to a smooth paste with a little cold water and stir into the sauce. Season to taste and bring to the boil, stirring.

Spoon a little of the tomato sauce over the base of the slow cooker pot and arrange one-third of the aubergine slices, overlapping, on top. Spoon over a thin layer of the sauce and sprinkle with a little grated Cheddar. Repeat to make 3 aubergine layers, finishing with a generous layer of sauce and grated Cheddar.

Cover and cook on high for 4–5 hours until the aubergines are soft. Sprinkle with the Parmesan and extra basil and serve.

FOR MUSHROOM PARMIGIANA, follow the recipe above to make the tomato sauce, then layer in the slow cooker pot with 8 large flat field mushrooms, in 2 layers, and the Cheddar. Cook and serve as above.

CHICKEN CACCIATORE ♥

Serves **4**
Preparation time **20 minutes**
Cooking temperature **low**
Cooking time **8–9 hours**

low-calorie cooking oil spray
500 g (1 lb) **boneless, skinless
    chicken thighs**, cubed
1 **onion**, chopped
2 **garlic cloves**, finely chopped
1 **red pepper**, cored, deseeded
    and diced
1 **orange pepper**, cored, deseeded
    and diced
2 **celery sticks**, diced
150 ml (¼ pint) **chicken stock**
400 g (13 oz) can **chopped tomatoes**
1 tablespoon **tomato purée**
1 tablespoon **balsamic vinegar**
leaves from 2 **rosemary
    sprigs**, chopped
200 g (7 oz) **dried tagliatelle**
salt and **pepper**
2 tablespoons chopped **parsley**,
    to garnish

Preheat the slow cooker if necessary. Spray a large frying pan with a little low-calorie cooking oil spray and place over a high heat until hot. Add the chicken a few pieces at a time until all the chicken is in the pan and cook for 3–4 minutes, stirring, until just beginning to brown. Add the onion and continue to cook until the chicken is golden and the onion has softened.

Stir in the garlic, peppers and celery, then add the stock, tomatoes, tomato purée, balsamic vinegar and rosemary. Season generously and bring to the boil, stirring. Transfer to the slow cooker pot, cover and cook on low for 8–9 hours until the chicken is tender and cooked through.

When almost ready to serve, cook the tagliatelle in a large saucepan of lightly salted boiling water according to the packet instructions until just tender. Drain, then toss with the chicken mixture and serve garnished with the parsley.

FOR POTATO-TOPPED CACCIATORE, follow the recipe above and place all the ingredients in the slow cooker pot. Thinly slice 625 g (1¼ lb) potatoes and arrange them on top of the chicken mixture, overlapping. Press the potatoes down into the liquid, then cover and cook on high for 5–6 hours until the potatoes and chicken are cooked through. If liked, lift the pot out of the housing using oven gloves, spray the potatoes with a little extra low-calorie cooking oil spray and place under a preheated hot grill until the potatoes are golden.

DESSERTS

CHERRY & COCONUT SPONGE PUDDING

Serves **4–6**
Preparation time **15 minutes**
Cooking temperature **high**
Cooking time **3–3½ hours**

butter, for greasing
40 g (1½ oz) **desiccated coconut**
400 g (13 oz) can **cherry pie filling**
500 g (1 lb) pack **Madeira cake mix**
4 tablespoons **sunflower oil** or
   1 **egg**, according to the cake
   mix instructions

Preheat the slow cooker if necessary. Lightly butter a 1.5 litre (2½ pint) pudding basin and base-line with a circle of nonstick baking paper, checking first that it will fit in the slow cooker pot. Sprinkle in a little of the coconut, then tilt and turn the basin until the buttery sides are lightly coated. Spoon half the cherry pie filling into the base of the basin.

Tip the cake mix into a bowl and mix in the oil or egg and water according to the pack instructions. Stir in the remaining coconut, then spoon the mixture into the basin and spread it level. Cover the top with buttered, domed foil and lower the basin into the slow cooker pot.

Pour boiling water into the pot to come halfway up the sides of the basin. Cover with the lid and cook on high for 3–3½ hours or until the sponge is well risen, feels dry and springs back when pressed with a fingertip.

Lift the basin out of the slow cooker pot using a tea towel and remove the foil. Loosen the edge of the pudding with a knife, turn out on to a plate and peel off the lining paper. Heat the remaining pie filling in a small saucepan or the microwave until hot. Serve the pudding in bowls with the warm cherries and scoops of vanilla ice cream, if liked.

FOR SPICED CHOCOLATE CHERRY SPONGE PUDDING, line the pudding basin with cherry pie filling as above, omitting the coconut. Make up a 500 g (1 lb) chocolate-flavoured Madeira cake mix with 1 teaspoon ground cinnamon and the sunflower oil or egg and continue as above.

HOT CHOCOLATE MOUSSES

Serves **4**
Preparation time **25 minutes**
Cooking temperature **high**
Cooking time **1–1¼ hours**

200 g (7 oz) **plain dark chocolate**,
    broken into pieces
50 g (2 oz) **butter**, plus extra
    for greasing
4 **eggs**, separated
4 tablespoons **caster sugar**
1 tablespoons warm **water**
sifted **icing sugar**, to decorate

MINT CREAM
6 tablespoons **double cream**
4 teaspoons chopped **mint**

Preheat the slow cooker if necessary. Put the chocolate and butter in a bowl set over a saucepan of very gently simmering water, making sure that the water does not touch the base of the bowl, and leave until just melted.

Meanwhile, butter 4 mugs, each 250 ml (8 fl oz), checking first that they will fit in the slow cooker pot.

Whisk the egg whites in a bowl until soft peaks, then gradually whisk in the sugar a teaspoonful at a time until it has all been added and the meringue is thick and glossy. Take the bowl of melted chocolate and butter off the saucepan, stir in the egg yolks and measurement warm water and gently fold in a spoonful of the egg whites to loosen the mixture. Fold in the remaining egg whites, then divide between the mugs.

Cover the tops with domed foil and put into the slow cooker pot. Pour boiling water into the pot to come halfway up the sides of the mugs. Cover with the lid and cook on high for 1–1¼ hours or until the puddings are softly set in the centre.

Lift the puddings out of the slow cooker pot using a tea towel and remove the foil. Mix the cream and mint together and pour into a jug. Dust the puddings with icing sugar and serve immediately with the mint cream.

FOR GINGERED MOUSSES WITH ORANGE CREAM, add 4 teaspoons drained, finely chopped stem ginger to the mousse mixture and cook as above. To serve with the hot puddings, stir an extra 2 teaspoons drained, finely chopped stem ginger and the finely grated rind of 1 orange into 6 tablespoons crème fraîche in a bowl.

APRICOT & ORANGE FOOL

Serves **6**
Preparation time **20 minutes**,
 plus cooling
Cooking temperature **low**
Cooking time **3–4 hours**

250 g (8 oz) **ready-to-eat**
 dried apricots
grated rind and juice of **1 orange**
2 tablespoons **caster sugar**
300 ml (½ pint) cold **water**
2 x 135 g (4½ oz) pots
 ready-made custard
500 ml (17 fl oz) **natural yogurt**

Preheat the slow cooker if necessary. Put the apricots, orange rind and juice and sugar into the slow cooker pot and pour over the measurement water. Cover and cook on low for 3–4 hours or until the apricots are plump.

Lift the pot out of the housing using oven gloves and leave the apricots to cool, then purée with a stick blender or transfer to a freestanding blender and whizz until smooth.

Fold the custard and yogurt together until just mixed, then add the apricot purée and very lightly mix for a marbled effect. Spoon into the glasses and serve with dainty biscuits, if liked.

FOR PRUNE & VANILLA FOOL, put 250 g (8 oz) ready-to-eat pitted prunes, 1 teaspoon vanilla extract, 2 tablespoons clear honey and 300 ml (½ pint) cold water in the slow cooker pot and then cook, cool and make up the fool as above.

ICED JAMAICAN GINGER CAKE

Serves **6**

Preparation time **25 minutes**, plus **cooling** and **setting**

Cooking temperature **high**

Cooking time **4½–5 hours**

100 g (3½ oz) **butter**, plus extra for greasing

100 g (3½ oz) **dark muscovado sugar**

100 g (3½ oz) **golden syrup**

100 g (3½ oz) **ready-chopped pitted dates**

100 g (3½ oz) **wholemeal plain flour**

100 g (3½ oz) **self-raising flour**

½ teaspoon **bicarbonate of soda**

2 teaspoons **ground ginger**

3 pieces of **stem ginger**, drained of syrup, 2 chopped and 1 cut into strips

2 **eggs**, beaten

100 ml (3½ fl oz) **milk**

125 g (4 oz) **icing sugar**

3–3½ teaspoons **water**

Preheat the slow cooker if necessary. Butter a soufflé dish 14 cm (5½ inches) in diameter and 9 cm (3½ inches) deep and base-line with a circle of nonstick baking paper, checking first that it will fit in the slow cooker pot.

Put the butter, sugar, syrup and dates into a saucepan and heat gently, stirring, until the butter and sugar have melted. Take the pan off the heat, add the flours, bicarbonate of soda, ground and chopped ginger, eggs and milk and beat until smooth. Pour into the lined dish and cover the top loosely with buttered foil.

Lower the dish carefully into the slow cooker pot. Pour boiling water into the pot to come halfway up the sides of the dish, cover with the lid and cook on high for 4½–5 hours or until a skewer comes out cleanly when inserted into the centre of the ginger cake.

Lift the dish out of the slow cooker pot using a tea towel and leave to stand for 10 minutes, then remove the foil and loosen the edge of the cake with a knife. Turn out on to a wire rack, peel off the lining paper and leave to cool.

Sift the icing sugar into a bowl and mix in just enough of the measurement water to make a smooth, thick icing. Spoon over the top of the cake, then decorate with the strips of ginger. Leave to set. Cut into wedges to serve.

FOR BANANA GINGER CAKE, omit the dates from the ginger cake and add 1 small mashed banana mixed with 1 tablespoon lemon juice when adding the chopped ginger. Cook and ice as above.

SAFFRON PEARS WITH CHOCOLATE

Serves **4**
Preparation time **20 minutes**
Cooking temperature **low**
Cooking time **3–4 hours**

300 ml (½ pint) **cloudy apple juice**
3 tablespoons **caster sugar**
large pinch of **saffron threads**
4 **cardamom pods**, roughly crushed
4 **firm, ripe pears**

CHOCOLATE SAUCE
4 tablespoons **chocolate and**
   hazelnut spread
2 tablespoons **double cream**
2 tablespoons **milk**

Preheat the slow cooker if necessary. Pour the apple juice into a small saucepan and add the sugar, saffron and cardamom pods and their black seeds. Bring to the boil, then tip into the slow cooker pot.

Cut each pear in half lengthways, leaving the stalk on, then cut away the skin. Remove the pear cores with a melon baller, if you have one, or a teaspoon. Add the pears to the slow cooker pot, pressing them beneath the surface of the liquid as much as you can. Cover with the lid and cook on low for 3–4 hours or until the pears are tender and pale yellow.

When ready to serve, put all the ingredients for the sauce into a small saucepan and warm together, stirring until smooth. Spoon the pears and some of the saffron sauce into shallow dishes, pour the chocolate sauce into a small jug and allow dinner guests to drizzle the sauce over the pears just before eating. Complete with a spoonful of ice cream or crème fraîche, if liked.

FOR SPICED PEARS WITH RED WINE warm 150 ml (¼ pint) red wine with 150 ml (¼ pint) water, 50 g (2 oz) caster sugar, the pared rind of ½ small orange, 1 small cinnamon stick, halved, and 4 cloves in a saucepan. Pour into the slow cooker pot, add 4 halved, peeled and cored pears, then cover and cook as above. Serve with spoonfuls of crème fraîche.

LEMON CUSTARD CREAMS

Serves **6**
Preparation time **15 minutes, plus
    cooling** and **chilling**
Cooking temperature **low**
Cooking time **2–2½ hours**

2 **eggs**
3 **egg yolks**
100 g (3½ oz) **caster sugar**
grated rind of 2 **lemons** and the juice
    of 1 **lemon**
300 ml (½ pint) **double cream**
150 g (5 oz) **blueberries**, to serve

Preheat the slow cooker if necessary. Put the whole eggs and egg yolks, sugar and lemon rind into a bowl and whisk together until just mixed.

Pour the cream into a small saucepan and bring just to the boil, then gradually whisk into the egg mixture. Strain the lemon juice and gradually whisk into the cream mixture.

Pour the mixture into 6 small coffee cups, checking first that they will fit in the slow cooker pot. Put them in the pot, then pour hot water into the pot so that it comes halfway up the sides of the cups. Loosely cover the tops of the cups with a piece of foil, cover with the lid and cook on low for 2–2½ hours or until the custards are just set.

Lift the cups carefully out of the slow cooker with a tea towel and leave to cool. Transfer to the refrigerator to chill for 3–4 hours or overnight.

Set the cups on their saucers and decorate the tops of the custard creams with the blueberries.

FOR LIME & ELDERFLOWER CUSTARD CREAMS, make the puddings as above but with the grated rind and juice of 2 limes and 2 tablespoons undiluted elderflower cordial instead of the lemon rind and juice. Cook in coffee cups as above, then serve chilled with fresh strawberries drizzled with a little extra elderflower cordial.

BAKED APPLES
WITH DATES

BAKED PEACHES
WITH GINGER ♥

Serves **4**
Preparation time **20 minutes**
Cooking temperature **low**
Cooking time **3–4 hours**

50 g (2 oz) **butter**, at room temperature
50 g (2 oz) **light muscovado sugar**
½ teaspoon **ground cinnamon**
grated rind of ½ small **orange**
1 tablespoon finely chopped **glacé** or drained
   stem ginger
50 g (2 oz) **ready-chopped pitted dates**
4 large **Braeburn** or other **firm dessert apples**
150 ml (¼ pint) **cloudy apple juice**
hot **custard** or **cream** to serve

Preheat the slow cooker if necessary. Mix together the butter, sugar, cinnamon and orange rind until smooth, then stir in the chopped ginger and dates.

Trim a thin slice off the bottom of the apples, if needed, so that they will stand up without rolling over, then cut a thick slice off the top of each and reserve for later. Using a small knife, cut away the apple core to leave a cavity for the stuffing.

Divide the date mixture into 4 and press a portion into each apple cavity, spreading it over the top cut edge of the apple if it won't all fit in. Replace the apple lids and then put the apples into the slow cooker pot. Pour the apple juice into the base of the pot, cover and cook on low for 3–4 hours or until the apples are tender.

Lift the apples carefully out of the slow cooker and serve in shallow dishes with the sauce spooned over and a drizzle of hot custard or cream.

FOR BAKED APPLES WITH GINGERED CHERRIES, follow the recipe as above, but omit the cinnamon, replace the orange rind with lemon rind and replace the dates with 50 g (2 oz) chopped glacé cherries.

Serves **4**
Preparation time **10 minutes**
Cooking temperature **low**
Cooking time **1½–2½ hours**

2.5 cm (1 inch) piece of **fresh root ginger**, peeled and
   finely chopped
6 **ripe peaches**, halved and stoned
6 tablespoons **cloudy apple juice**
1 tablespoon **caster sugar**
75 g (3 oz) **blueberries**
150 ml (¼ pint) **0% fat Greek yogurt**

Preheat the slow cooker if necessary. Arrange the chopped ginger over the base of the slow cooker pot, then place the peaches, cut sides down, on top in a single layer. Pour over the apple juice, then sprinkle with the sugar and blueberries.

Cover and cook on low for 1½–2½ hours until the peaches are piping hot and the juices are beginning to run from the blueberries. Spoon into serving bowls and serve warm or cold with the Greek yogurt.

FOR BAKED PEACHES WITH ROSÉ WINE, arrange 8 peach halves, cut sides down, in the base of the slow cooker pot and pour over 6 tablespoons rosé wine, 1 tablespoon caster sugar and 125 g (4 oz) raspberries instead of the blueberries. Cover, cook and serve as above.

MINI BANANA & DATE PUDDINGS

Serves **4**
Preparation time **20 minutes**
Cooking temperature **high**
Cooking time **2–3 hours**

100 g (3½ oz) **butter**, at room temperature, plus extra
　for greasing
100 g (3½ oz) **light muscovado sugar**
2 **eggs**, beaten
125 g (4 oz) **self-raising flour**
1 small **ripe banana**
75 g (3 oz) **ready-chopped pitted dates**
250 g (8 oz) **ready-made toffee sauce**
50 g (2 oz) **plain dark chocolate**, broken into pieces

Preheat the slow cooker if necessary. Butter 4 metal
pudding moulds, each 250 ml (8 fl oz), and base-line
each with a circle of nonstick baking paper, checking
first that they will fit in the slow cooker pot. Beat
the butter and sugar in a bowl with a wooden spoon
or hand-held electric whisk until soft and creamy.
Gradually add alternate spoonfuls of egg and flour until
both have all been added and the mixture is smooth.
Mash the banana on a plate, then beat into the pudding
mix. Stir in the dates, then divide between the moulds.

Cover each one with a square of foil and stand in the
slow cooker pot. Pour boiling water into the pot to come
halfway up the sides of the moulds. Cover with the lid
and cook on high for 2–3 hours or until the tops of the
puddings spring back when pressed with a fingertip. Lift
the moulds from the slow cooker pot using a tea towel
and remove the foil. Loosen the edges with a knife, turn
out on to plates and peel off the lining paper. Pour the
toffee sauce into a small saucepan, add the chocolate
and warm through, stirring, until the chocolate has just
melted. Drizzle over the puddings and serve.

FOR MINI CHOCOLATE & BANANA PUDDINGS,
make up the puddings with the butter, sugar and
eggs as above. Substitute 15 g (½ oz) cocoa powder
for the same weight of flour, then add with the
remaining flour, mashed banana and dates. Cook as
above. Warm 4 tablespoons chocolate and hazelnut
spread with 2 tablespoons each double cream and milk
in a saucepan, stirring until smooth, and serve with
the puddings.

PLUM & BLUEBERRY SWIRL ♥

Serves **4**
Preparation time **15 minutes**, **plus cooling** and **chilling**
Cooking temperature **high**
Cooking time **2¼–2¾ hours**

300 g (10 oz) **ripe red plums**, halved, stoned and
　cut into chunks
150 g (5 oz) **blueberries**
1 tablespoon **granular sweetener**
juice of ½ **orange**
3 tablespoons **water**
1 tablespoon **cornflour**

YOGURT
200 ml (7 fl oz) **0% fat Greek yogurt**
finely grated rind of ½ **orange**
1 tablespoon **granular sweetener**

Preheat the slow cooker if necessary. Place the plums
and blueberries in the slow cooker pot, sprinkle
with the sweetener, then add the orange juice and
measurement water. Cover and cook on high for
2–2½ hours until the fruit is soft.

Mix the cornflour to a smooth paste with a little cold
water and stir into the pot. Cover again and cook, still
on high, for a further 15 minutes until thickened. Stir
the fruit and leave to cool.

Mix the yogurt with the orange rind and sweetener.
Divide the fruit between 4 serving glasses, top with the
yogurt, then swirl together with a teaspoon. Chill until
ready to serve.

FOR MINTED STRAWBERRY & BLUEBERRY SWIRL, place
300 g (10 oz) ripe strawberries, hulled, in the slow
cooker pot with 150 g (5 oz) blueberries, 1 tablespoon
granular sweetener and the juice of ½ orange. Cook
as above, then thicken with the cornflour, cook for a
further 15 minutes and leave to cool. Mix 200 ml
(7 fl oz) 0% fat Greek yogurt with 1 tablespoon
chopped mint and 1 tablespoon granular sweetener,
then swirl with the fruit as above.

STRAWBERRY CHEESECAKE

Serves **4–5**
Preparation time **30 minutes**,
   plus cooling and **chilling**
Cooking temperature **high**
Cooking time **2–2½ hours**

4 **trifle sponges**
300 g (10 oz) **full-fat**
   cream cheese
75 g (3 oz) **caster sugar**
150 ml (¼ pint) **double cream**
3 **eggs**
grated rind and juice of ½ **lemon**
butter, for greasing

TOPPING
2 tablespoons **strawberry jam**
1 tablespoon **lemon juice**
200 g (7 oz) **strawberries**, hulled
   and sliced

Preheat the slow cooker if necessary. Line the base and sides of a soufflé dish 14 cm (5½ inches) in diameter and 9 cm (3½ inches) deep with nonstick baking paper, checking first that it will fit in the slow cooker pot. Line the base with the trifle sponges, trimming them to fit in a single layer.

Put the cream cheese and sugar in a bowl, then gradually whisk in the cream until smooth and thick. Gradually whisk in the eggs 1 at a time, then mix in the lemon rind and juice. Pour the mixture into the dish and spread it level.

Cover the top with buttered foil and lower it into the slow cooker pot. Pour boiling water into the pot to come halfway up the sides of the dish. Cover with the lid and cook on high for 2–2½ hours or until the cheesecake is well risen and softly set in the centre.

Lift the dish out of the slow cooker pot using a tea towel and leave to cool and firm up. The cheesecake will sink quickly as it cools to about the size that it was before cooking. Transfer to the refrigerator and chill for at least 4 hours.

When ready to serve, loosen the edge of the cheesecake with a knife, turn out on to a serving plate, peel off the lining paper and turn it the right way up. Mix the jam and lemon juice in a bowl until smooth, add the sliced strawberries and toss together. Spoon on top of the cheesecake and serve.

CHOCOLATE BROWNIE PUDDINGS

Serves **4**
Preparation time **20 minutes**
Cooking temperature **high**
Cooking time **1¼–1½ hours**

125 g (4 oz) **plain dark chocolate**,
 plus 8 extra small squares
75 g (3 oz) **butter**
2 **eggs**
2 **egg yolks**
75 g (3 oz) **caster sugar**
½ teaspoon **vanilla extract**
40 g (1½ oz) **plain flour**

TO DECORATE
sifted **icing sugar**
mini **pastel-coloured marshmallows**
vanilla ice cream or **crème fraîche**

Preheat the slow cooker if necessary. Break the 125 g (4 oz) chocolate into pieces, put into a saucepan with the butter and heat gently, stirring occasionally, until melted. Take off the heat and set aside. Meanwhile, butter 4 individual metal pudding moulds, each 250 ml (8 fl oz), and base-line with circles of nonstick baking paper, first checking that they will fit in the slow cooker pot.

Whisk together the whole eggs, egg yolks, sugar and vanilla extract in a large mixing bowl with a hand-held electric whisk for 3–4 minutes or until light and frothy. Gradually whisk in the melted chocolate mixture.

Sift the flour into the chocolate mixture and fold together. Divide between the pudding moulds. Press 2 squares of chocolate into the centre of each, then loosely cover the tops with squares of buttered foil. Transfer the pudding moulds to the slow cooker pot and pour boiling water into the pot to come halfway up the sides of the moulds. Cover and cook on high for 1¼–1½ hours until well risen and the tops spring back when lightly pressed with a fingertip.

Lift the moulds out of the pot using a tea towel. Loosen the puddings with a knife, turn out into shallow serving dishes and remove the lining paper. Sprinkle with sifted icing sugar. Serve with marshmallows and spoonfuls of vanilla ice cream or crème fraîche.

FOR BRANDIED CHERRY BROWNIE PUDDINGS, soak 8 drained, canned pitted black cherries in 1 tablespoon brandy for at least 2 hours, longer if possible. Make up the brownie mixture as above and drop 2 cherries into the centre of each instead of the squares of chocolate.

BLUEBERRY & PASSION FRUIT CHEESECAKE ♥

Serves **4**

Preparation time **25 minutes, plus
    cooling** and **chilling**

Cooking temperature **high**

Cooking time **2–2½ hours**

1 tablespoon **sunflower margarine**,
    plus extra for greasing

75 g (3 oz) **reduced-fat digestive
    biscuits**, finely crushed

300 g (10 oz) **extra-light soft cheese**

175 ml (6 fl oz) **0% fat Greek yogurt**

1 tablespoon **cornflour**

finely grated rind and juice of ½ **lime**

1 teaspoon **vanilla extract**

3 tablespoons **granular sweetener**

3 tablespoons **caster sugar**

2 **eggs**

125 g (4 oz) **blueberries**

2 **passion fruits**, halved

Preheat the slow cooker if necessary. Grease the base and sides of a 15 cm (6 inch) round ovenproof dish, about 6 cm (2½ inches) deep, with a little margarine and base-line with a circle of nonstick baking paper.

Melt the margarine in a small saucepan and stir in the crushed biscuits. Spoon into the dish and press down firmly to make a thin, even layer. Place the cheese, yogurt and cornflour in a mixing bowl and whisk until smooth. Add the lime rind and juice, vanilla, sweetener, sugar and eggs and whisk again until smooth.

Pour the mixture into the dish and smooth the surface. Cover with greased foil and put in the slow cooker pot. Pour boiling water into the slow cooker pot to come halfway up the sides of the dish, cover and cook on high for 2–2½ hours or until the cheesecake is set but with a slight wobble in the centre. Lift the dish out of the slow cooker pot using a tea towel and leave to cool, then chill in the refrigerator for 3–4 hours or overnight.

Loosen the edge of the cheesecake with a knife, turn out of the dish and peel away the lining paper. Place on a serving plate, pile the blueberries on top, then scoop the passion fruit seeds out of the halved fruits with a teaspoon over them. Serve cut into wedges.

FOR SUMMER BERRY CHEESECAKE, follow the recipe above to make the cheesecake, using the grated rind and juice of ½ lemon instead of the lime. Gently toss 100 g (3½ oz) hulled, sliced strawberries and 100 g (3½ oz) raspberries with 2 tablespoons reduced-sugar strawberry jam and 1 tablespoon lemon juice instead of the blueberries and passion fruits. Turn out the cheesecake and top with the berry mixture just before serving.

GINGERED DATE & SYRUP PUDDINGS ♥

Serves **4**
Preparation time **20 minutes**
Cooking temperature **high**
Cooking time **3½–4 hours**

125 g (4 oz) **pitted dates**, chopped
125 ml (4 fl oz) boiling **water**
¼ teaspoon **bicarbonate of soda**
4 tablespoons **golden syrup**
50 g (2 oz) **sunflower margarine**,
   plus extra for greasing
50 g (2 oz) **light muscovado sugar**
100 g (3½ oz) **self-raising flour**
1 **egg**
1 teaspoon **vanilla extract**
1 teaspoon **ground ginger**
2 small scoops of **low-fat vanilla
   ice cream**

Preheat the slow cooker if necessary. Place the chopped dates, measurement boiling water and bicarbonate of soda in a bowl, stir and leave to soak for 10 minutes.

Meanwhile, lightly grease 4 metal pudding basins, each 200 ml (7 fl oz), and base-line with circles of nonstick baking paper. Divide the golden syrup between the basins.

Place the margarine, sugar, flour, egg, vanilla and ginger in a food processor and blend until smooth. Drain the dates, add to the processor and blend briefly to mix. Divide the mixture between the pudding basins, cover the tops with greased foil and put in the slow cooker pot.

Pour boiling water into the slow cooker pot to come halfway up the sides of the basins, cover and cook on high for 3½–4 hours until the sponge is well risen and springs back when pressed with a fingertip.

Lift the basins out of the pot using a tea towel. Remove the foil, loosen the edges of the puddings with a knife and turn out into shallow bowls. Peel away the lining paper and serve immediately with the ice cream.

FOR GINGERED BANANA PUDDINGS, omit the dates, boiling water and bicarbonate of soda. Follow the recipe above, adding 1 ripe banana to the food processor with the remaining ingredients. Blend and continue as above.

PLUM & POLENTA CAKE

Serves **6**
Preparation time **30 minutes**
Cooking temperature **high**
Cooking time **3–3½ hours**

200 g (7 oz) **sweet red plums**,
    stoned and halved
150 g (5 oz) **butter**, at room
    temperature, plus extra
    for greasing
150 g (5 oz) **caster sugar**
2 **eggs**, beaten
100 g (3½ oz) **ground almonds**
50 g (2 oz) **fine polenta (cornmeal)**
½ teaspoon **baking powder**
grated rind and juice of ½ **orange**

TO DECORATE
2 tablespoons toasted
    flaked almonds
sifted **icing sugar**

Preheat the slow cooker if necessary. Butter a 1.2 litre (2 pint) oval or round heatproof dish that will fit comfortably in your slow cooker pot and base-line with a circle of nonstick baking paper. Arrange the plum halves, cut side down, in rings in the base of the dish.

Cream together the butter and caster sugar in a mixing bowl until light and fluffy. Gradually beat the eggs and ground almonds alternately into the mixture. Stir in the polenta, baking powder and orange rind and juice and beat until smooth.

Spoon the mixture over the plums and smooth with a knife. Cover the dish with buttered foil, then stand it on an upturned saucer or 2 individual flan rings in the slow cooker pot. Pour boiling water into the pot to come halfway up the sides of the dish. Cover with the lid and cook on high for 3–3½ hours or until the top of the cake is dry and springs back when pressed with a fingertip.

Remove the dish carefully from the slow cooker using a tea towel. Take off the foil and leave to cool slightly. Run a knife around the inside edge of the dish to loosen the cake and turn it out on to a serving plate. Remove the lining paper, sprinkle the top with toasted flaked almonds and dust with a little sifted icing sugar to decorate. Cut into wedges and serve warm or cold with spoonfuls of whipped cream, if liked.

FOR APPLE & POLENTA CAKE, follow the recipe as above, but replace the plums with 2 Braeburn dessert apples, peeled, cored and thickly sliced, then tossed with the grated rind and juice of ½ lemon.

SPICED PEARS ♥

Serves **4**
Preparation time **15 minutes**
Cooking temperature **low**
Cooking time **3–4 hours**

300 ml (½ pint) hot **water**
4 **cardamom pods**, crushed
7 cm (3 inch) **cinnamon stick**, halved
2.5 cm (1 inch) piece of **fresh root ginger**, peeled and
    thinly sliced
2 teaspoons **granular sweetener**
4 **pears with stalks**, peeled, halved lengthways and cored
pared rind and juice of 1 **lemon**
pared rind and juice of 1 **orange**

Preheat the slow cooker if necessary. Pour the measurement hot water into the slow cooker pot, then stir in the cardamom pods and their black seeds, the cinnamon, ginger and sweetener.

Add the pears and the lemon and orange juice, then gently turn the pears in the liquid to coat and arrange them, cut sides down, in a single layer. Cut the pared lemon and orange rind into very thin strips and sprinkle on top.

Cover and cook on low for 3–4 hours until the pears are tender. The cooking time will depend on their ripeness. Serve warm.

FOR MULLED WINE PEARS, follow the recipe above, using 150 ml (¼ pint) red wine and 150 ml (¼ pint) hot water instead of 300 ml (½ pint) hot water, and using 4 cloves instead of the cardamom pods. Increase the granular sweetener to 3 teaspoons, or to taste, and cook as above.

HOT TODDY ORANGES

Serves **4**
Preparation time **15 minutes**
Cooking temperature **low**
Cooking time **2–3 hours**

8 **clementines**
50 g (2 oz) **clear honey**
75 g (3 oz) **light muscovado sugar**
grated rind and juice of ½ **lemon**
4 tablespoons **whisky**
300 ml (½ pint) boiling **water**
15 g (½ oz) **butter**

Preheat the slow cooker if necessary. Peel the clementines, leaving them whole. Put the remaining ingredients in the slow cooker pot and mix together.

Add the clementines. Cover with the lid and cook on low for 2–3 hours or until piping hot. Spoon into shallow bowls and serve with just-melting scoops of vanilla ice cream, if liked.

FOR HOT TODDY APRICOTS, put all the ingredients, omitting the clementines and sugar, into the slow cooker pot as above. Add 300 g (10 oz) ready-to-eat dried apricots and continue as above. Serve warm with crème fraîche or vanilla ice cream.

CHOCOLATE CROISSANT PUDDING

Serves **4**

Preparation time **15 minutes**,
plus soaking

Cooking temperature **low**

Cooking time **4–4½ hours**

50 g (2 oz) **butter**

4 **chocolate croissants**

50 g (2 oz) **caster sugar**

¼ teaspoon **ground cinnamon**

40 g (1½ oz) **pecan nuts**,
roughly crushed

300 ml (½ pint) **milk**

2 **eggs**

2 **egg yolks**

1 teaspoon **vanilla extract**

sifted **icing sugar**, to decorate

Butter the inside of a 1.2 litre (2 pint) straight-sided heatproof dish with a little of the butter, checking first that it will fit into the slow cooker pot.

Slice the chocolate croissants thickly and spread 1 side of each slice with the remaining butter. Mix together the caster sugar and cinnamon. Arrange the croissants in layers in the dish, sprinkling each layer with the spiced sugar and the pecans.

Whisk the milk, whole eggs, egg yolks and vanilla extract together in a mixing bowl. Pour into the dish and leave to soak for 15 minutes. Meanwhile, preheat the slow cooker if necessary.

Cover the top of the dish loosely with buttered foil and lower it into the slow cooker pot. Pour boiling water into the pot to come halfway up the sides of the dish, cover with the lid and cook on low for 4–4½ hours or until the custard is set and the pudding well risen. Lift the dish out of the slow cooker pot using a tea towel. Dust with sifted icing sugar. Scoop into bowls and serve with cream, if liked.

FOR BREAD & BUTTER PUDDING, spread 40 g (1½ oz) butter over 4 thick slices of bread, cut into triangles and layer in the buttered dish with 3 tablespoons luxury mixed dried fruit and the caster sugar. Pour the custard over the bread and continue as above.

STICKY TOFFEE APPLE PUDDING

Serves **4–5**
Preparation time **30 minutes**
Cooking temperature **high**
Cooking time **3–3½ hours**

150 g (5 oz) **self-raising flour**
50 g (2 oz) **butter**, diced, plus
 extra for greasing
100 g (3½ oz) **dark
 muscovado sugar**
2 **eggs**
2 tablespoons **milk**
1 **dessert apple**, cored and
 finely chopped
crème fraîche, **vanilla ice cream**
 or **pouring cream**, to serve

SAUCE
125 g (4 oz) **dark muscovado sugar**
25 g (1 oz) **butter**, diced
300 ml (½ pint) boiling **water**

Preheat the slow cooker if necessary. Butter the inside of a soufflé dish 14 cm (5½ inches) in diameter and 9 cm (3½ inches) deep, checking first that it will fit into the slow cooker pot. Put the flour in a bowl, add the measured butter and rub in with the fingertips until the mixture resembles fine breadcrumbs. Stir in the sugar, then mix in the eggs and milk until smooth. Stir in the apple.

Spoon the mixture into the soufflé dish and spread it level. Sprinkle the sugar for the sauce over the top and dot with the butter. Pour the measurement boiling water over the top, then cover loosely with foil.

Lower the dish carefully into the slow cooker pot. Pour boiling water into the pot so that it comes halfway up the sides of the soufflé dish. Cover with the lid and cook on high for 3–3½ hours or until the sponge is well risen and the sauce is bubbling around the edges.

Lift the dish out of the slow cooker using a tea towel. Remove the foil and loosen the edge of the sponge. Cover with a dish that is large enough to catch the sauce, then invert and remove the soufflé dish. Serve with spoonfuls of vanilla ice cream, crème fraîche or pouring cream.

FOR STICKY BANANA PUDDING, prepare the pudding as above, but replace the chopped apple with 1 small ripe and roughly mashed banana and ½ teaspoon ground cinnamon. Make up the sauce and cook as above.

DARK CHOCOLATE & COFFEE POTS

Serves **4**
Preparation time **25 minutes,**
  plus cooling and **chilling**
Cooking temperature **low**
Cooking time **3–3½ hours**

450 ml (¾ pint) **milk**
150 ml (¼ pint) **double cream**
200 g (7 oz) **plain dark chocolate**,
  broken into pieces
2 **eggs**
3 **egg yolks**
50 g (2 oz) **caster sugar**
¼ teaspoon **ground cinnamon**
chocolate curls, to decorate

TOPPING
150 ml (¼ pint) **double cream**
75 ml (3 fl oz) **coffee cream liqueur**

Preheat the slow cooker if necessary. Pour the milk and cream into a saucepan and bring just to the boil. Remove from the heat, add the chocolate pieces and set aside for 5 minutes, stirring occasionally, until the chocolate has melted.

Put the whole eggs, egg yolks, sugar and cinnamon in a mixing bowl and whisk until smooth. Gradually whisk in the warm chocolate milk, then strain the mixture into 4 heatproof pots or mugs, each 250 ml (8 fl oz).

Cover the tops of the pots or mugs with foil and stand them in the slow cooker pot. Pour hot water into the slow cooker pot to come halfway up the sides of the pots or mugs. Cover with the lid and cook on low for 3–3½ hours or until set.

Lift the dishes carefully out of the slow cooker pot using a tea towel. Leave to cool at room temperature, then transfer to the refrigerator for at least 4 hours until well chilled.

Just before serving, whip the cream for the topping until soft swirls form. Gradually whisk in the liqueur, then spoon the flavoured cream over the tops of the desserts. Sprinkle with chocolate curls and serve.

FOR CAPPUCCINO POTS WITH COFFEE CREAM LIQUEUR, add 2 teaspoons instant coffee to the just-boiled cream and milk when adding the chocolate. Continue as above, but omit the cinnamon.

EVE'S PUDDING ♥

Serves **4**
Preparation time **25 minutes**
Cooking temperature **high**
Cooking time **3–3½ hours**

50 g (2 oz) **sunflower margarine**,
  plus extra for greasing
50 g (2 oz) **caster sugar**
50 g (2 oz) **self-raising flour**
25 g (1 oz) **ground almonds**
¼ teaspoon **baking powder**
1 **egg**
grated rind and juice of 1 **lemon**
1 **dessert apple**, quartered, cored
  and sliced
1 tablespoon **apricot jam**
75 g (3 oz) **instant powdered
  custard with sweetener to serve**

Preheat the slow cooker if necessary. Grease the base and sides of a 15 cm (6 inch) round ovenproof dish, about 6 cm (2½ inches) deep, with a little margarine, checking first that it will fit in the slow cooker pot. Place the margarine, sugar, flour, almonds and baking powder in a food processor, add the egg and lemon rind and blend until smooth. Spoon into the dish and spread level.

Toss the apple slices with the lemon juice, then overlap in a ring on top of the pudding mixture. Cover the dish with greased foil and put in the slow cooker pot. Pour boiling water into the slow cooker pot to come halfway up the sides of the dish, cover and cook on high for 3–3½ hours until a knife comes out cleanly when inserted into the centre.

Dot the top of the pudding with the apricot jam, then gently spread into an even layer. Place under a preheated hot grill for 3–4 minutes until the top is lightly caramelized. Make the custard with boiling water according to packet instructions and serve with the pudding.

FOR CHOCOLATE & PEAR PUDDING, follow the recipe above to make the pudding base, using 1 tablespoon cocoa powder instead of the lemon rind. Quarter, core and slice 1 small pear, toss with the lemon juice, then arrange over the pudding mixture. Cover and bake as above, then dust the top with a little sifted icing sugar before serving.

JAM ROLY-POLY PUDDING

Serves **4**
Preparation time **25 minutes**
Cooking temperature **high**
Cooking time **3½–4 hours**

300 g (10 oz) **self-raising flour**, plus
    extra for dusting
150 g (5 oz) **shredded**
    vegetable suet
50 g (2 oz) **caster sugar**
grated rind of 2 **lemons**
pinch of **salt**
200–250 ml (7–8 fl oz) **milk** or **milk**
    and water mixed
4 tablespoons **strawberry jam**
hot **custard**, to serve

Preheat the slow cooker if necessary. Put the flour, suet, sugar, lemon rind and a pinch of salt in a bowl and mix well. Gradually stir in the milk or milk and water to make a soft but not sticky dough. Knead lightly, then roll out on a piece of floured nonstick baking paper to a rectangle about 23 x 30 cm (9 x 12 inches). Turn the paper so that the shorter edges are facing you.

Spread the jam over the pastry, leaving 2 cm (¾ inch) around the edges. Roll up, starting at a shorter edge, using the paper to help. Wrap in the paper, then in a sheet of foil. Twist the ends together tightly, leaving space for the pudding to rise.

Transfer the pudding to the slow cooker pot and raise off the base by standing it on 2 ramekin dishes. Pour boiling water into the pot to come a little up the sides of the pudding, being careful that the water cannot seep through any joins. Cover with the lid and cook on high for 3½–4 hours or until the pudding is light and fluffy. Lift out of the pot, then unwrap and cut into thick slices. Serve with hot custard.

FOR SPOTTED DICK, grate the rind of 1 large orange and reserve. Squeeze the juice into a saucepan, bring to the boil, add 150 g (5 oz) raisins and leave to soak for 30 minutes. Make up the pastry as above, adding the orange rind, the grated rind of 1 lemon and the soaked raisins before mixing with enough milk to make a soft dough. Shape into a log 23 cm (9 inches) long. Wrap in nonstick baking paper and foil, then cook as above.

TOPSY TURVY PLUM PUDDING

Serves **6**
Preparation time **25 minutes**
Cooking temperature **high**
Cooking time **4–5 hours**

100 g (3½ oz) **blackberries**, thawed
   if frozen
200 g (7 oz) **ripe red plums**, halved,
   stoned and sliced
2 tablespoons **red berry jam**
100 g (3½ oz) **butter**, at room
   temperature, plus extra
   for greasing
100 g (3½ oz) **caster sugar**
100 g (3½ oz) **self-raising flour**
2 **eggs**, beaten
50 g (2 oz) **ground almonds**
few drops of **almond extract**
toasted **flaked almonds**, to decorate

Preheat the slow cooker if necessary. Lightly butter a 1.2 litre (2 pint) soufflé dish and base-line with a circle of nonstick baking paper, checking first that the dish will fit in the slow cooker pot. Arrange the blackberries and plums in the base, then dot with the jam.

Cream together the butter and sugar in a mixing bowl with a wooden spoon or hand-held electric whisk until soft and creamy. Gradually mix in alternate spoonfuls of the flour and beaten egg, and continue adding and beating until the mixture is smooth. Stir in the almonds and almond extract. Spoon the mixture over the fruit, spread it level and cover the top with foil.

Lower the dish into the slow cooker pot and pour boiling water into the pot to come halfway up the sides of the dish. Cover with the lid and cook on high for 4–5 hours or until the sponge is well risen and springs back when pressed with a fingertip.

Lift the dish out of the slow cooker pot using a tea towel and remove the foil. Loosen the edges of the pudding with a knife, turn out on to a plate with a rim and remove the lining paper. Decorate with toasted flaked almonds and serve hot with custard, if liked.

FOR PEACH & CHOCOLATE PUDDING, arrange 2 (or 1 if very large) halved, stoned and sliced ripe peaches in the base of the dish and dot with 2 tablespoons apricot jam. Make up the sponge mixture as above, adding 25 g (1 oz) cocoa powder and an extra 25 g (1 oz) self-raising flour instead of the ground almonds and almond extract. Continue as above.

LEMON & POPPY SEED DRIZZLE CAKE

Serves **6–8**
Preparation time **25 minutes**, plus
   cooling and **soaking**
Cooking temperature **high**
Cooking time **4½–5 hours**

125 g (4 oz) **butter**, at room
   temperature, plus extra
   for greasing
125 g (4 oz) **caster sugar**
125 g (4 oz) **self-raising flour**
2 **eggs**, beaten
2 tablespoons **poppy seeds**
grated rind of 1 **lemon**
lemon rind curls, to decorate
crème fraîche, to serve

LEMON SYRUP
juice of 1½ **lemons**
125 g (4 oz) **caster sugar**

Preheat the slow cooker if necessary. Lightly butter a soufflé dish 14 cm (5½ inches) in diameter and 9 cm (3½ inches) deep, and base-line with a circle of nonstick baking paper, checking first that it will fit in the slow cooker pot.

Cream together the butter and sugar in a mixing bowl with a wooden spoon or hand-held electric whisk until soft and creamy. Gradually mix in alternate spoonfuls of the flour and beaten egg, and continue adding and beating until the mixture is smooth. Stir in the poppy seeds and lemon rind, then spoon the mixture into the soufflé dish and spread the top level. Cover the top of the dish loosely with buttered foil and then lower into the slow cooker pot.

Pour boiling water into the slow cooker pot so that it comes halfway up the sides of the dish. Cover with the lid and cook on high for 4½–5 hours or until the cake is dry and springs back when pressed with a fingertip.

Lift the dish carefully out of the slow cooker using a tea towel, remove the foil and loosen the edge of the cake with a knife. Turn out on to a plate or shallow dish with a rim and remove the lining paper. Quickly warm the lemon juice and sugar together for the syrup, and as soon as the sugar has dissolved, pour the syrup over the cake. Leave to cool and for the syrup to soak in. Cut into slices and serve with spoonfuls of crème fraîche, decorated with lemon rind curls.

FOR CITRUS DRIZZLE CAKE, omit the lemon rind and poppy seeds from the cake mixture and stir in the grated rind of ½ lemon, ½ lime and ½ small orange. Bake as above. Make the syrup using the juice of the grated fruits and sugar as above.

CHERRY & CHOCOLATE PUDDINGS

Serves **4**
Preparation time **25 minutes**
Cooking temperature **high**
Cooking time **1½–2 hours**

50 g (2 oz) **butter**, plus extra
   for greasing
50 g (2 oz) **caster sugar**
50 g (2 oz) **self-raising flour**
1 **egg**
1 tablespoon **cocoa powder**
¼ teaspoon **baking powder**
¼ teaspoon **ground cinnamon**
425 g (14 oz) can **pitted black
   cherries**, drained

CHOCOLATE SAUCE
100 g (3½ oz) **white chocolate**,
   broken into pieces
150 ml (¼ pint) **double cream**

Preheat the slow cooker if necessary. Butter the inside of 4 metal pudding moulds, each 250 ml (8 fl oz), and base-line with circles of nonstick baking paper, checking first that they will fit in the slow cooker pot.

Put the butter, sugar, flour, egg, cocoa, baking powder and cinnamon in a mixing bowl and beat them together with a wooden spoon until smooth.

Arrange 7 cherries in the base of each pudding mould. Roughly chop the remainder and stir them into the pudding mixture. Spoon the mixture into the pudding moulds and level the tops. Loosely cover the tops of the moulds with foil and put them in the slow cooker pot. Pour boiling water into the pot so that it comes halfway up the sides of the moulds, cover with the lid and cook on high for 1½–2 hours or until the puddings are well risen and the tops spring back when pressed with a fingertip. Lift the puddings out of the slow cooker pot using a tea towel.

Put the chocolate and cream in a small saucepan and heat gently, stirring occasionally, until melted. Loosen the edges of the puddings, turn them out into shallow bowls, peel away the lining paper and pour the sauce around them before serving.

FOR CHERRY & ALMOND PUDDINGS, prepare the sponge as above, omitting the cocoa and ground cinnamon and instead adding 2 tablespoons ground almonds and a few drops of almond extract. Cook as above, turn out and serve with spoonfuls of vanilla ice cream.

RASPBERRY & RHUBARB OATY CRUMBLE

Serves **4–5**
Preparation time **15 minutes**
Cooking temperature **low**
Cooking time **2–3 hours**

400 g (13 oz) trimmed **rhubarb**
150 g (5 oz) **frozen raspberries**
50 g (2 oz) **caster sugar**
3 tablespoons **water**

TOPPING
15 g (½ oz) **butter**
3 tablespoons **flaked almonds**
200 g (7 oz), **ready-made flapjacks**
   (about 4)

Preheat the slow cooker if necessary. Cut the rhubarb into 2.5 cm (1 inch) thick slices and add to the slow cooker pot with the still-frozen raspberries, the sugar and measurement water. Cover with the lid and cook on low for 2–3 hours or until the rhubarb is just tender.

When almost ready to serve, heat the butter in a frying pan, add the almonds and crumble in the flapjacks. Fry, stirring, for 3–4 minutes or until hot and lightly browned. Spoon the fruit into bowls, sprinkle the crumble over the top and serve with thick cream, if liked.

FOR PEACH & MIXED BERRY CRUMBLE, dice 3 fresh peaches, discarding the stones, and add to the slow cooker pot with 150 g (5 oz) mixed still-frozen summer fruits, the sugar and water as above. Cook and sprinkle with the flapjack topping as above.

COMPOTE WITH MASCARPONE

Serves **4**
Preparation time **20 minutes**
Cooking temperature **high**
Cooking time **1–1¼ hours**

4 **nectarines**, halved, stoned and diced
250 g (8 oz) **strawberries**, hulled, halved or quartered
   depending on size
50 g (2 oz) **caster sugar**, plus 2 tablespoons
finely grated rind and juice of 2 **oranges**
125 ml (4 fl oz) cold **water**
150 g (5 oz) **mascarpone cheese**
40 g (1½ oz) **amaretti biscuits**

Preheat the slow cooker if necessary. Put the fruit in the slow cooker pot with the 50 g (2 oz) sugar, the rind of 1 orange, the juice of 1½ oranges and the measurement water. Cover and cook on high for 1–1¼ hours or until the fruit is tender. Serve warm or cold.

When almost ready to serve, mix the mascarpone with the remaining 2 tablespoons sugar and orange rind and juice. Reserve some of the amaretti biscuits for decoration. Crumble the rest with your fingertips into the bowl with the mascarpone and stir until mixed. Spoon the fruit into tumblers, top with spoonfuls of the orange mascarpone mixture and decorate with a sprinkling of amaretti biscuit crumbs.

FOR PLUM & CRANBERRY COMPOTE WITH ORANGE MASCARPONE, replace the nectarines and strawberries with 625g (1¼ lb) plums, quartered and stoned, and 125 g (4 oz) cranberries (no need to thaw if frozen). Increase the sugar to 75 g (3 oz), then follow the recipe above, using cranberry and raspberry juice instead of water, if liked.

STICKY MARMALADE SYRUP PUDDING

Serves **4–5**
Preparation time **20 minutes**
Cooking temperature **high**
Cooking time **3–3½ hours**

butter, for greasing
4 tablespoons **golden syrup**
3 tablespoons **orange marmalade**
175 g (6 oz) **self-raising flour**
75 g (3 oz) **shredded vegetable suet**
50 g (2 oz) **light muscovado sugar**
1 teaspoon **ground ginger**
grated rind and juice of 1 **orange**
2 **eggs**
2 tablespoons **milk**

Preheat the slow cooker if necessary. Lightly butter a 1.2 litre (2 pint) pudding basin and base-line with a circle of nonstick baking paper, checking first that it will fit in the slow cooker pot. Spoon the golden syrup and 2 tablespoons of the marmalade into the basin.

Put the flour, suet, sugar and ginger in a bowl and mix together. Add the remaining marmalade, orange rind and juice, the eggs and milk and beat until smooth. Spoon the mixture into the basin, spread it level and cover the top with buttered foil.

Lower the basin into the slow cooker pot and pour boiling water into the pot to come halfway up the sides of the basin. Cover with the lid and cook on high for 3–3½ hours or until the pudding is well risen and feels firm and dry when the top is pressed with a fingertip. Lift the basin out of the slow cooker pot using a tea towel and remove the foil. Loosen the edge of the pudding with a knife, turn out on to a plate and peel off the lining paper. Serve scoops of the pudding in bowls with custard or vanilla ice cream, if liked.

FOR STICKY BANANA PUDDING, spoon 4 tablespoons golden syrup and 3 tablespoons light muscovado sugar into the base of the lined basin. Cut 2 bananas in half lengthways, then in half again crossways. Toss in the juice of ½ lemon and arrange, cut side down, in the bottom of the basin. Make up the pudding mixture, spoon over the bananas and continue as above.

COCONUT & ROSE RICE PUDDING ♥

Serves **4**
Preparation time **10 minutes**
Cooking temperature **high**
Cooking time **2½–3 hours**

65 g (2½ oz) **pudding rice**, rinsed and drained
50 g (2 oz) **caster sugar**
25 g (1 oz) **desiccated coconut**, plus 2 teaspoons
600 ml (1 pint) **semi-skimmed milk**
½–1 teaspoon **rosewater**, to taste
125 g (4 oz) **raspberries**, to serve

Preheat the slow cooker if necessary. Place the rice, sugar and the 25 g (1 oz) coconut in the slow cooker pot, add the milk and stir well. Cover and cook on high for 2½–3 hours until the rice is tender.

Stir well, then add the rosewater. Spoon into bowls, top with the raspberries and the remaining 2 teaspoons coconut and serve immediately.

FOR VANILLA & ORANGE RICE PUDDING, split 1 vanilla pod lengthways and scrape out the seeds with a small knife. Follow the recipe above, adding the vanilla seeds to the rice and milk in the slow cooker pot with the vanilla pod and the finely grated rind of ½ orange. Stir well, cover and cook as above. Stir again and remove the vanilla pod before serving with raspberries and a sprinkling of coconut.

PEPPERMINT & RASPBERRY BRÛLÉE

Serves **4**
Preparation time **30 minutes**, **plus cooling** and **chilling**
Cooking temperature **low**
Cooking time **2½–3½ hours**

4 **egg yolks**
40 g (1½ oz) **caster sugar**
400 ml (14 fl oz) **double cream**
¼ teaspoon **peppermint extract**
150 g (5 oz) **raspberries**
2 tablespoons **icing sugar**

Preheat the slow cooker if necessary. Whisk the egg yolks and sugar in a bowl for 3–4 minutes until frothy, then gradually whisk in the cream. Stir in the peppermint extract. Strain the mixture into a jug.

Pour into 4 ramekin dishes, each 150 ml (¼ pint), checking first that they will fit in the slow cooker pot. Put the dishes into the slow cooker pot, pour boiling water into the pot to come halfway up the sides of the dishes, then loosely cover the top of each dish with foil.

Cover with the lid and cook on low for 2½–3½ hours or until the custard is set with a slight quiver to the middle. Lift the dishes carefully out of the slow cooker and leave to cool. Transfer to the refrigerator to chill for 4 hours.

When ready to serve, pile a few raspberries in the centre of each dish and sift over the icing sugar. Caramelize the sugar with a cook's blowtorch.

FOR PEPPERMINT & WHITE CHOCOLATE BRÛLÉE, bring 350 ml (12 fl oz) double cream just to the boil in a saucepan, then take off the heat, add 100 g (4 oz) good-quality white chocolate, broken into pieces, and leave until melted. Whisk the egg yolks with 25 g (1 oz) caster sugar, then gradually mix in the chocolate cream and the peppermint extract. Continue as above. Replace the raspberries with blueberries and serve as above.

DRINKS

SKIER'S HOT CHOCOLATE

Serves **4**
Preparation time **10 minutes**
Cooking temperature **low**
Cooking time **2–3 hours**

100 g (3½ oz) **good-quality chocolate**
25 g (1 oz) **caster sugar**
750 ml (1¼ pints) **milk**
few drops of **vanilla extract**
little **ground cinnamon**
3 tablespoons **Kahlúa coffee
   liqueur** (optional)
mini marshmallows, to serve

Preheat the slow cooker if necessary. Put the chocolate and sugar in the slow cooker pot, then add the milk, vanilla extract and cinnamon.

Cover with the lid and cook on low for 2–3 hours, whisking once or twice, until the chocolate has melted and the drink is hot. Stir in the Kahlúa, if using. Ladle into mugs and top with a few mini marshmallows.

FOR HOT CHOCOLATE WITH BRANDY CREAM, make up the hot chocolate as above, replacing the Kahlúa with 3 tablespoons brandy. Whip 125 ml (4 fl oz) double cream with 2 tablespoons sifted icing sugar until soft peaks form, then gradually whisk in 3 tablespoons brandy. Pour the hot chocolate into mugs, then top with spoonfuls of the whipped cream and dust lightly with drinking chocolate powder or grated chocolate.

FOR MEXICAN HOT CHOCOLATE, put 50 g (2 oz) cocoa powder and 4 teaspoons instant coffee into the slow cooker pot. Measure 1 litre (1¾ pint) boiling water. Make a smooth paste by mixing a little of the boiling water with the cocoa and coffee. Add the rest of the water, 150 ml (¼ pint) rum, 100 g (3½ oz) caster sugar, ½ teaspoon ground cinnamon and 1 dried red chilli, cut in half. Cover and cook on low for 3–4 hours. Discard the chilli and ladle into 4 cups. Top with 150 ml (¼ pint) double cream.

LEMON CORDIAL

HOT JAMAICAN PUNCH

Serves about **20**
Preparation time **10 minutes**, plus cooling
Cooking temperature **high** and **low**
Cooking time **3–4 hours**

3 **lemons**, washed and thinly sliced, pips discarded
625 g (1¼ lb) **granulated sugar**
900 ml (1½ pints) boiling **water**
25 g (1 oz) **tartaric acid**
ice cubes, to serve

Preheat the slow cooker if necessary. Add the lemon slices to the slow cooker pot with the sugar and measurement boiling water and stir well until the sugar is almost all dissolved. Cover with the lid and cook on high for 1 hour.

Reduce the heat and cook on low for 2–3 hours or until the lemons are almost translucent. Switch off the slow cooker and stir in the tartaric acid. Leave to cool.

Remove and discard some of the sliced lemons using a slotted spoon. Transfer the cordial and remaining lemon slices to 2 sterilized screw-topped, wide-necked bottles or storage jars. Seal well, label and store in the refrigerator for up to 1 month.

Dilute the cordial with water in a ratio of 1:3, adding a few of the sliced lemons for decoration, ice cubes and mint or lemon balm sprigs, if liked.

FOR LEMON & LIME CORDIAL, prepare the cordial using 2 lemons and 2 limes, washed and thinly sliced, instead of 3 lemons. Serve diluted with sparkling mineral water and mint sprigs.

Serves **6**
Preparation time **10 minutes**
Cooking temperature **high** and **low**
Cooking time **3–4 hours**

juice of 3 **limes**
300 ml (½ pint) **dark rum**
300 ml (½ pint) **ginger wine**
600 ml (1 pint) cold **water**
75 g (3 oz) **caster sugar**

TO DECORATE
1 **lime**, thinly sliced
2 slices of **pineapple**, cored but skin left on and cut into pieces

Preheat the slow cooker if necessary. Strain the lime juice into the slow cooker pot and discard the pips. Add the rum, ginger wine, measurement water and sugar, cover and cook on high for 1 hour.

Reduce the heat and cook on low for 2–3 hours until the punch is piping hot or until you are ready to serve. Stir well, then ladle into heatproof glasses and add a slice of lime and 2 pieces of pineapple to each glass.

FOR RUM TODDY, put the grated rind of 1 lemon and 1 orange and the juice of 3 lemons and 3 oranges into the slow cooker. Add 125 g (4 oz) set honey and 75 g (3 oz) caster sugar. Increase the water to 750 ml (1¼ pints) and reduce the rum to 150 ml (¼ pint). Cook and serve as above.

MULLED CRANBERRY & RED WINE

Makes **8–10 glasses**
Preparation time **10 minutes**
Cooking temperature **high** and **low**
Cooking time **4–5 hours**

75 cl bottle **inexpensive red wine**
600 ml (1 pint) **cranberry juice**
100 ml (3½ fl oz) **brandy**, **rum**, **vodka** or **orange liqueur**
100 g (3½ oz) **caster sugar**
1 **orange**, cut into segments
8 **cloves**
1–2 **cinnamon sticks** (depending on size)

TO SERVE
1 **orange**, cut into segments
2–3 **bay leaves**
few **cranberries**

Preheat the slow cooker if necessary. Pour the red wine, cranberry juice and brandy or other alcohol into the slow cooker pot. Stir in the sugar.

Stud each orange segment with a clove. Break the cinnamon sticks into large pieces and add to the pot with the orange pieces. Cover with the lid and cook on high for 1 hour. Reduce the heat and cook on low for 3–4 hours.

Replace the orange segments with new ones and add the bay leaves and cranberries. Ladle into heatproof glasses, keeping back the fruits and herbs, if liked.

FOR MULLED ORANGE & RED WINE, prepare the wine as above, but omit the cranberry juice and instead add 300 ml (½ pint) orange juice from a carton and 300 ml (½ pint) water. Serve the mulled wine decorated with extra herbs and fruit.

HOT SPICED BERRY PUNCH

Serves **6**
Preparation time **10 minutes**
Cooking temperature **high** and **low**
Cooking time **3–4 hours**

1 litre (1¾ pints) **cranberry and raspberry drink**
250 g (8 oz) **frozen berry fruits**
50 g (2 oz) **caster sugar**
4 tablespoons **crème de cassis** (optional)
4 small **star anise**
1 **cinnamon stick**, halved
raspberries, to decorate (optional)

Preheat the slow cooker if necessary. Pour the cranberry and raspberry drink into the slow cooker pot. Add the frozen fruits, sugar and crème de cassis, if using. Stir together, then add the star anise and cinnamon.

Cover with the lid and cook on high for 1 hour. Reduce the heat and cook on low for 2–3 hours, or set to auto for 3–4 hours, until piping hot.

Strain, if liked, then put the star anise and cinnamon into small heatproof glasses. Ladle the hot punch into the glasses and add a few raspberries, if liked.

FOR BOOZY BERRY PUNCH, replace the crème de cassis with 150 ml (¼ pint) vodka and then make up the recipe as above.

FOR SPICED BERRY AND PEAR COMPOTE, make up the punch as above. Peel, core and slice 4 ripe pears and arrange in a heatproof serving dish. Pour over 300 ml (½ pint) of the hot punch and leave to cool. Serve as a dessert or breakfast accompaniment topped with spoonfuls of Greek yogurt flavoured with a little honey. Serve the remaining punch in glasses as above.

HOT MEXICAN COFFEE

Serves **4**
Preparation time **10 minutes**
Cooking temperature **low**
Cooking time **3–4 hours**

50 g (2 oz) **cocoa powder**
4 teaspoons **instant coffee granules**
1 litre (1¾ pints) boiling **water**
150 ml (¼ pint) **dark rum**
100 g (3½ oz) **caster sugar**
½ teaspoon **ground cinnamon**
1 large **dried** or **fresh red chilli**, halved
150 ml (¼) pint **double cream**

TO DECORATE
2 tablespoons grated **plain dark chocolate**
4 **dried red chillies** (optional)

Preheat the slow cooker if necessary. Put the cocoa and instant coffee in a bowl and mix to a smooth paste with a little of the measurement boiling water.

Pour the cocoa paste into the slow cooker pot. Add the remaining measurement boiling water, the rum, sugar, cinnamon and red chilli and mix together. Cover with the lid and cook on low for 3–4 hours until piping hot or until the coffee is required.

Stir well, then ladle into heatproof glasses. Whip the cream until it is just beginning to hold its shape and spoon a little into each glass. Decorate each drink with a little of the grated chocolate and a dried chilli, if liked.

FOR HOT MOCHA COFFEE, reduce the amount of boiling water to 900 ml (1½ pints) and use 1 teaspoon vanilla extract instead of the rum and chilli. Cook as above, then whisk in 300 ml (½ pint) milk. Pour the drink into heatproof glasses, top with cream as above and decorate each glass with a few mini marshmallows.

CIDER TODDY

Serves **6**
Preparation time **10 minutes**
Cooking temperature **high** and **low**
Cooking time **3–4 hours**

1 litre (1¾ pints) **dry cider**
125 ml (4 fl oz) **whisky**
125 ml (4 fl oz) **orange juice**
4 tablespoons **set honey**
2 **cinnamon sticks**
orange wedges and curls,
    to decorate (optional)

Preheat the slow cooker if necessary. Add all the ingredients to the slow cooker pot, cover with the lid and cook on high for 1 hour.

Reduce the heat and cook on low for 2–3 hours, or set to auto for 3–4 hours, until piping hot. Stir, then ladle into heatproof tumblers. Add orange wedges and curls to decorate, if liked.

FOR GINGERED CIDER TODDY, replace the whisky with 125 ml (4 fl oz) ginger wine and 2 tablespoons drained, finely chopped stem ginger and make up the recipe as above.

FOR CITRUS TODDY, pour 150 ml (¼ pint) whisky into the slow cooker pot, add 125 g (4 oz) set honey, 100 g (3½ oz) caster sugar and 750 ml (1¼ pints) cold water, then add the grated rind of 1 orange, the juice of 3 oranges, the grated rind of 1 lemon and the juice of 3 lemons. Roughly crush 8 cardamom pods and add the pods and their black seeds to the slow cooker pot. Cover and cook as above.

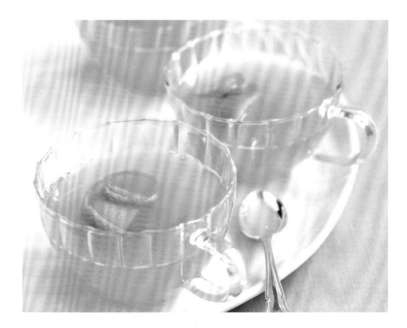

HOT BUTTERED RUM

Serves **6**
Preparation time **5 minutes**
Cooking temperature **high** and **low**
Cooking time **3–4 hours**

1 litre (1¾ pints) **clear apple juice**
150 ml (¼ pint) **dark rum**
2 tablespoons **set honey**
2 tablespoons **dark muscovado sugar**
25 g (1 oz) **butter**
6 **cloves**
1 **dessert apple**, cored and thickly sliced, to decorate

Preheat the slow cooker if necessary. Put all the ingredients into the slow cooker pot, cover with the lid and cook on high for 1 hour. Reduce the heat and cook on low for 2–3 hours, or set to auto for 3–4 hours, until piping hot.

Stir, scoop out the cloves, then ladle the punch into heatproof tumblers. Decorate with the apple slices.

FOR HOT BUTTERED CALVADOS, replace the rum with 150 ml (¼ pint) calvados (apple brandy) and make up the recipe as above.

FOR POACHED APPLES WITH BUTTERED RUM, once the punch is made, pour into a serving jug, keeping 300 ml (½ pint) in the slow cooker pot. Add 4 cooking apples that have been quartered, cored and peeled, cover with the lid and cook on high for 1–1½ hours until the apples are tender. Serve as a dessert with scoops of vanilla ice cream.

BLACKBERRY MULLED WINE

Serves **6**
Preparation time **5 minutes**
Cooking temperature **high** and **low**
Cooking time **3–4 hours**

75 cl bottle **red wine**
150 ml (¼ pint) **dark rum**
200 ml (7 fl oz) **orange juice**
400 ml (14 fl oz) cold **water**
150 g (5 oz) **caster sugar**
200 g (7 oz) **blackberries**
1 **cinnamon stick**, halved
1 **orange**, halved and sliced, to serve

Preheat the slow cooker if necessary. Pour the wine, rum, orange juice and measurement water into the slow cooker pot. Add the sugar, blackberries and cinnamon and stir together.

Cover with the lid and cook on high for 1 hour, then reduce the heat and continue to cook on low for 2–3 hours. Ladle into heatproof glasses and serve each with a half slice of orange.

FOR TRADITIONAL MULLED WINE, omit the blackberries and rum. Heat the red wine, orange juice and water with the sugar and 2 cinnamon sticks, adding 1 orange, cut into chunks and spiked with 4 cloves, plus a little grated nutmeg and a 2.5 cm (1 inch) piece of fresh root ginger, peeled and thinly sliced. Cook as above.

MULLED WINE

Serves **6**
Preparation time **5 minutes**
Cooking temperature **high** and **low**
Cooking time **3–4 hours**

75 cl bottle **inexpensive red wine**
300 ml (½ pint) **clear apple juice**
300 ml (½ pint) cold **water**
juice of 1 **orange**
1 **orange**, sliced
½ **lemon**, sliced
1 **cinnamon stick**, halved
6 **cloves**
2 **bay leaves**
125 g (4 oz) **caster sugar**
150 ml (¼ pint) **brandy**

Preheat the slow cooker if necessary. Pour the wine, apple juice, measurement water and orange juice into the slow cooker pot.

Add the orange and lemon slices, the cinnamon stick, cloves and bay leaves, then mix in the sugar and brandy.

Cover with the lid and cook on high for 1 hour. Reduce the heat and cook on low for 2–3 hours, or set to auto for 3–4 hours, until piping hot. Ladle into heatproof glasses.

FOR CRANBERRY MULLED WINE, replace the apple juice with 300 ml (½ pint) cranberry juice and 125 g (4 oz) cranberries and make up the recipe as above.

FOR MULLED WINE JELLY, cook the mulled wine as above. Spoon 6 tablespoons cold water into a bowl, sprinkle over 30 g (1 oz) powdered gelatine and leave to soak for 5 minutes. Strain the mulled wine, stir in the gelatine mixture until dissolved and leave to cool. Pour into 8 wine glasses and chill in the refrigerator until set. Top each of the mulled wine jellies with whipped cream.

PRESERVES

APPLE, THYME & ROSEMARY JELLY

Makes **3 jars of assorted sizes**
Preparation time **40 minutes**
Cooking temperature **high**
Cooking time **2–3 hours**

1 kg (2 lb) **cooking apples** (not peeled
  or cored), washed and diced
125 ml (4 fl oz) **red wine** or
  cider vinegar
600 ml (1 pint) boiling **water**
about 625 g (1¼ lb) **granulated sugar**
1 tablespoon **thyme leaves**, stripped
  from the stems
2 tablespoons finely chopped
  rosemary leaves

Preheat the slow cooker if necessary. Put the apples and wine or vinegar into the slow cooker pot and pour over the measurement boiling water. Cover with the lid and cook on high for 2–3 hours or until the apples are tender. Don't worry if the apples discolour.

Hang a jelly bag from a frame or upturned stool and set a bowl beneath it. Ladle the apples and their juices into the bag and allow to drip through.

Measure the liquid and pour it into a large saucepan; for every 600 ml (1 pint) liquid add 500 g (1 lb) sugar. Heat gently, stirring occasionally, until the sugar has dissolved, then boil rapidly for about 15 minutes until setting point is reached. Check with a jam thermometer or spoon a little of the jelly on to a saucer that has been chilled in the refrigerator. Leave for 1–2 minutes, then run a finger through the jelly. If a finger space is left and the jelly has wrinkled, it is ready; if not, boil for 5–10 minutes more and then retest. Skim off any scum with a slotted spoon, then stir in the herbs. Leave the jelly to stand for 5 minutes.

Warm 3 sterilized jars in a low oven for 5 minutes. Ladle the jelly into the warm jars, cover the surface with waxed discs, add cellophane jam pot covers and secure with elastic bands or screw the jar lids in place. Label and leave to cool. Store in a cool place until required. Once opened, store in the refrigerator. Serve with lamb.

FOR APPLE & BLACKBERRY JELLY, put 750 g (1½ lb) cooking apples, washed and diced, into the slow cooker pot with 250 g (8 oz) blackberries, 125 ml (4 fl oz) lemon juice and the boiling water. Continue as above, omitting the herbs. Serve with scones.

TANGY CITRUS CURD

Makes **2 × 400 g (13 oz) jars**
Preparation time **25 minutes**
Cooking temperature **low**
Cooking time **3–4 hours**

125 g (4 oz) **unsalted butter**
400 g (13 oz) **caster sugar**
grated rind and juice of 2 **lemons**
grated rind and juice of 1 **orange**
grated rind and juice of 1 **lime**
4 **eggs**, beaten

Preheat the slow cooker if necessary. Put the butter
and sugar in a saucepan, add the fruit rinds, then
strain in the juice. Heat gently for 2–3 minutes, stirring
occasionally, until the butter has melted and the sugar
has dissolved.

Pour the mixture into a basin that will fit comfortably
in your slow cooker pot. Leave to cool for 10 minutes,
then gradually strain in the eggs and mix well. Cover
the basin with foil and lower into the slow cooker
pot. Pour hot water into the slow cooker pot to come
halfway up the sides of the basin. Cover with the lid
and cook on low for 3–4 hours or until the mixture is
very thick. Stir once or twice during cooking if possible.

Warm the 2 sterilized jars in a low oven for 5 minutes.
Spoon in the citrus curd, place a waxed disc on top and
leave to cool. Seal each jar with a screw-top lid or a
cellophane jam pot cover and an elastic band, label and
store in the refrigerator. Use within 3–4 weeks.

FOR LEMON CURD, prepare as above, but omit the
orange and lime and use 3 lemons rather than 2. Cook
and store as above.

APRICOT CONSERVE

Makes **3 jars of assorted sizes**
Preparation time **15 minutes**
Cooking temperature **high**
Cooking time **3–5 hours**

300 g (10 oz) **ready-to-eat dried apricots**, diced
4 **peaches**, halved, stoned and diced
250 g (8 oz) **caster sugar**
300 ml (½ pint) boiling **water**

Preheat the slow cooker if necessary. Put all the
ingredients into the slow cooker pot and stir together.

Cover with the lid and cook on high for 3–5 hours,
stirring once during cooking and then again at the end,
until the fruit is soft and the liquid thick and syrupy,
with a texture like chutney.

Warm 3 sterilized jars in a low oven for 5 minutes.
Ladle the conserve into the warm jars. Cover the
surface with waxed discs, add cellophane jam pot
covers and secure with elastic bands or screw the jar
lids in place. Label and leave to cool. The conserve can
be stored for up to 2 months in the refrigerator.

FOR APRICOT & ORANGE CONSERVE, put 400 g (13 oz)
ready-to-eat dried apricots, the grated rind and juice of
1 large orange, the sugar and the boiling water in the
slow cooker, omitting the peaches. Continue as above.

CHILLIED TOMATO & GARLIC CHUTNEY

Makes **5 × 400 g (13 oz) jars**
Preparation time **30 minutes**
Cooking temperature **high**
Cooking time **6–8 hours**

1 kg (2 lb) **tomatoes**, skinned and
    roughly chopped
1 large **onion**, chopped
2 **cooking apples**, about 500 g (1 lb),
    peeled, cored and chopped
2 **red peppers**, cored, deseeded
    and diced
75 g (3 oz) **sultanas**
100 ml (3½ fl oz) **distilled
    malt vinegar**
250 g (8 oz) **granulated sugar**
2–3 large **mild red chillies**, halved,
    deseeded and finely chopped
6–8 **garlic cloves**, finely chopped
1 **cinnamon stick**, halved
½ teaspoon **ground allspice**
1 teaspoon **salt**
pepper

Preheat the slow cooker if necessary. Put all the ingredients in the slow cooker pot and mix together. Cover with the lid and cook on high for 6–8 hours or until thick and pulpy, stirring once or twice.

Warm the 5 sterilized jars in a low oven for 5 minutes. Spoon in the chutney, place a waxed disc on top and leave to cool. Seal each jar with a screw-top lid, then label. Store in a cool place for up to 2 months. Once opened, store in the refrigerator.

FOR SPICED GREEN TOMATO CHUTNEY, replace the tomatoes with 1 kg (2 lb) green tomatoes (chopped but not skinned) and replace the onion and peppers with 3 onions weighing 500 g (1 lb) in total. Mix the tomatoes and onions with the cooking apples, vinegar, sugar, chillies and salt. Decrease the garlic cloves to 2 and replace the cinnamon and allspice with 1 teaspoon each ground ginger and ground turmeric and 1 teaspoon roughly crushed cloves. Cook and store as above.

ORANGE MARMALADE

Makes **6 jars of assorted sizes**
Preparation time **45 minutes, plus overnight cooling**
Cooking temperature **low**
Cooking time **8–10 hours**

1 kg (2 lb) **Seville oranges**
1.2 litres (2 pints) boiling **water**
2 kg (4 lb) **preserving** or granulated sugar

Preheat the slow cooker if necessary. Put the whole oranges into the slow cooker pot, cover with the measurement boiling water and put an upturned saucer on top of the oranges to stop them from floating.

Cover with the lid and cook on low for 8–10 hours or until the oranges are tender. Lift the pot out of the housing using oven gloves and leave to cool overnight. The next day, lift the oranges out of the slow cooker pot, draining well. Cut into quarters, scoop out and discard the pips, then thinly slice the oranges.

Put the sliced oranges and the liquid from the slow cooker pot into a preserving pan or large saucepan, add the sugar and heat gently, stirring occasionally, until the sugar has completely dissolved. Increase the heat, and boil for 20–30 minutes or until setting point is reached (*see* page 277).

Warm 6 sterilized jars in a low oven for 5 minutes. Ladle the hot marmalade into the warm jars, cover the surface with waxed discs, add cellophane jam pot covers and secure with elastic bands or screw the jar lids in place. Label and leave to cool. Store in a cool place until required.

FOR DARK GINGER ORANGE MARMALADE, cook the Seville oranges with 75 g (3 oz) peeled and finely chopped fresh root ginger in the slow cooker as above. Make up the marmalade with the sliced oranges and ginger as above, using 1.5 kg (3½ lb) preserving or granulated sugar and 500 g (1 lb) light muscovado sugar.

PICKLED PLUMS

Makes **2 × 750 ml (1¼ pint)**
  and **1 × 500 ml (17 fl oz)**
  preserving jars
Preparation time **20 minutes**
Cooking temperature **high**
Cooking time **2–2½ hours**

750 ml (1¼ pints) **white wine vinegar**
500 g (1 lb) **caster sugar**
7 **rosemary sprigs**
7 **thyme sprigs**
7 small **bay leaves**
4 **lavender sprigs** (optional)
4 **garlic cloves**, unpeeled
1 teaspoon **salt**
½ teaspoon **black peppercorns**
1.5 kg (3 lb) **firm red plums**, washed
  and pricked

Preheat the slow cooker if necessary. Pour the vinegar and sugar into the slow cooker pot, then add 4 sprigs each of the rosemary and thyme and the bay leaves, all the lavender, if using, the garlic cloves, salt and peppercorns. Cover with the lid and cook on high for 2–2½ hours, stirring once or twice.

Warm the 3 sterilized jars in a low oven for 5 minutes. Pack the plums tightly into the jars. Tuck the remaining fresh herbs into the jars. Strain in the hot vinegar, making sure that the plums are completely covered, then seal tightly with the rubber seals and jar lids.

Label the jars and leave to cool. Transfer to a cool, dark cupboard and store for 3–4 weeks before using. Once opened, store in the refrigerator.

FOR PICKLED SHALLOTS, trim a little off the tops and roots of 1.25 kg (2½ lb) small shallots. Put them in a bowl and cover with boiling water, leave to soak for 3 minutes, then pour off the water and re-cover with cold water. Lift the shallots out 1 at a time and peel off the brown skins. Drain and layer in a second bowl with 40 g (1½ oz) salt. Leave overnight. Make up the vinegar mixture in the slow cooker as above, but using 250 g (8 oz) caster sugar and 250 g (8 oz) light muscovado sugar and omitting the lavender. Tip the shallots into a colander and drain off as much liquid as possible. Rinse with cold water, drain and pat dry with kitchen paper. Pack tightly into the warmed jars, adding a few extra herbs. Pour over the hot, strained vinegar, add crumpled greaseproof paper to keep the shallots beneath the surface of the vinegar and finish as above.

PASSION FRUIT & LIME CURD

Makes **3 small jars**
Preparation time **15 minutes**
Cooking temperature **low**
Cooking time **3–4 hours**

125 g (4 oz) **unsalted butter**, diced
400 g (13 oz) **caster sugar**
4 **eggs**, beaten
grated rind and juice of 2 **limes**
grated rind of 2 **lemons**
juice of 1 **lemon**
3 **passion fruit**, halved

Preheat the slow cooker if necessary. Put the butter and sugar in a large basin, checking first that it will fit into the slow cooker pot, then heat in the microwave until the butter has just melted. Alternatively, heat the butter and sugar in a saucepan and pour into the basin.

Stir the sugar mixture, then gradually whisk in the eggs, and then the fruit rind and juice. Cover the basin with foil and lower into the slow cooker pot. Pour boiling water into the pot to come halfway up the sides of the basin. Cover with the lid and cook on low for 3–4 hours, stirring once during cooking, until thick.

Stir once more, then scoop the passion fruit seeds out of the halved fruit with a teaspoon and stir them into the preserve.

Warm the 3 sterilized jars in a low oven for 5 minutes. Ladle the preserve into the warm jars, cover the surface with waxed discs, add cellophane jam pot covers and secure with elastic bands or screw the jar lids in place. Label and leave to cool. The preserve can be stored for up to 2 weeks in the refrigerator.

FOR LEMON CURD, make up as above, using the rind and juice of 3 lemons and omitting the lime rind and juice and passion fruit.

FIERY TROPICAL CHUTNEY

Makes **4 x 375 g (12 oz) jars**
Preparation time **25 minutes**
Cooking temperature **high**
Cooking time **4–5 hours**

250 ml (8 fl oz) **distilled malt vinegar**
250 g (8 oz) **granulated sugar**
2 large **red chillies**, halved, deseeded and finely chopped
3.5 cm (1½ inch) piece of **fresh root ginger**, peeled and finely chopped
2 teaspoons **black mustard seeds**
1 teaspoon **cumin seeds**, roughly crushed
1 teaspoon **coriander seeds**, roughly crushed
½ teaspoon **ground turmeric**
½ teaspoon **salt**
2 large **mangoes**, peeled, stoned and diced
1 large **pineapple**, peeled, cored and diced
2 **onions**, finely chopped
pepper

Preheat the slow cooker if necessary. Put the vinegar and sugar in a non-reactive saucepan and heat gently, stirring, until the sugar has dissolved. Mix in the red chillies, ginger, mustard seeds, crushed spices, turmeric, salt and pepper to taste.

Put the mangoes, pineapple and onions into the slow cooker pot, pour over the hot vinegar mixture, then cover and cook on high for 4–5 hours until the fruit is almost translucent.

Warm the 4 sterilized jars in a low oven for 5 minutes. Mash the fruit slightly, if liked, then ladle the chutney into the warm jars to the very top and press down well, making sure there are no air pockets. Seal each jar with a screw-top lid, label and leave to cool. Store in a cool, dry place for up to 3 months. Once opened, store in the refrigerator and consume within 2 weeks.

FOR SWEET TROPICAL MANGO & PINEAPPLE CHUTNEY, omit the chillies and continue as above.

SPICY TOMATO 'SANDWICH' CHUTNEY

Makes **5 x 375 g (12 oz) jars**
Preparation time **20 minutes**
Cooking temperature **high**
Cooking time **6–7 hours**

500 g (1 lb) **cooking apples**, peeled, cored and diced
500 g (1 lb) **butternut squash**, peeled, deseeded
    and diced
500 g (1 lb) **onions**, finely chopped
500 g (1 lb) **tomatoes**, roughly chopped (no need to skin,
    unless preferred)
125 g (4 oz) **sultanas**
1 teaspoon **crushed dried red chillies**
1 teaspoon **ground ginger**
1 teaspoon **ground turmeric**
1 teaspoon **cumin seeds**, roughly crushed
1 teaspoon **salt**
250 g (8 oz) **light muscovado sugar**
250 ml (8 fl oz) **red wine vinegar**

Preheat the slow cooker if necessary. Add the apples, vegetables and sultanas to the slow cooker pot. Sprinkle over the spices, salt and sugar and stir together.

Pour over the vinegar, cover with the lid and cook on high for 6–7 hours, stirring the chutney once and again at the end, until the vegetables are soft. If you prefer a fine-textured chutney, mash the cooked chutney.

Warm the 5 sterilized jars in a low oven for 5 minutes. Spoon the hot chutney into the warm jars to the very top and press down well, making sure there are no air pockets. Seal each jar with a screw-top lid, label and leave to cool. Store in a cool, dry place for up to 3 months. Leave the chutney to stand for at least 2–3 days before serving so that the flavours can mellow. Once opened, store in the refrigerator and consume within 2 weeks. Add to cheese and salad or ham sandwiches, or try in hot toasted sandwiches, if liked.

FOR SPICY TOMATO & COURGETTE CHUTNEY, omit the butternut squash and replace with 375 g (12 oz) diced courgette and 1 red pepper, cored, deseeded and diced. Continue as above.

BEST-EVER BARBECUE SAUCE

Makes **about 1 kg (2 lb)**
Preparation time **15 minutes**
Cooking temperature **high**
Cooking time **5–6 hours**

2 **onions**, finely chopped
2 small **cooking apples**, 450 g (14½ oz) in total,
    peeled, cored and finely chopped
500 g (1 lb) **passata**
4 tablespoons **dark muscovado sugar**
2 tablespoons **sherry vinegar**
1 tablespoon **Worcestershire sauce**
1 teaspoon **mustard powder**
salt and **pepper**

Preheat the slow cooker if necessary. Add all the ingredients to the slow cooker pot. Stir together, then cover with the lid and cook on high for 5–6 hours, stirring once during cooking and again at the end.

Warm sterilized jars in a low oven for 5 minutes. Pour the sauce into the warm jars to the very top. Seal each jar with a screw-top lid, then label and leave to cool. Store in the refrigerator for up to 1 month. Alternatively, pack into plastic containers and freeze for up to 3 months. Thaw in the refrigerator overnight. Serve with burgers, sausages or steak, if liked.

FOR CAJUN SAUCE, add 1 teaspoon each ground allspice and cinnamon, ½ teaspoon smoked hot paprika and 1 teaspoon crushed dried red chillies to the other barbecue sauce ingredients. Cook as above.

INDEX

ACKNOWLEDGEMENTS

Senior Commissioning Editor: Eleanor Maxfield
Editorial Assistant: Natalie Bradley
Design: Tracy Killick and Jaz Bahra
Production Controller: Allison Gonsalves

Photography: Fotolia Barbara Dudzińska 5, 238; Claudia
Paulussen 132; daffodilred 14; Daria Minaeva 56, 92; dusk 268;
geargodz 28; Jiri Hera 164; juliasudnitskaya 220; katrinshine 42;
marylooo 182; strixcode 202; victoria p 150; weyo 276; zzayko 112.
iStock twohumans 76. **Octopus Publishing Group** Stephen
Conroy 2, 6 left, 10 left, 10 right, 11 left, 11 right, 17, 19, 22, 24, 25,
26, 31, 33, 37, 38, 39, 40, 41, 45, 46, 47, 51, 52, 54, 55, 57, 59, 62, 63,
64, 65, 67, 68, 69, 70, 71, 72, 73, 75, 77, 80, 82, 87, 89, 93, 97, 98, 99,
103, 104, 105, 107, 110, 111, 113, 115, 116, 117, 118, 123, 124, 125,
126, 127, 129, 136, 137, 138, 139, 140, 141, 143, 144, 145, 146, 147,
149, 153, 155, 159, 163, 165, 170, 171, 172, 173, 175, 176, 177, 178,
179, 185, 186, 187, 188, 189, 191, 193, 194, 195, 199, 208, 209, 214,
215, 216, 217, 219, 223, 224, 225, 226, 227, 228, 232, 233, 239, 241,
242, 243, 244, 245, 249, 250, 253, 255, 257, 258, 260, 261, 263, 264,
265, 269, 272, 273, 275, 277, 279, 280, 281; William Shaw 6 right, 7, 9
left, 9 right, 12, 15, 21, 23, 27, 29, 32, 34, 43, 49, 53, 79, 81, 83, 84, 85,
88, 91, 95, 96, 101, 106, 119, 130, 131, 133, 135, 151, 154, 156, 157,
160, 161, 167, 168, 169, 181, 183, 196, 197, 198, 203, 205, 206, 207,
210, 211, 213, 221, 229, 231, 234, 235, 237, 251, 252, 259.